# The Israel of God in Prophecy

Principles of Prophetic Interpretation

D1707590

Andrews University Monographs, Studies in Religion, Volume XIII

# The Israel of God
# in Prophecy

## Principles of Prophetic Interpretation

by Hans K. LaRondelle

 Andrews University Press, Berrien Springs, Michigan

Dedicated to every person who searches
for the basic unity and harmony of the
progressive revelation of God in the
Holy Scriptures

Andrews University Press
Sutherland House
Berrien Springs, MI 49104-1700
Telephone: 269-471-6134
FAX: 269-471-6224
Email: aupo@andrews.edu
Website: http://www.universitypress.andrews.edu

ISBN: 0-943872-14-6
Library of Congress Catalog Card Number: 82-74358

# Contents

# Foreword

Correct Bible interpretation presupposes correct principles of Bible interpretation. Perhaps nowhere has faulty hermeneutic led to greater confusion and misunderstanding of Scripture than in prophetic interpretation pertaining to the culminating events of this earth's history. It is clear that the Middle East is a major focus of attention in the political world today — as it has been down through the centuries. Is it equally clear, however, that this geographical region is also a chief focus of Bible prophecies pertaining to the last days?

The present volume gets at the heart of the issues on this important subject through an approach which seeks out, first of all, the fundamentals of proper Bible interpretation. The author, Dr. Hans K. LaRondelle, is an expert in the field. His present volume, *The Israel of God in Prophecy,* is the product of several years of careful research and reveals not only a broad and deep understanding of Scripture itself, but also manifests a comprehensive knowledge of pertinent up-to-date secondary literature.

This book is a vital and vibrant corrective to a view proclaimed widely and loudly today by a dominant segment of evangelical Christianity — namely, the dispensationalist focus on modern political events in the Middle East as being the core of the eschatological message of the Bible. LaRondelle appropriately turns our attention to Scripture as its own interpreter, noting the importance of both the immediate and wider scriptural contexts. He also places appropriate stress on the "remnant" concept (basic to both Old Testament and New

Testament theology), on the New Testament's christological and ecclesiological applications of Old Testament prophecies, on its universalization of the territorial promises to Israel, and on related matters that are essential for a proper understanding of the Bible's own message.

It may just be noted that chapter 10 in this volume has a useful treatment of several "problem texts" (texts frequently used by modern dispensationalists for support of their theories concerning a political Israel), and that chapters 11 and 12 deal with two particular areas closely related to the book's main theme, namely, the dispensationalist placement of the "seventieth week" of Daniel 9 as still future at the end of the age, and the so-called "secret rapture" or "double-second-advent" theory. These latter two chapters represent an adaptation (with some additional material) from three articles within a longer series published by Dr. LaRondelle in *Ministry* magazine during the years 1980 and 1981.

It should also be mentioned that this volume contains a certain amount of redundancy or repetition of coverage. In some instances, this is a necessity in order to maintain coherence and a logical sequence for a particular line of argument. There are places where the pressure of meeting publication deadlines has precluded the amount of attention to repetition that might have been desirable. However, this has not impaired the content of the book.

LaRondelle's *Israel of God in Prophecy* is, in my view, an excellent work. It is an essential tool that should be in the hands of every Christian minister and of all laymen who need to deal with the present-day issues relating to Israel and prophecy. In short, I can say that it is the best I have seen on the subject.

Andrews University  
Berrien Springs, Michigan  
December 1982

KENNETH A. STRAND  
Professor of  
Church History

# Acknowledgments

I wish to thank the administrators of Andrews University and the Seventh-day Adventist Theological Seminary in Berrien Springs, Michigan, for their support in preparing this manuscript. I am also indebted to Dr. Adrio König, Professor of Systematic Theology, Theological Studies, and Practical Theology at the University of South Africa in Pretoria; to Dr. Kenneth A. Strand, Professor of Church History, and Dr. Gerhard F. Hasel, Dean, both of the Theological Seminary of Andrews University, for their constructive criticisms of the manuscript and their encouragement; and to Dr. Robert Firth, Director of the Andrews University Press, for his editing work which made this a much more readable book.

I thank the editors of *Ministry* magazine for their permission to use my articles on dispensationalism published between May 1981 and July 1982. I am grateful to Mr. and Mrs. Donald E. Loveridge for providing me with a quiet place to work on this investigation in Melbourne, Florida, and especially to Barbara, my wife, for her loving support and cooperation in this extensive project.

—Hans K. LaRondelle

# Glossary of Technical Terms

apocalyptic — related to the final Judgment and glorious second advent of Christ

christological — fulfillment or realization in Christ

ecclesiological — fulfillment or realization in the Church of Christ

eschatology — study of final events centered in both advents of Christ

exegesis — science of the meaning of a text in its own literary and historical contexts

hermeneutics — science of interpretation and application

*parousia* — the second coming of Christ

theological — related to the God of Holy Scripture

# List of Abbreviations

| | |
|---|---|
| *AUSS* | *Andrews University Seminary Studies* |
| *BSac* | *Bibliotheca Sacra* |
| BKAT | Biblischer Kommentar Altes Testament. Neukirchen-Vluyn: Neukirchener Verlag. |
| BWANT | Beitrage zur Wissenschaft vom Alten und Neuen Testament. Stuttgart: W. Kohlhammer. |
| *EOTH* | *Essays on Old Testament Hermeneutics.* Edited by C. Westermann. English translation edited by James L. Mays. Richmond, Va.: John Knox Press, 1963. |
| *ISBE* | *International Standard Bible Encyclopedia.* Grand Rapids, Mich.: Wm. B. Eerdmans Pub. Co., 1979. |
| *JBL* | *Journal of Biblical Literature* |
| *JETS* | *Journal of the Evangelical Theological Society* |
| *JTS* | *Journal of Theological Studies* |
| KJV | King James Version |
| NASB | New American Standard Bible |
| NICNT | New International Commentary on the New Testament. Grand Rapids, Mich.: Wm. B. Eerdmans Pub. Co. |

| | |
|---|---|
| *NIDNTT* | *New International Dictionary of New Testament Theology.* Edited by Colin Brown. 3 vols. Grand Rapids, Mich.: Zondervan, 1975-78. |
| NIV | New International Version |
| *NSRB* | *The New Scofield Reference Bible* (1967) |
| *NTS* | *New Testament Studies* |
| OTS | Oudtestamentische Studien. Leiden: E. J. Brill. |
| RSV | Revised Standard Version |
| *SDABC* | *Seventh-day Adventist Bible Commentary.* Edited by Francis D. Nichol. 7 vols. Washington, D.C.: Review and Herald Pub. Assn., 1957. |
| *TDNT* | *Theological Dictionary of the Old Testament.* Edited by G. Johannes Botterweck and Helmer Ringgren. Translated by John T. Willis and G. W. Bromiley. Grand Rapids, Mich.: Wm. B. Eerdmans Pub. Co., 1974-. |
| *ThLZ* | *Theologische Literatur Zeitung* |
| ThStKr | Theologische Studien und Kritiken. Berlin: Ev. Verlagsanstalt. |
| *TSF* | *Theological Students Fellowship (Bulletin)* |
| *WTJ* | *Westminster Theological Journal* |
| *ZAW* | *Zeitschrift für die alttestamentliche Wissenschaft* |

# Introduction

Modern interpreters of apocalyptic prophecies often do not recognize the hermeneutical problems involved in prophetic interpretation because of their literalistic presupposition. Our aim is not to attempt an exhaustive treatment of all biblical prophecies and issues of eschatology, but rather to seek to discover and apply theological principles or guidelines fundamental to proper prophetic interpretation. Correct biblical principles of interpretation are ultimately far more crucial than the exegesis of isolated texts and words, not only because such principles affect and guide all exegesis, but also because they determine how false exegesis and misinterpretation can be corrected.

It is widely recognized today that one's philosophical and theological presuppositions substantially affect one's conclusions. Of vital importance, therefore, is one's idea of divine inspiration and of the mode of prophetic transmittance of divine revelation, whether one starts from literalistic assumptions of biblical terms or allows God to communicate His revelations through "borrowed" cultural symbols and contemporary thought processes with *added* depth and *new* content to old words.

Our purpose focuses on the interrelationship of the Old Testament prophecies and their New Testament fulfillments or further applications. We wish to search for those theological principles that underlie the interpretative approach of the New Testament writers to the Hebrew Scriptures and to establish the New Testament patterns of fulfillment. We aim to analyze

1

how Old Testament prophecies have been fulfilled already in past history, in order to use these principles of fulfillment as the guideline and norm for interpreting the yet-unfulfilled prophecies.

Our deep concern in accepting the Bible as an organic unity in Christ is to recapture the proper historical perspective on the rise and development of Israel's prophetic utterances. The reconstruction of the historical context is essential to establish the exegetical foundation of each prophetic interpretation. History and prophetic interpretation cannot be separated or compartmentalized.

A major problem in applying the ancient prophetic messages to our times is that many modern interpreters manifest a total disregard for the essential theological—specifically the christological—dimensions of the Old Testament prophecies. The prophetic view of history was never directed to secular events of a political nature, disconnected from the Messiah and His people.

Each Bible prophet kept his promises of blessing or threats of doom solidly and consistently in the focus of redemptive history. To interpret the prophetic messages as mere predictions of current social and political events in the Middle East would essentially transform the God of Israel into a soothsayer. The hallmark of soothsaying has always been to predict future events outside redemptive history, disconnected from the true Messiah and the messianic people. When God speaks, His Name is at stake in being faithful to His holy covenant which is centered in and confirmed by Jesus Christ as the one and only Mediator between God and man, between God and Israel. Never is God interested in trying to convince man of His divine existence and truthfulness by a mere exhibition of His foreknowledge in isolation from His plan of salvation. From Genesis to Revelation the focus of all biblical prophecies is consistently on God's eternal purpose for the reconciliation of heaven and earth through Christ Jesus (Ephesians 1:4-19). Prophets and apostles alike insist on the sovereignty of God in all affairs of salvation history, on the continuity of God's purpose through Christ in particular. "For no matter how many promises God has made, they are 'Yes' in Christ" (2 Corinthians 1:20, NIV).

This study is based on the assumption of faith that both the Old and the New Testaments are not purely historical documents, but religious writings which are inspired by the Spirit of God and therefore the authoritative Word of God. We accept it to be our task to interpret the ancient texts of Holy Scripture as we find them; that is, we focus on the canonical text in its present form as the finished literary product. We apply to these texts the inductive principle of the *analogy of Scripture,* which carefully relates those passages of Scripture which reveal the same terminology, imagery, or comparable redemptive events, recognizing that Christ alone is the true Interpreter of Israel's sacred Scriptures.

This consideration has led us to take the traditional Christian position that the New Testament is the authorized and authoritative interpreter of the Old Testament. Our study can be considered also an ongoing dialogue with dispensational theologians and their eschatology, with its exclusive focus on the Jewish people and the Middle East territory, based on their strict application of the principle of literalism.

If not indicated otherwise, quotations from Scripture are taken from the New International Version (Zondervan Bible Publishers).

# 1

## The Christocentric Focus

## of all Holy Scripture

The Bible is unique in human literature. There is not a second book like it, in which the Creator of heaven and earth has revealed Himself and His will for mankind in the way of promise and fulfillment, as outlined in the Old and the New Testaments. The Bible is basically a spiritual book because God, who discloses Himself in it, is Spirit. Man, originally created in God's image and likeness, has fallen away from God in futility of thinking and distrust of God's revealed word. Paul describes the mental, moral, and religious destitution of fallen men:

> They are darkened in their understanding and separated from the life of God because of the ignorance that is in them due to the hardening of their hearts (Ephesians 4:18; cf. also 2:1-3).

No wonder that Jesus Christ pointed out to Nicodemus, a leading interpreter of the Hebrew Scriptures in Jerusalem, that one "cannot see the kingdom of God" — that is, one cannot understand the nature or share the blessedness of God's kingdom — "unless a man is born again" (John 3:3). Christ explained that rebirth is not the result of man's own doing but a supernatural act and gift of God: "Flesh gives birth to flesh, but the Spirit gives birth to spirit" (John 3:6). Christ thus taught that man's experience of *rebirth* by the Holy Spirit is an essential condition for the understanding of the Old Testament in its true, spiritual intent, in its theological message of salvation and the kingdom of God.

Peter reminds us that the prophecies of the Hebrew Scriptures originated, not in the prophet's own foresight or invention, but "men spoke from God as they were carried along by the Holy Spirit" (2 Peter 1:21). The Old Testament prophecies possess, therefore, a moral purpose: salvation through the Messiah.

> And we have the word of the prophets made more certain, and you will do well to pay attention to it, as to a light shining in a dark place, until the day dawns *and the morning star rises in your hearts* (2 Peter 1:19; emphasis added).

The bright Morning Star is Christ (Revelation 22:16). This christological focus of the Hebrew Bible in its two dimensions of a suffering Servant-Messiah and of the exalted royal Messiah is not obvious or plain to the natural mind, as Jesus' rejection by the Jewish leaders shows. One should not conclude from this that the Old Testament does not sufficiently reveal the truth of the Messiah's atoning suffering and death or that Christ proclaimed a Kingdom and a Messiah which were completely different from what the Jews expected. The problem was not the darkness or incomprehensibility of the divine revelation in the Hebrew Scriptures, but rather the stubbornness of the unspiritual mind. Jesus reproved even His own followers:

> How foolish you are, and how slow of heart to believe all that the prophets have spoken! Did not the Christ have to suffer these things and then enter his glory? And beginning with Moses and all the Prophets, he explained to them what was said in all the Scriptures concerning himself (Luke 24:25-27).

This Old Testament explanation by the risen Christ brought a new vision of messianic truth to the Jewish mind, which resulted in a new love for God. The disciples testified, "Were not our hearts burning within us while he talked with us on the road and *opened the Scriptures to us?*" (Luke 24:32; emphasis added). Christ *"opened their minds so they could understand the Scriptures"* (Luke 24:45; emphasis added). We conclude, therefore: because Jesus Christ is the divine Interpreter of the Old Testament, He must open the Scriptures to us; by Him our minds must be opened to see the messianic light in Israel's Scriptures. This conclusion implies that faith in Jesus as the Christ, the Messiah of Israel's prophecies, is an essential qualification for the Christian interpreter of the Hebrew Scriptures.

Those interpreters who cannot see Christ at the heart of all the Old Testament writings will not be able to explain the real thrust of Israel's prophecies.

Paul said of the Christ-rejecting Jews:

> But their minds were made dull, for to this day the same veil remains when the old covenant is read. It has not been removed, because only in Christ is it taken away (2 Corinthians 3:14).

For the apostle Paul the central truth of the Hebrew Bible was not about Israel and its national future, but rather about Messiah Jesus, the Lord of Israel, the Redeemer of the world (Romans 16:25-27; Galatians 3:16, 29; Philippians 3:3-10).

The apostle says that none of the rulers of this age had understood God's hidden wisdom in the Scriptures. Nevertheless,

> God has revealed it to us by his Spirit. The Spirit searches all things, even the deep things of God. . . . We have not received the spirit of the world but *the Spirit who is from God, that we may understand what God has freely given us.* This is what we speak, not in words taught us by human wisdom but in words taught by the Spirit, expressing spiritual truths in spiritual words. The man without the Spirit of God does not accept the things that come from the Spirit for they are foolishness to him, and he cannot understand them, because they are spiritually discerned (1 Corinthians 2:10, 12-14; emphasis added).

These words of Paul are full of promise for the student of the prophetic word. Ellen G. White even assures us today: "There are veins of truth yet to be discovered; but spiritual things are spiritually discerned."[1] The Bible student must be willing, however, to consider the prophetic Word in the spirit of a humble, constant learner under the guidance of the Holy Spirit, always willing to hide self in Christ and to bring new treasures out of the old storeroom (Matthew 13:52).

### The Need for the Christocentric Focus
### in Prophetic Interpretations

The widespread confusion evident among modern interpreters of biblical prophecies which pertain to last-days' events is largely due to a lack of clearly-defined principles of prophetic interpretation. The need for sound hermeneutical principles for Bible interpretation is generally recognized today. It is manifest in the recent development of the theological science of hermeneutics, the study of the methodology of interpreting the Holy Scriptures; in short, the science and art of the correct interpretation of the Bible. The basic task of biblical hermeneutics is to determine what God has said in sacred Scripture and what it means for us today. "Hermeneutics is a *science* in that it can determine certain principles for discovering the meaning of a document, and in that these principles are not a mere list of rules but bear *organic* connection to each other."[2]

The skillful application of the principles of biblical hermeneutics is the task of the theological discipline of exegesis. Exegesis is thus applied hermeneutics. Comparatively little has been published, however, on the special hermeneutics of prophetic principles that disclose the nature of the progressive revelation of God's eternal purpose in the apocalyptic parts of Scripture. In other words, valid hermeneutical rules of Scripture interpretation must be "inspired principles" which are legitimately and systematically derived from the Scriptures themselves and constitute, within the living organism of the Bible, the inherent, unifying structure of the total body of Holy Writ. It is irresponsible to jump unprepared into the area of end-time prophecies of Scripture. By considering such apocalyptic portions of Holy Scripture by themselves, in isolation from the total prophetic-messianic framework, one will necessarily fall into the pitfall of a geographic and ethnic literalism. Such interpreters are not ashamed to compare the biblical prophecies to a "jigsaw puzzle" (H. Lindsey). But without the Spirit the letter remains unspiritual, and blessed hope turns into idle speculation and future time settings. More than a historical-grammatical exegesis of isolated parts of Scripture is needed. Every proof-text method that appeals to the letters of Scripture verses, not considering their immediate and wider theological contexts and consequently not relating the verses to God's holy covenant with its messianic framework, denies the theological unity of God's Word and obscures the religious-moral issue of the apocalyptic war between heaven and earth.

"Method" as such is too limited an instrument to grasp deep theological truth. More basic are the spiritual perspective and theological presuppositions with which the interpreter approaches the prophetic texts of Scripture. The Christian interpreter comes to the Old Testament with a different theological perspective than the Jewish expositor. Their conclusions will be utterly different concerning the final war in prophecy.

The Christian understanding of the Old Testament is determined by the christocentric focus by which the New Testament writers interpreted the Hebrew Scriptures. Therefore it is essential for a Christian to discover the principles and procedures according to which Christ and His apostles understood and expounded the writings of Moses, the Psalms, and the Hebrew prophets. Otherwise he is in grave danger of reading the Old Testament prophecies in an *un*christian way and hence of misinterpreting and distorting the biblical prophecies simply by not interpreting the Old Testament by the New Testament key. The Old Testament is no longer the last word on end-time prophecies since the Messiah of prophecy Himself has come as the last Word. The New Testament has been written as the ultimate norm for the fulfillment and interpretation of Israel's prophecies. A Christian would deny his Christian faith and Lord if he reads the Old Testament as a closed entity, as the full and final message of God for Jews irrespective of the cross and resurrection of Jesus, the Messiah, and apart from the New Testament explanation of the Hebrew writings.

It is of vital importance, therefore, to prepare ourselves for the study of the unfulfilled prophecies of the Old Testament by first analyzing the patterns of promise and fulfillment in fulfilled prophecies. A clear understanding of these New Testament patterns of fulfillment is essential to the adequate interpretation of all the symbols and images of prophecy. We must proceed from the known to the unknown.

A practical knowledge of the New Testament principles of applying the Old Testament is indispensable for the accurate understanding of the Scriptures as a whole. Our fundamental Christian presupposition is the historic Protestant confession of the spiritual unity in Christ of God's plan and covenants in both Testaments. For both Luther and Calvin, eschatology was essentially christocentric, with the message of Christ as the central truth of Holy Scripture. Although the eschatology of these reformers largely lacks the cosmic breadth and grandeur of the biblical hope because of neglect of certain aspects of the prophetic content, the christological perspective of the evangelical theology of the reformers is a valid safeguard against all speculative interpretation of both exegetical literalism and allegorism. We need biblical principles, derived from the fullness of Scripture itself, in order to detect any speculative approach to the prophetic imagery and symbols.

The apostle Paul urges his younger associate Timothy to do his best to present himself to God as an approved workman "who does not need to be ashamed and who correctly handles the word of truth" (2 Timothy 2:15). Those modern interpretations of the prophetic Word which exclude Christ, His saving grace, and His new-covenant people from the center of Israel's end-time prophecies basically miss the divine mark and exalt a torch of false prophecy. Christ is "the Alpha and the Omega, the First and the Last, the Beginning and the End" (Revelation 22:13) of the whole prophetic Word. Christ is the shining Morning Star, who illuminates each covenant promise and prophecy with His saving presence. Christ is "the Root and Offspring of David" (Revelation 22:16), which means that He is the Lord of David as well as the Son of David. He represents Yahweh, the God of Israel, in all that He says and does (John 12:44-50). Christ, the Holy Spirit, and God the Father are united so intimately that the christocentric focus is the inalienable hallmark of a biblical-theological exposition of Israel's prophetic Word.

Seventh-day Adventists have received special counsel to draw all eyes to Christ as the center of hope in their prophetic interpretations:

> Let Daniel speak, let the Revelation speak, and tell what is truth. But whatever phase of the subject is presented, uplift Jesus as the center of all hope, "the Root and the Offspring of David, and the bright and morning Star."[3]

> Of all professing Christians, Seventh-day Adventists should be foremost in uplifting Christ before the world.[4]

### Notes on Chapter 1

[1]Ellen G. White, *Fundamentals of Christian Education* (Nashville, Tenn.: Southern Pub. Assn., 1923), p. 188.

[2]Bernard Ramm, *Protestant Biblical Interpretation*, 3d ed. (Grand Rapids, Mich.: Baker Book House, 1970), p. 11.

[3]Ellen G. White, *Testimonies to Ministers* (Mountain View, Calif.: Pacific Press, 1923), p. 118.

[4]Ellen G. White, *Evangelism* (Washington: Review & Herald Pub. Assn., 1946), p. 188.

# 2

## The Key to the Old Testament:

## Literalism or the New Testament?

Dispensationalism represents that system of Bible interpretation which maintains that the terms "Israel" and "Church" in Scripture always stand for two essentially different covenant peoples of God: Israel stands for an earthly national-theocratic kingdom, but the Church for a spiritual and heavenly people. As Lewis S. Chafer puts it:

> The dispensationalist believes that throughout the ages God is pursuing two distinct purposes: one related to the earth with earthly people and earthly objectives involved, while the other is related to heaven with heavenly people and heavenly objectives involved.[1]

Daniel P. Fuller therefore concluded: "The basic premise of Dispensationalism is two purposes of God expressed in the formation of two peoples who maintain their distinction throughout eternity."[2] In other words, dispensationalism maintains different eschatologies for "Israel" and the "Church," each having its own, contrasting, covenant promises. The essence of dispensationalism thus consists in "rightly dividing" the Scriptures, not merely into compartments of time or dispensations, but also into sections of Scripture which apply *either* to Israel *or* to the Church *or* to the Gentiles, a division derived from 1 Corinthians 10:32. Chafer went so far as to teach that the only Scriptures addressed specifically to Christians are the Gospel of John, the book of Acts, and the New Testament Epistles.[3] The final conflict or tribulation in Revelation 6-20 is claimed to be between the antichrist and godly Jews, not between

10

antichrist and the Church of Christ, because "the book as a whole is not occupied primarily with God's program for the church" (J. F. Walvoord).[4]

The fundamental principle from which this compartmentalizing of Scriptures stems is called a "consistent literalism." One of its modern spokesmen, Charles C. Ryrie, categorically states:

> Since consistent literalism is the logical and obvious principle of interpretation, dispensationalism is more than justified.[5]

> Dispensationalism is a result of consistent application of the basic hermeneutical principle of literal, normal, or plain interpretation. No other system of theology can claim this.[6]

> Consistent literalism is at the heart of dispensational eschatology.[7]

The implications of this predetermined principle of literalism are far-reaching in theology, especially in eschatology. It demands the literal fulfillment of Old Testament prophecies, which therefore must take place during some future period in Palestine, "for the Church is not now fulfilling them in any literal sense."[8] Thus literalism leads necessarily to dispensational futurism in prophetic interpretation.

According to dispensationalism, the Church of Christ, which was born on the day of Pentecost as recorded in Acts 2, is definitely *not* a part of God's covenants with Abraham and David. The Christian Church with its gospel of grace is only an "interruption" of God's original plan with Israel, a "parenthesis" (H. Ironside) or "intercalation" (L. S. Chafer), unforeseen by the Old Testament prophets and having no connection with God's promises of an earthly kingdom to Abraham, Moses, and David.

Basic to the dispensational system is the assumption that Christ offered Himself to the nation of Israel as the messianic King to establish the glorious, *earthly* kingdom which was promised to David. On this supposition rests the inference that Christ "postponed" His kingdom offer when Israel rejected Him as her rightful King. Instead, Christ began to offer His kingdom of grace (from Matthew 13 onward) as a temporary covenant of grace that would terminate as soon as He would again establish the Jewish nation as His theocracy.

The church of reborn believers must therefore first be taken out of this world through a sudden, invisible "rapture" to heaven before God can fulfill His "unconditional" Old Testament promises to Israel.

Dispensationalism asserts that the Old Testament covenant promises to Israel can only be fulfilled to the Jewish nation (in all details as written) during the future Jewish millennium of Revelation 20. Only then will God's distinctive and unconditional purposes with "Israel" be gloriously consummated. This implies the rebuilding of the temple in Jerusalem and the reinstitution of animal sacrifices, in "commemoration" of the death of Christ. All the nations will then acknowledge Israel as the favored people of God. Ryrie says, "This millennial culmination is the climax of history and the great goal of God's program for the ages."[9] Thus it is quite clear that dispensationalism separates the Church of Christ from the total redemptive plan of God for Israel and mankind and restricts the future kingdom of God to a restoration of a strictly Jewish kingdom — the so-called millennial kingdom.

This dichotomy between Israel and the Church, between the kingdom of God on earth and the Church, between Jesus' gospel of the kingdom and Paul's gospel of grace, is the logical outgrowth of the adopted principle of literalistic interpretation of the prophetic Word of God.

This system of literalism has no roots in the historic Christian faith but was created around 1830 in reaction against the spiritualizations of the liberal theology of the nineteenth century. Modern dispensationalism arose basically in the teachings of the former lawyer John N. Darby (1800-1882), leader of a Christian group called the Plymouth Brethren (in England), and is popularized in the footnotes of the *Scofield Reference Bible* (1917) and the *New Scofield Reference Bible* (New York: Oxford University Press, 1967). Dispensational theology is worked out systematically by Lewis Sperry Chafer (successor of C. I. Scofield) in his apologetic work *Systematic Theology* (8 vols.) and in the writings of John F. Walvoord, president of Dallas Theological Seminary. Dispensationalism is taught on principle at Moody Bible Institute (Chicago) and in an estimated two hundred Bible institutes in the U.S.A. The dispensational magazine is *Bibliotheca Sacra* (inherited by Dallas Theological Seminary in 1934). Popular authors like Hal Lindsey,

Salem Kirban, and others influence millions through their writings and motion pictures to accept the dispensational interpretation as the true prophetic picture of God's plan for the Jewish people: a Middle-East Armageddon war and a Jewish millennium.

### The Key to the Old Testament:
### The New Testament

Is the dispensationalist hermeneutic of "consistent literalism" the genuine key to interpreting the future fulfillment of Old Testament prophecies? Is the hermeneutic of dispensational literalism organically (i.e., genuinely and intrinsically) related to the Holy Scriptures themselves, or is it a presupposition forced upon God's Word from the outside as an "objective standard"[10] in order to safeguard the Bible against unwarranted spiritualizations and allegorizations? Should not the "objective" principle for understanding the Word of God be derived inductively from the inspired record itself?

The cardinal point is this: Is the Christian believer permitted to take the writings of the Old Testament as a closed unit by themselves, in isolation from the New Testament witness of their fulfillment, or must he accept the Old Testament and the New Testament *together* as one organic revelation of God in Christ Jesus?

In the first place, the Old Testament by itself lacks the guiding norm of Jesus Christ and His apostles for the Christian understanding of the Hebrew Scriptures. The principle of "literalism" is then introduced into this vacuum of an unfinished canon of Scripture to supply the guiding norm of interpretation that Christ and the New Testament were appointed by God to fulfill. The term "literalism" itself becomes dubious in meaning if one defines it as the literal or normal grammatico-historical exegesis of the Old Testament but then immediately exalts this Old Testament exegesis as the final truth within the total canon of the Bible, so that Christ and the apostolic gospel have no authority to unfold, modify, or (re)interpret the Old Testament promises. Charles C. Ryrie states that the dispensational view of progressive revelation can accept additional light but not that the term "Israel" can mean the "Church." This would mean an unacceptable "contradiction" of terms and concepts.[11] Dispensationalism denies an organic relationship between Old Testament prophecy and the Church of Christ Jesus. It rejects the traditional application of the Davidic kingdom promises to Christ's spiritual rulership over His Church, because such an application would be interpreting prophecy allegorically, not literally, and therefore illegitimately.

A crucial question then becomes: Do dispensationalists really accept the organic character of the Bible *as a whole*, that is, the spiritual and theological unity of the Old and New Testament revelation? Is the Christian expositor allowed to interpret the Old Testament as a *closed* canon, as the complete and final revelation of God to the Jewish people, without letting Jesus Christ be the true Interpreter of Moses and the prophets, without letting the New Testament have the supreme authority to apply the Old Testament prophecies?

The Christian interpreter cannot interpret the Old Testament in the final and ultimate sense as if Christ has not yet come and as if the New Testament has not yet been written. Would not that rather be the position of Christ-rejecting Judaism and Zionism?[12]

### Literalism in Late Judaism

It is abundantly clear from the Christian perspective that the Jewish leaders in Jesus' time had a confused and one-sided understanding of the promised Messiah. They misinterpreted the prophetic Word by their literalism, overlooking the conditional character of the promised covenant blessing to Israel.[13] The Jews were not looking for a suffering Messiah; not even Christ's disciples were (Luke 24:20-27; Matthew 16:21-22). In all the Jewish apocryphal writings, which reflect various concepts of the expected Messiah and the kingdom of God, not once is a Messiah foreseen who would die for the sins of Israel in fulfillment of Isaiah 53.[14] What the Jewish theology of late Judaism taught about the Messiah and His kingdom can therefore never be a safe guide or a Christian norm for understanding what the Old Testament prophecies really meant.

The disciples of Christ, including John the Baptist (Matthew 11:2-6), discovered a new and deeper understanding of what the messianic mission and the kingdom of God involved. Jesus did not come to offer Himself to Israel as the King of glory or His kingdom as an earthly, political power. When the Jews tried to "make him king by force" (John 6:15), Jesus refused to become the king of Israel, *as they interpreted the kingship of Israel,* and "withdrew into the hills by himself." And to Pilate, the Roman governor, Jesus clarified, *"My kingdom is not of this world.* If it were, my servants would fight to prevent my arrest by the Jews. But now *my kingdom is from another place"* (John 18:36; emphasis added). Here appears the reason why the Jews, as a nation, rejected Christ as their King. They had fundamentally misinterpreted the mission of the Messiah and the deep, religious nature of His kingdom or reign.[15] By concentrating primarily on the earthly-political glory of the coming Messiah and His kingdom, to the neglect of the basically religious picture of the messianic mission and reign, rabbinic Judaism had come to expect a political Messiah who would deliver the Jewish nation from the Roman oppression.[16] The Jewish expectation of the coming messianic kingdom was therefore the opposite of that which Jesus came to introduce in Israel. He who came, first of all, to overcome Satan and his enslaving power over Jewish hearts through His victory in the wilderness and to redeem Israelites by exorcising demons from their souls was denounced by the Jews as doing the work of Beelzebub (Matthew 12:22-28), as having "an evil spirit" (Mark 3:30). Christ, however, interpreted the exercise of his saving power for Israel as the true reign of God: "If I drive out demons by the Spirit of God, then *the kingdom of God has come upon you"* (Matthew 12:28, emphasis added; cf. Luke 17:21 in RSV).

Even Christ's own disciples had not understood the spiritual nature of God's kingdom or reign. When Peter wanted to prevent Jesus from being a suffering and dying Messiah, Christ rebuked Peter sharply: "Out of my sight, Satan! You do not have in mind the things of God, but the things of men" (Mark 8:33). As T. W. Manson renders it freely: "Out of my way, Satan! You are a stumbling-block to me; for you are more concerned for a human empire than for the kingdom of God."[17] Jesus offered Himself to Israel, exactly as the prophetic Word had determined, not first as the King of glory but as the Servant-Messiah. It is clearly not so that Jesus offered Israel a glorious Davidic empire. He rather rejected the political messianism of the Jewish hope, even of His own disciples (Luke 19:41-42; Matthew 23:37-38). G. E. Ladd has concluded:

> The very fact that he did not come as the glorious King, but as the humble Savior, should be adequate evidence by itself to prove that his offer of the kingdom was not the outward, earthly kingdom, but one which corresponded to the form in which the King himself came to men.[18]

What, then, was the cause of the Jewish rejection of Jesus as the Prince of peace, of His spiritual reign as the kingdom of God? From the very start of His public ministry Christ disappointed the Jewish expectation of a glorious worldly Messiah and their hope that Israel as a nation was to be exalted as the head of a universal kingdom (Luke 4:16-30; Matthew 5:1-12). However, the underlying cause may be found in a frequently applied *literalism* in the Jewish exegesis of the first century.[19] This form of atomistic treatment of the Scriptures took the letters and words of Moses and the prophets very seriously, yet it dissected and compartmentalized the Scriptures by neglecting to relate the prophetic words to salvation history and to the theological center of Scripture. That unifying center of the Old Testament is the living God of Israel,[20] from whom all revelation of truth issues and to whom all revelation must be related in order to understand God's eternal purpose for the world and His covenant people. Jewish literalism or letterism can therefore be described as a form of legalism.

A peculiar form of Jewish literalism and compartmentalizing of prophetic Scripture was employed by the Qumran sect or Dead Sea covenanters. Not only did they explain parts of the Mosaic law in a more dissected way than Pharisaic Judaism (e.g., on Exodus 16:29),[21] but their interpretations of the prophetic Scriptures (e.g., Habakkuk) show that they completely ignored the historical and literary context of the Old Testament prophecies. They interpreted the prophetic passages as being exclusively concerned with their own time as the time of the end and their own Jewish sect as the faithful remnant of Israel.[22] Their conviction of possessing the only true insight in Scripture was built on their implicit confidence in the divine guidance of the "Teacher of Righteousness," the founder of the Qumran community. To him God had unquestionably revealed the true meaning of the prophecies, the key to unlock all the mysteries of prophecy, and the touchstone for all applications to the impending crisis. The Qumran sect therefore completely identified the Scripture interpretations of their "righteous" teacher with divine revelation and took his specific word as the absolute norm of interpretation.[23]

This form of apocalypticism with its exclusive claims of the "literal" meaning of the prophecies and its neglect of the historical-grammatical exegesis was really only a form of speculative literalism, a caricature of the genuine literal interpretation. Needless to say, its misguided hope ended in a catastrophic disappointment for its believers. Qumran literalism started from a wrong point of departure; more interested in the *application* of the prophetic word than in the original meaning of the biblical text — its exegesis — it led its believers to uncritically accept the claims of a contemporary charismatic teacher as the superior norm of Scripture interpretation.

### The Key to the Old Testament: Christ in the New Testament

God Himself is the interpreter of His Word. The words of Scripture receive their meaning and message from their divine Author and must constantly be related to His dynamic and progressive will and purpose in order to hear God's own unfolding interpretation of His earlier promises in a "Thus says the Lord." Promises concerning Israel as a people, dynasty, land, city, and mountain are not self-contained, isolated promises for the sake of Israel, but are integral parts of God's progressive plan of salvation for the world and the human race. The Old Testament reveals such a universal plan. It can be detected by a diachronic, longitudinal (long-cut) approach which pays attention to the chronological sequence of the prophetic messages in the Old Testament.

In our day, Walter C. Kaiser, Jr., has conducted such an inductive search of the Old Testament in his scholarly book *Toward an Old Testament Theology* (Grand Rapids, Mich.: Zondervan, 1978). He concludes that the focal center of the Old Testament as an organic unity is *the promise of God* to bless all peoples through the seed of Abraham, also summarized in the tripartite formula: "I will be your God, and you shall be My people, and I will dwell in the midst of you" (pp. 12, 32-35). This all-inclusive, single plan of God, *this promise,* is the fixed core in the progressive revelation of all Israel's covenants. It is clearly not an "abstract divining rod" foisted over the texts of the Old Testament but provides "its own pattern for a permanent, normative standard by which to judge that day and all other days by a yardstick which claims to be divinely laid on the writer of Scripture and all subsequent readers simultaneously" (p. 14).

Kaiser shows that the *messianic* promise is the central focus of all God's covenants with man from the beginning. This promise relates to all divine predictions in the Old Testament. The writers of the New Testament recognize Christ as the perfect fulfillment of God's promises to the patriarchs and Israel. Paul sums up the whole messianic hope in one definite promise:

> And now it is because of my hope in what God has promised our fathers that I am on trial today. This is the promise our twelve tribes are hoping to see fulfilled as they earnestly serve God day and night. O king, it is because of this hope that the Jews are accusing me (Acts 26:6-7).

> We tell you the good news: What God promised our fathers he has fulfilled for us, their children, by raising up Jesus (Acts 13:32-33).

> If you belong to Christ, then you are Abraham's seed and heirs according to the promise (Galatians 3:29).

Christ is the goal of the mission of Abraham and Israel. Christ came to redeem the world and the human race as a whole. Salvation is from the Jews but not for the Jews only.

> The Scripture declares that the whole world is a prisoner of sin, so that what was promised, being given through faith in Jesus Christ, might be given to those who believe (Galatians 3:22).

The New Testament emphasizes the truth that God has fulfilled the Abrahamic promise in Jesus of Nazareth and has renewed His covenant with Israel through Jesus Christ in a "better covenant" (Hebrews 7:22), introducing a "better hope" (Hebrews 7:19) for all Christ-believing Israelites and Gentiles (Hebrews 8). Thus the New Testament testifies to a basic fulfillment of the Old Testament promise in Messiah Jesus. In the words of the apostle Paul, "For no matter how many promises God has made, they are 'Yes' in Christ" (2 Corinthians 1:20). To Paul, every interpretation that centers on national Israel by itself, on its earthly and political covenant promises, fails to grasp the real heart and theological center of God's promise.

Without recognizing Jesus Christ as the Key, the Root, and the Center to all God's covenants with Israel (Revelation 22:16), any "literal" understanding of God's ancient covenants would only be a dramatic misunderstanding, any claim to its promised blessings, a presumption. "Even to this day when Moses is read, a veil covers their hearts. But whenever anyone turns to the Lord, the veil is taken away" (2 Corinthians 3:15-16). Without Christ or the Spirit, the application of Israel's covenant only hardens the heart. "The letter kills, but the Spirit gives life" (2 Corinthians 3: 6). Only when the Jew accepts the New Testament message that Jesus is the Messiah of prophecy and receives Christ as the Lord and Savior of his heart, will the darkening veil be removed from the Old Testament letters and will he be able to understand the true literal meaning of Scripture, the original truth-intention of the Old Testament. It is therefore necessary to make a fundamental distinction between a genuine literal interpretation and literalism or letterism. The key to the Old Testament is not a rationalistic method or principle, be it literalism or allegorism, but Christ Jesus, the Son of God, as revealed in the New Testament.

The Christian interpreter of the Old Testament is once and for all obliged to read the Hebrew Scriptures in the light of the New Testament as a whole, because the Old is interpreted authoritatively, under divine inspiration, in the New Testament as God's continuous history of salvation. Historic Christianity has always confessed that the New Testament is the goal and fulfillment of the Old.[24] G. E. Ladd represents the position of the Church of the ages when he states: "Our point of departure must be the way the New Testament interprets the Old Testament."[25] F. F. Bruce declares more specifically: "Our Lord's use of the OT may well serve as our standard and pattern in biblical interpretation; and Christians may further remind themselves that part of the Holy Spirit's present work is to open the Scriptures for them as the risen Christ did for the disciples on the Emmaus road."[26]

The Ecumenical Study Conference, held at Oxford, England, in 1949, accepted as "Guiding Principles for the Interpretation of the Bible," among others, this necessary theological presupposition:

> It is agreed that the unity of the Old and the New Testament is not to be found in any naturalistic development or in any static identity, but in the ongoing redemptive activity of God in the history of one people, reaching its fulfillment in Christ.

Accordingly it is of decisive importance for hermeneutical method to interpret the Old Testament in the light of the total revelation in the person of Jesus Christ, the Incarnate Word of God, from which arises the full Trinitarian faith of the Church.[27]

And regarding the theological interpretation of a passage, after the grammatical and historical exegesis is completed:

It is agreed that in the case of an Old Testament passage, one must examine and expound it in relation to the revelation of God to Israel both before and after its own period. Then the interpreter should turn to the New Testament in order to view the passage in that perspective. In this procedure the Old Testament passage may receive limitation and correction, and it may also disclose in the light of the New Testament a new and more profound significance, unknown to the original writer.

It is agreed that in the case of a New Testament passage one should examine it in the light of its settings and context; then turn to the Old Testament to discover its background in God's former revelation. Returning again to the New Testament one is able to see and expound the passage in the light of the whole scope of *Heilsgeschichte*. Here our understanding of a New Testament passage may be deepened through our apprehension of the Old.[28]

### Notes on Chapter 2

[1]Lewis S. Chafer, "Dispensationalism," *BSac* 93 (1936):448.

[2]Daniel P. Fuller, "The Hermeneutics of Dispensationalism" (dissertation, Northern Baptist Theological Seminary, Chicago, Ill., 1957), p. 25.

[3]Chafer, "Dispensationalism," pp. 406-407.

[4]John F. Walvoord, *The Revelation of Jesus Christ* (Chicago: Moody Press, 1967), p. 103.

[5]Charles C. Ryrie, *Dispensationalism Today* (Chicago: Moody Press, 1965), p. 97.

[6]Ibid., p. 96.

[7]Ibid., p. 158.

[8]Ibid.

[9]Ibid., p. 104.

[10]Ryrie (ibid., p. 88) states: "What check would there be on the

variety of interpretations which man's imagination could produce if there were not an objective standard which the literal principle provides?"

[11]Ibid., p. 94.

[12]"The aim of Zionism is to create for the Jewish people a home in Palestine secured by public law" (The Basel Program for World Jewry, 1897). The "Proclamation of Independence" of the State of Israel (1948) declares that the National Council of Palestinian Jews and the World Zionist Movement together appeal to "the natural and historic gifts of the Jewish people" to Palestine as their homeland and refers to their "great struggle for the fulfillment of the dream of generations for the redemption of Israel." See F. H. Epp, *Whose Land is Palestine?* (Grand Rapids, Mich.: Wm. B. Eerdmans Pub. Co., 1974), pp. 117, 191, 192.

[13]See S. Mowinckel, *He That Cometh* (Nashville, Tenn.: Abingdon Press, 1954), chapter 9, "The National Messiah."

[14]G. E. Ladd, *Crucial Questions About the Kingdom of God* (Grand Rapids, Mich.: Wm. B. Eerdmans Pub. Co., 1961), p. 115. Ladd shows that not even the *dying* Messiah in IV Ezra 7:27-31 has a vicarious purpose. Also G. Scholem, *The Messianic Idea in Judaism* (New York: Schocken Books, 1974), pp. 17-18.

[15]See the excellent treatise "Kingdom of God" by G. E. Ladd in *Baker's Dictionary of Theology,* ed. E. F. Harrison (Grand Rapids, Mich.: Baker Book House, 1973). Also his *A Theology of the New Testament* (Grand Rapids, Mich.: Wm. B. Eerdmans Pub. Co., 1974), chapter 4.

[16]T. W. Manson, *The Servant Messiah* (Grand Rapids, Mich.: Baker Book House, 1977; reprint of 1953 ed.), chapter 1, referring especially to the nature of the messianic hope in the *Psalms of Solomon* (8 and 17).

[17]Ibid., p. 36, note 3.

[18]Ladd, *Crucial Questions About the Kingdom of God,* p. 117.

[19]See R. Longenecker, *Biblical Exegesis in the Apostolic Period* (Grand Rapids, Mich.: Wm. B. Eerdmans Pub. Co., 1977), chapter 1, "Jewish Hermeneutics in the First Century," for some examples of "hyperliteralism." The literalist interpretation "was considered basic to all further exegetical developments" (p. 29). Cf. also Ramm, *Protestant Biblical Interpretation,* p. 45-48, who concludes: "There is one major lesson to be learned from rabbinical exegesis: the evils of *letterism.* In the exaltation of the very letters of the Scripture the true meaning of the Scripture was lost" (p. 48). Cf. G. F. Moore, *Judaism* (Cambridge: Harvard University Press, 1932), vol. 1, p. 248.

[20]See G. F. Hasel, "The Problem of the Center in the OT Theology Debate," *ZAW* 86 (1974):65-82.

[21]The extreme literalistic interpretation of Exodus 16:29 appears in the report of Flavius Josephus that on the Sabbath the Essenes even refused "to remove any vessel out of its place, nor go to stool thereon" (*Wars* II, 8, 9 [Josephus, *Complete Works*, trans. W. Whiston (Grand Rapids, Mich.: Kregel Publ., 1966)]).

[22]See F. F. Bruce, *Biblical Exegesis in the Qumran Texts* (Grand Rapids, Mich.: Wm. B. Eerdmans Pub. Co., 1959), pp. 9f., 15-17.

[23]See H. K. LaRondelle, *Perfection and Perfectionism*, Andrews University Monographs, Studies in Religion, Vol. 3, 3d ed. (Berrien Springs, Mich.: Andrews University Press, 1979), pp. 272-275.

[24]For the latest official Roman Catholic confession of the progressive unity of both Testaments, see *The Documents of Vatican II*, W. M. Abbott and J. Gallagher, eds. (New York: Guild Press, 1966), chapter 4, section 16, "Dogmatic Constitution on Divine Revelation."

[25]Ladd, *Crucial Questions About the Kingdom of God*, p. 139. Also his *The Last Things* (Grand Rapids, Mich.: Wm. B. Eerdmans Pub. Co., 1978), pp. 18, 19.

[26]F. F. Bruce in *Baker's Dictionary of Theology* (1973), p. 293.

[27]In G. Ernest Wright, "The Problem of Archaizing Ourselves," *Interpretation* 3 (1949):457f.

[28]In Wright, "The Problem of Archaizing Ourselves," *Interpretation* 3 (1949):458.

# 3

## The Literal and
## Allegorical Interpretations

We need to define as precisely as possible what we mean by the theological terms we employ. Such terms as "literalism," "allegorism," "literal," "allegorical," and "typological" are not used in the same sense by all parties. This causes confusion in the communication of ideas.

### *The Literal Interpretation*

First, what is meant by "literal" interpretation and by "literalism"? Dispensationalists define it as "giving to language its reasonable and grammatical meaning" or "the natural, literal, and grammatical way which the predictions imply" (Chafer[1]); as "the literal, normal, or plain meaning" (Ryrie[2]), the "primary, ordinary, normal, literal meaning" (D. Cooper as quoted and accepted by Hal Lindsey[3]).

There is here, however, a secret assumption implied which has axiomatic and fundamental value for dispensationalism: that literal exegesis of an Old Testament prophecy "demands" an identical or absolutely *literal fulfillment.* J. D. Pentecost declares, "According to the established principles of interpretation the Davidic covenant demands a literal fulfillment. This means that Christ must reign on David's throne on the earth over David's people forever."[4] Such a conclusion would seem to be valid only if the Old Testament is taken by itself, apart from the New Testament. The Christian interpreter, however, is bound by his faith in Christ to acknowledge the New Testament as the authoritative interpretation of the Old Testament promises. Here we already observe that the

23

scope of prophetic Bible interpretation for the Christian is larger than the task of Old Testament exegesis. It also includes, for the Christian interpreter, the study of the essential unity of the whole Bible and the patterns of promise and fulfillment in the interrelationships of the two Testaments.

The evangelical scholar B. Ramm calls the term "literalism" an ambiguous term because to some it stands negatively for "letterism." He therefore distinguishes literalism from the "literal" interpretation by taking "literal" in its dictionary (Webster's) designation as "the customary, the usual, the socially-acknowledged designations" of words.[5] He calls the literal method the "historico-grammatical" or "philological" method. Its goal is only *exegesis*, "to discover the original meaning and intention of the text"[6] in the light of the situation in which it was first written; it does *not* include the field of application and fulfillment. This distinction between exegesis and application is crucial, because they are not necessarily completely identical.

The *words* of Scripture are not intended to be an end in themselves but rather to serve as an instrument to convey a *meaning* or message. Words and meaning are not always synonymous, as is clear in figures of speech or in symbolic language. The essential point is therefore "to take the meaning of the Bible literally. Our conscience is to be bound by the Word of God! . . . It is the meaning of these Words, therefore, which we are to seek."[7] The literal or normal interpretation recognizes poetic symbolism in its attempt "to assign to Scripture its original, divinely intended meaning", that "which God willed for the passages to designate at the time in which He had it written."[8]

The literal or philological interpretation will not do justice to a piece of literature as a matter of course. But the literal exegesis must always be the necessary point of departure in both biblical and extra-biblical literature. All secondary meanings of documents, as figures of speech, allegories, types, parables, etc., find their basic control and meaning in the literal stratum of language. The literal interpretation will recognize the peculiar nature of each genre or type of literature with which it deals.

Ramm understands the "literal" interpretation of Scripture to stand independently between the extremes of literalism (or letterism) and allegorism (an uncontrolled allegorical method). He does not accept the dispensationalist assumption that the literal interpretation of the Old Testament predictions demands also a literal fulfillment. He explains: "In our use of the word *literal* we have in mind *literal* in the philological sense."[9] In this respect there is no difference between dispensational and reformation evangelicals. "The real issue in prophetic interpretation among evangelicals is this: *can prophetic literature be interpreted by the general method of grammatical exegesis, or is some special principle necessary?*"[10] This "special principle" has been commonly called by reformation evangelicals the "theological interpretation." These scholars state that it is absolutely necessary to complement the usual grammatical and historical interpretations with a third (the theological interpretation) in order to maintain the theological unity and spiritual dimension of both Testaments. L. Berkhof calls this theological dimension "the deeper sense of Scripture,"[11] which is not a second sense added to the grammatical meaning, but is the proper sense of Scripture. He states:

> The real meaning of Scripture does not always lie on the surface. There is no truth in the assertion that the intent of the secondary authors [God being the primary author], determined by the grammatico-historical method, always exhausts the sense of Scripture, and represents in all its fullness the meaning of the Holy Spirit.[12]

Other Bible scholars also stress that an "exegesis that stops short of the theology of the text is an incomplete exegesis"[13] and that even Israel's prophets themselves attempted to fathom their own predictions (1 Peter 1:10, 11), compelled to confess ignorance over their own visions (Daniel 8:27, Zechariah 4:13) or words (Daniel 12:8).[14] In other words, grammatico-historical exegesis is not sufficient for the interpretation of Holy Scripture. Theological exegesis is also necessary.[15]

Dispensationalism, however, categorically rejects such a "theological" principle of hermeneutics because it would allow a blending of Israel and the Church, placing a non-literal application beside a literal exegesis of Old Testament prophetic Scripture. We need to consider, however, the fact "that identity of phrase [in the NT quotations of OT prophecy] does not necessarily imply absolute identity of meaning."[16]

Dispensationalism does not want to deny the unity of the Scriptures, but starts from another assumption. Not the plan of salvation, but "the glory of God is the governing principle and overall purpose."[17] On the basis of the primacy of this doxological principle, with its compartmentalized purposes for Israel and the Church, dispensationalists accuse all other evangelicals of a "reductive error" (Walvoord) and of compromising the principle of literalism, especially in the realm of prophetic interpretation.

C. I. Scofield stated unambiguously that the specific *prophetic* sections of Scripture must be interpreted and applied with absolute literalism: "Prophecies may never be spiritualized, but are always literal."[18] Such an absolute literalism in prophetic interpretation, however, leads irrevocably to a forced interpretation. Not only must Israel be restored as a national theocracy, but also Edom, Moab, and Ammon must then be restored as nations, because the prediction reads: "They [Israelites] will lay hands on Edom and Moab, and the Ammonites will be subject to them" (Isaiah 11:14). Such a consistent literalism may not unjustly be called "the insanity of literalism."[19] The historic Christian position recognizes that the literal exegesis of Old Testament Scripture permits the typological application as employed by Christ and His apostles in the New Testament. This acknowledges that the Old Testament is "a Christian book."[20]

Dispensational literalism does not allow that Jesus Christ provided a new perspective for interpreting the Old Testament. Dispensationalism is therefore basically oriented to the Old Covenant instead of to the Cross.[21]

### The Allegorical Interpretation

Regarding the terms "allegory," "allegorism," and "allegorical," we observe no uniform understanding and use among Christian interpreters. General agreement prevails in defining an allegory as a more extensive form of a metaphor or figure of speech. An allegory is a story which contains several points of comparison. It tells a truth in terms of a narrative. Some biblical examples are: the allegories of old age under the figure of a deteriorating house, in Ecclesiastes 12:3-7; of Israel as a vine brought from Egypt, in Psalm 80:8-15; of the false prophets in Israel who built flimsy walls, in Exodus 13:8-16.[22]

Christ used allegories in his parables of the good shepherd in John 10:1-16 and of the vine in John 15:1-8. Paul writes a profound allegory about the armor of the Christian, in Ephesians 6:11-17. All these are intended to be allegories and recognized as such, as a legitimate way of teaching truth.

It is a different story if an interpreter would *allegorize* a plainly historical narrative in the Bible. Such allegorizing transforms the narrative into a springboard for teaching an idea which is different from that intended by the Bible writer. Whenever an allegorical interpretation arbitrarily converts a historical narrative into teaching a spiritual or theological truth, such a speculative allegorizing is negatively called an *"allegorism."* It imposes a meaning on the Bible text that is not really there. It is added to the text by the interpreter only for the purpose of edification and finding spiritual truths and deep meanings. Allegorizing was the popular method among Jewish expositors (especially Philo), the early Christian church fathers, and the medieval scholastic theologians.[23] B. Ramm rejects such allegorizations because they assume a "plural meaning of Scripture. The unity of the sense of Scripture eliminates all allegorizing of Scripture, ancient and modern."[24]

It is, however, a fact that Paul uses an allegorical application when he deals with the story of Sarah and Hagar of Genesis 21 in Galatians 4:24-31, in order "to heighten the contrast for his readers between bondage and freedom."[25] Paul indeed declares in Galatians 4:24 that he interprets the Genesis narrative "allegorically," which is "figuratively" (NIV). In 1 Corinthians 9:9 Paul gives an allegorical interpretation of a legal text in Deuteronomy 25:4. Even when this procedure admittedly is rare in the New Testament, it should keep us from condemning each allegorical interpretation of a historical narrative or legal text. Paul declares that he now gives an allegorical application which he builds on, not exchanges for, the historical truth of a particular narrative in Genesis. Allegorical interpretation as such cannot be described as "anti-historical in character."[26] It should not be defined by its aberrations in Philo but rather by its homogeneous allegorizing which remains in basic harmony with the general Christian doctrines.

Criticism of the allegorical method should therefore concentrate on its misuse, which has lost its respect for the historical reality and form of the original texts.[27] If one defines allegorizing as "the interpretation of a text in terms of something else, irrespective of what that something else is,"[28] no norm or standard is set by which one can determine what constitutes a legitimate or an illegitimate spiritualizing. One scholar has therefore argued that valid allegorical interpretation must rest on "a *genuine analogy*" between the original meaning and the given application.[29] Such allegorizing presupposes the unity and continuity of biblical revelation. In other words, in false allegorizing there is no organic relationship, no analogical basis, no existing harmony between the Scripture text and its mystical "something else" to which it is related. Philo's allegorizing and rabbinic allegorizing were illegitimate because they related the Scripture text to the oral traditions of the fathers. Jesus condemned such allegorizing when he said to the religious leaders of His day that they had nullified the Word of God by their tradition (Matthew 15:6). Likewise the patristic and medieval allegorizing of Scripture was illegitimate because it did not establish an organic relationship between the Bible text and the Roman Catholic traditions. This is the reason why Luther and Calvin explicitly rejected the method of allegorizing as their principle of Scripture interpretation. The Reformers started from the assumption that the Old Testament and the New Testament are organically related to each other. In spite of the differences in the forms of administering God's grace, the two Testaments are substantially the same, both teaching redemption by one and the same Mediator and Redeemer, both having one hope and one fellowship with the same covenant God, summed up in the words, "I will be your God and you shall be my people."

Because of this fundamental unity in Christ and this theological analogy or correspondence, it is legitimate to interpret the Old in terms of the New. Some refuse to distinguish, therefore, between an allegorical interpretation which is homogeneous with the total Scripture and a typological interpretation. It seems more correct, however, to conclude that Paul's incidental allegorizing "rests in a typological framework and is not allegory in the usual Jewish or Hellenistic sense."[30] In Paul's allegorizing of the Sarah-Hagar stories (of Genesis 21) in Galatians 4:24-31, he points out the theological meaning which is *common*—the analogical basis—to both the Old Testament stories and the historical situation of present Jerusalem (Judaism) and the Church.

What does dispensationalism teach with regard to allegorical interpretations? It charges the non-dispensationalists

with allegorizing or spiritualizing when it comes to the interpretation of prophecy and, consequently, being inconsistent in
their use of the literal interpretation of Scripture. Ryrie asserts,
"The dispensationalist claims to apply his literal principle to all
Scripture, including prophecy, while the non-dispensationalist
does not apply it to prophecy."[31]

Is it really true that dispensationalism consistently applies
its principle of literalism "to all Scripture"? The annotations of
the *Scofield Reference Bible* frequently apply allegorical
(figurative) and typological interpretations to the Old Testament narratives. The following examples are found in the *New
Scofield Reference Bible* (1967). The whole Old Testament
book Song of Solomon (or Song of Songs) has a threefold interpretation: (1) of Solomon's love for a Shulamite girl; (2) *"as a
figurative revelation* of God's love for His covenant people,
Israel, the wife of the Lord (Is 54:5-6; Jer 2:2 . . .)"; (3) *"as an
allegory of Christ's love for His heavenly bride, the Church* (2
Cor 11:1-2; Eph 5:25-32)" (p. 705; emphasis added).

Here dispensationalism officially and explicitly adopts the
principle of *allegorizing* an Old Testament narrative, even a
whole book. As its justification for this wholesale allegorizing of
eight chapters of Song of Songs, it states that the love of the
divine Bridegroom, "symbolized here by Solomon's love," follows "the *analogy* of the marriage relationship" (p. 705, emphasis added). Thus dispensationalism does adopt an allegorical or
spiritualizing interpretation of a whole Old Testament historical
book on the basis of a twofold analogy: (1) the analogy between
the marriage covenant and God's covenant with Israel; and (2)
the analogy between God's covenant with Israel and Christ's love
for His Church. This is a twofold allegorizing of a historical love
story: first, with regard to Israel; secondly, with regard to the
Church of Christ. The given Scripture references support this
double allegorical interpretation as a legitimate hermeneutic.
But this means the acceptance of a basic theological analogy
between the old and the new dispensation, the old and the new
covenant, the Old and New Testament. These are therefore
theologically, not heterogeneous or dissimilar, but homogeneous or similar to one another.

The *New Scofield Reference Bible* also interprets other
Old Testament passages allegorically. The scarlet line which
Rahab bound in the window of her home at Jericho (Joshua

2:21) is applied allegorically because of its red color "of safety through sacrifice (Heb 9:19-22)" (p. 261). Most interpreters reject this allegorism as an illegitimate spiritualizing. The passage of Israel through the Jordan River (in Joshua 3) is said to be "a figure of our death with Christ (Rom 6:3-4, 6-11)" (p. 261).

The story of Joseph in Genesis 37-45 is allegorized because of its "many analogies" between Joseph's history and Christ's, with the conclusion "that Joseph was a type of Christ" (p. 53). Joseph's Egyptian wife Asenath then "portrays the Church" (p. 59, on Genesis 41:45). The wife of Isaac, Rebekah, is considered "a type of the Church" (p. 34).

In the book of Ruth, Boaz "points to Christ; Ruth portrays those who enter into a new life through trust in Him" (p. 317). Eve, whom Adam called "Woman" to indicate that she was taken "out of Man" (Genesis 2:23), is given the interpretation: "The woman is a type of the Church, the bride of Christ (Eph 5:25-32)" (p. 6).

It becomes quite clear that dispensationalism constantly acknowledges christological and ecclesiological types and analogies in the Old Testament narratives, with an appeal to the New Testament for support.[32] It is highly remarkable that dispensationalism accepts the christological-ecclesiological principle of typology and allegorizing for Old Testament interpretation, while its own dogmatic axiom declares that Israel and the Church are basically *dissimilar* and *incongruous* to each other. It considers the Church of Christ, therefore, merely as an interim phenomenon which was *not foreseen* and intended by the Old Testament. Dispensationalism tries to harmonize this apparent inconsistency of opposite principles — that the Church of Christ is *not predicted* in the Old Testament, while nevertheless the Church is *prefigured* in the Old Testament — by the device of compartmentalizing Scripture into two separate sections which would require two different principles of interpretation: *history* and *prophecy* within the Old Testament. The history of Israel must be interpreted typologically and allegorically in view of Christ and the Church. The prophecy of Israel must be interpreted exclusively by a literalism which refuses to recognize any type or figure of the Church. While dispensationalists boast of their literalism, they prove to be inconsistent.[33] Dispensationalism operates with two basically different canons of interpreting the Old Testament:

the christological-ecclesiological principle on the basis of New Testament authority for the historical part; the principle of literalism for the prophetic parts, which fundamentally denies the christological-ecclesiological fulfillment.

What causes this inconsistent and conflicting double hermeneutic for the Old Testament in dispensationalism? What is the basis for this (New-Testament-authority-defying) literalism regarding Israel's prophecy. It is dispensationalism's unique view of the revelation and inspiration of Israel's prophecy: "prophecy is prewritten history"[34], or, in the words of C. I. Scofield, "Historical Scriptures have an allegorical or spiritual significance . . . [In prophetic Scriptures] we reach the ground of *absolute literalness.*"[35]

Here we face the frank admission that the principle of literalism is not applied consistently "to all Scripture" by dispensationalism, as Ryrie asserted, but only to a selected part of Scripture: to prophecy. What is the justification for this switch to absolute literalness in the realm of fulfillment of each prophetic word in the Old Testament? Is this use of a double hermeneutic taught in the New Testament?

Dispensationalism accepts a theological, organic relationship between the Old Testament history of Israel (persons, redemptive events, etc., as types of the Church) and the Church of Christ, yet rejects this organic relationship between Israel's prophecy and the Church. The assertion is made, "The Davidic covenant demands a literal fulfillment. This means that Christ must reign on David's throne on the earth over David's people forever."[36] The application of the Davidic covenant to Christ's present messianic reign over the Church from His heavenly throne of grace (cf. Acts 2:30-36; 1 Corinthians 15:25; Ephesians 1:20-23) is rejected by dispensationalism as an allegorization or wrong hermeneutic for prophetic interpretation. For the historical and poetic books of the Old Testament the allegorical and typological method is adequate because there is an admitted analogical basis. But for prophetic interpretation this New Testament method is sharply rejected, because here is supposedly no longer any analogical basis between Israel and the Church. Dispensationalism cannot admit an organic relationship between prophecy and the Christian Church. The consequences of dispensational literalism can be summarized as follows:

In short, Paul's words must be interpreted in such a way as not to conflict with the hopes and claims of the Zionists! The present glorious age of the preaching of the gospel of the grace of God to every creature must be regarded as a merely temporal interruption in the Old Testament program for the glorification of Israel.[37]

The question is therefore: Does the New Testament use the christological typological method only for the *historical* parts of the Old Testament and switch to the method of "absolute literalness" for the *prophetic* parts of the Old Testament? How does the New Testament interpret the prophetic perspectives of the Abrahamic, Mosaic, and Davidic covenants? Only when these questions have been answered correctly has one received the "objective standard" to judge whether the dispensationalist double hermeneutic is adequate or whether it is a speculative, modern construction which exalts its extra-biblical canon of interpretation above the authority of the New Testament.

In summary, we maintain the validity of the grammatical-historical and the theological principles of exegesis for all Scripture interpretation. Recognizing the principles of progressive revelation, specifically between the Old Testament prophets and the New Testament witness of Jesus Christ (Hebrews 1:1-2; John 1:7-18), we accept the essential unity of both Testaments which allows the meaning of any part of Scripture—including the prophetic parts—to be ultimately determined by the totality of Scripture. This classical Protestant hermeneutic, known as the *sola Scriptura* principle, seems to be accepted as an axiom of faith by all conservative evangelical Christians.[38]

### Notes on Chapter 3

[1]L. S. Chafer, *Systematic Theology* (Dallas: Dallas Seminary Press, 1947), vol. 4, pp. 259, 288.

[2]Ryrie, *Dispensationalism Today*, p. 96.

[3]Hal Lindsey, *The Late Great Planet Earth* (New York: Bantam, 1973), p. 40; quoting David Cooper, *When Gog's Armies Meet the Almighty in the Land of Israel.*

[4]J. D. Pentecost, *Things to Come* (Findlay, Ohio: Dunham Pub. Co., 1961), p. 112.

[5]Ramm, *Protestant Biblical Interpretation*, pp. 114, 119ff.

[6]Ibid., p. 115.

[7]R. H. Stein, *The Method and Message of Jesus' Teachings* (Philadelphia: Westminster Press, 1978), p. 10.

[8]J. Barton Payne, *Encyclopedia of Biblical Prophecy* (New York: Harper and Row, 1973), p. 43.

[9]Ramm, *Protestant Biblical Interpretation*, p. 241.

[10]Ibid., p. 244 (italics of B. Ramm).

[11]See discussion by L. Berkhof, *Principles of Biblical Interpretation* (Grand Rapids, Mich.: Baker Book House, 1964), chapter 7, pp. 133-166. Quotation is from p. 134.

[12]Ibid., pp. 59, 60.

[13]J. Bright, *The Authority of the Old Testament* (Grand Rapids, Mich.: Baker Book House, 1977), p. 171.

[14]Payne, *Encyclopedia of Biblical Prophecy*, p. 5; cf. p. 45.

[15]F. F. Bruce in *Baker's Dictionary of Theology*, p. 293.

[16]R. B. Girdlestone, *A Systematic Guide to Biblical Prophecy* (Grand Rapids, Mich.: Kregel, 1955), p. 87. See chapter 7 for examples.

[17]Ryrie, *Dispensationalism Today*, p. 102.

[18]Quoted in C. B. Bass, *Backgrounds to Dispensationalism* (Grand Rapids, Mich.: Baker, 1977; reprint of 1960), p. 150.

[19]A. B. Davidson, *Old Testament Prophecy* (Edinburgh: T. & T. Clarke, 1905), p. 476.

[20]Ramm, *Protestant Biblical Interpretation*, p. 258.

[21]See Bass, *Backgrounds to Dispensationalism*, p. 151.

[22]See M. S. Terry, *Biblical Hermeneutics* (New York: Eaton & Mains, 1890), pp. 214ff.

[23]See examples of Rabbi Aqiba who believed on principle that a mystical meaning was to be found in every letter of Scripture, in F. W. Farrar, *History of Interpretation* (New York: E. P. Dutton, 1886), pp. 71-77; on Philo's allegorizing, see pp. 139-152; on Scholasticism, pp. 266-274.

[24]Ramm, *Protestant Biblical Interpretation*, pp. 111, 223.

[25]A. B. Michelson, *Interpreting the Bible* (Grand Rapids, Mich.: Wm. B. Eerdmans Pub. Co., 1963), p. 231.

[26]See J. Barr, *Old and New in Interpretation* (New York: Harper and Row, 1966), pp. 103ff. He argues that allegorical interpretation is not basically different from typological interpretation within the New Testament. Cf. also F. F. Bruce in *Baker's Dictionary*

*of Theology* (1973), p. 293, "One form of allegorization is typological interpretation . . ."

[27]Barr, *Old and New in Interpretation*, pp. 115-117. Also C. H. Dodd, *The Bible Today* (Cambridge: Cambridge University Press, 1946), p. 16. Also C. H. Dodd, *The Old Testament in the New* (Philadelphia: Fortress Press, Facet Books BS 3, 1971), pp. 5-8.

[28]H. A. Wolfson, *Philo*, vol. 1 (Cambridge: Harvard University Press, 1947), p. 134.

[29]P. K. Jewett, "Concerning the Allegorical Interpretation of Scripture," *WTJ* 17 (1954):1-20. Quotation on p. 13.

[30]E. E. Ellis, *The Pauline Use of the Old Testament* (Grand Rapids, Mich.: Wm. B. Eerdmans Pub. Co., 1957), p. 127; cf. pp. 5ff.

[31]Ryrie, *Dispensationalism Today*, p. 90.

[32]See *NSRB*, p. 6, for the dispensational definition of a biblical type, based on "explicit N.T. authority."

[33]See O. T. Allis, *Prophecy and the Church* (Philadelphia: Presbyterian and Reformed Pub. Co., 1974; reprint of 1947), p. 21.

[34]A. C. Gaebelein, *The Prophet Daniel*, pp. 1, 166; as quoted in Allis, *Prophecy and the Church*, p. 26.

[35]*Scofield Bible Correspondence Course* (Chicago: Moody Bible Institute), pp. 45-46, as quoted in Bass, *Backgrounds to Dispensationalism*, p. 150.

[36]Pentecost, *Things to Come*, p. 112. See, however, G. E. Ladd's more biblical interpretation in *The Last Things*, pp. 17-18.

[37]Allis, *Prophecy and the Church*, p. 50.

[38]E.g., B. Ramm, *Protestant Biblical Interpretation*, p. 105, states: "The entire Holy Scripture is the context and guide for understanding the particular passages of Scripture." J. W. Wenham, *Christ and the Bible* (Downers Grove, Ill.: Inter-Varsity Press, 1973), p. 10: "Both in the case of the Bible and in the case of the world of nature, the parts must be understood from the whole, not the whole from the parts. A God-created theology demands a God-centered methodology." C. C. Ryrie, *The Basis of the Premillennial Faith* (Neptune, N.J.: Loiseaux Brothers, 1966), p. 37: "It [the analogy of faith in Scripture] not only uses parallel passages in Scripture but also regulates the interpretation of each passage in conformity with the whole tenor of revealed truth. . . . The application of this principle of hermeneutics means the harmonization of all the Bible." For the Seventh-day Adventist position on the *"sola Scriptura,"* see L. E. Froom, *Movement of Destiny* (Washington, D.C.: Review and Herald Pub. Assn., 1971), chapter 5.

# 4

# The Typological
# Interpretation

Typological interpretation is distinct from both the grammatical-historical method and the allegorical approach. Grammatical-historical exegesis focuses exclusively on one period of time as the context of Scripture. It must be asked, however, whether the meaning of an Old Testament event or prophecy can be determined fully by the original historical situation. The meaning of single events can often be fully understood only in the light of their consequences in later history.

From the start, Israel's faith in Yahweh as sovereign Lord of history contained a fundamental hope for the future (Genesis 3:15; 12:2-3). This hope was concentrated, not on national exaltation and material prosperity as such, but on the coming presence of God in glory among Israel (Isaiah 40:5) and on His final intervention to restore paradise lost for His people and for the whole earth (Isaiah 2; 9; 11; 52; Psalms 2; 46; 48; 72). Israel's hope was built on the promise of the coming kingdom of God: "Your God reigns!" (Isaiah 52:7). Among all the nations of the Oriental world, only Israel developed an eschatology, a hope in which God gradually unfolded His promise, corrected false, nationalistic hopes, and constantly transcended Israel's concepts of His kingdom by pointing to a future fulfillment that would exceed all Israel's earthly expectations (Isaiah 64:4; cf. 1 Corinthians 2:9).[1] In its communal worship Israel sang of its God as the Savior and Hope of the world: "O God our Savior, the hope of all the ends of the earth and of the farthest seas . . ." (Psalm 65:5; cf. Deuteronomy 7:9-10; Isaiah 2:1-4).

As soon as Jesus of Nazareth was born and dedicated to God in the temple of Jerusalem, a certain Simeon, who "was waiting for the consolation of Israel," took the baby Jesus in his arms and praised God:

> Sovereign Lord, as you have promised,
>   you now dismiss your servant in peace.
> For my eyes have seen your salvation,
>   which you have prepared in the sight of all people,
> a light for revelation to the Gentiles
>   and for glory to your people Israel.
>                                     —Luke 2:29-32

The earliest Jewish Christians believed that Jesus was the Messiah of prophecy, the goal and fulfillment of the Old Testament promise. The New Testament is the fruit of their conviction that God had fulfilled His promise in Christ Jesus (2 Corinthians 1:20). The arrival of the Davidic king and the outpouring of the Spirit of God, as promised for the last days by the prophets (Joel 2:28f.; Isaiah 32:15; Zechariah 12:10), meant to the apostles that the end of the old age had come (1 Corinthians 10:11) and the predicted era of the messianic reign, or "last days," had now begun (Acts 2:16ff.). A profound sense of the dramatic unity of God's saving work for Israel in the past (the exodus deliverances from Egypt and Babylon) and the resurrection and present reign of Christ, took hold of the apostles. They began to read the whole Old Testament in a new light—in the light of its fulfillment in Jesus Christ and His own Israel. For the early Christians, Christ and His Church became the full historical context of the Old Testament! Through the Spirit of God the apostles' eyes were opened to the dimly understood meanings of the sanctuary ritual and the redemptive acts of Israel's history. The New Testament writers, under divine inspiration, disclosed surprising correspondences between God's redemptive acts in the Old Testament and the salvation they had beheld in Jesus Christ. The study of such historical correspondences is called *Christian typology*.

A valid definition of a biblical type may be seen in the following description:

> A type is an institution, historical event, or person, ordained by God, which effectively prefigures some truth connected with Christianity.[2]

This theological definition draws a clear line of demarcation between typology and allegory in that biblical types are not fictitious, but real and meaningful in Israel's salvation history, e.g., the sanctuary, the exodus, Abraham, and others.

But how does it become evident that we have to do here with prefigurative types of Christ and His salvation? Is it the fact that there are some striking resemblances and similarities with the life and work of Christ Jesus? C. T. Fritsch answers, "No." "Typology is not just a matter of collecting all the resemblances between the Old and New Testaments, but rather of understanding the underlying redemptive and revelational process which begins in the Old Testament and finds its fulfillment in the New."[3] As an example he mentions that "the covenant of Sinai becomes a type of that perfect covenant relation between God and man in Christ, clearly adumbrated in the new Covenant of Jeremiah 31." In other words, an Old Testament institution, event, or person only becomes a clear and understandable type in the light of Christ and His covenant people as the antitype. This conclusion exposes the dispensational compartmentalizing of Israel and the Church as a forced literalism. It is the authority of the New Testament which establishes the divinely *pre-ordained* connection between a type and antitype and discloses the *predictive* nature of the type. Typology is based on the Christian conviction of faith that Jesus is the Messiah of Israel's prophecy and that the New Testament is a living continuation and completion of the Hebrew Scriptures. Consequently: "The organic relationship between the type and antitype is just one of the many evidences of the organic relationship between the Old and New Testaments."[4]

Our primary inquiry is concerned with the question whether Christ and the New Testament writers were in principle engaged in typological thinking. It seems clear that it was Jesus Himself who introduced into Judaism the new idea that the time of the antitypes had arrived by His startling claims that His messianic mission was "greater than" Jonah's prophetic mission (Matthew 12:41); "greater than" Solomon's wisdom (Matthew 12:42); greater than David's kingship (cf. Mark 2:25-28). He even stated, "I tell you that one greater than the temple is here" (Matthew 12:6). In this respect He declared that His self-sacrificial death would provide the "blood of the (new) covenant, which is poured out for many" (Mark 14:24). In all these sayings Jesus presented himself as the ultimate reality to which all types, symbols, and messianic prophecies in Israel's salvation economy had pointed. Seeing Himself as the antitype of Israel's sacred temple ritual and of its anointed public officers, Jesus announced also the fulfillment of the messianic age (Luke 4:16-21), of the arrival of the kingdom or reign of God (Matthew 12:28), and of the outpouring of the Spirit of God (Luke 24:49; Acts 1:8); in short, of the eschatological time. Jesus' typology, just as Israel's prophecy, is characterized by its climactic fulfillment in eschatological time, in the "last days" (cf. Hebrew 1:1-2).[5] To Jesus, His mission to fulfill the Hebrew Scriptures and Israel's historical types possessed both a redemptive and an eschatological significance.

The New Testament writers continued Jesus' typological thinking in their applications of the Old Testament to their own apostolic mandate and gospel mission.

The whole New Testament is essentially characterized by the typological and eschatological application of the Old Testament, motivated and directed by the Holy Spirit.[6] Although L. Goppelt recognizes different lines of connection between the Old and the New Testaments, he comes to the conclusion: "Among the various ways in which the New Testament applies the Old Testament, typology ranks as its predominant and most characteristic way of interpretation."[7] In the epistles of Paul—especially Romans 5:12-19 and 1 Corinthians 10: 1-11—and in the Letter to the Hebrews, Goppelt observes the typological pattern most prominently and systematically. He notes, however, that Paul's theology of the Old Testament history is determined by his faith experience with the risen and glorified Christ Jesus. In other words, the full sense of the Old Testament Scriptures and types is disclosed and can be grasped only from the position of faith in Christ. As Paul declares of his Jewish contemporaries:

> Even to this day when Moses is read, a veil covers their hearts. But whenever anyone turns to the Lord [Jesus], the veil is taken away . . . Only in Christ is it taken away (2 Corinthians 3:15-16, 14).

It seems generally agreed that Paul uses the term *typos* in a historically new sense for typology in Romans 5:14, where he calls Adam literally *"a type of the one to come."* Paul interprets the narrative of Genesis 3 concerning the fallen Adam in the light of the risen Christ and announces, under the Holy

Spirit, a typological relation between Adam and Christ. This means that Adam stands as an advance presentation of the future Adam, Christ Jesus (see 1 Corinthians 15:45, 47). The correspondence between Adam and Christ is of an antithetical nature which nevertheless maintains one basic similarity: both men were appointed by God as heads of the human race and lived a life which was of decisive and universal significance for mankind. The *New Scofield Reference Bible* acknowledges (in a note on Genesis 5:1), "Adam, as the natural head of the race (Luke 3:38) is a contrasting type of Christ, the Head of the new creation." While Adam caused the universal fall of man in sin and death, Christ's victory over Satan availed for man "much more" (Romans 5:17) than Adam lost: righteousness (justification) and life eternal (resurrection; 1 Corinthians 15:22; Romans 5:17-19).

In addition, Paul thinks typologically when he interprets God's acts in Israel's past history in the light of Christ and His Church in 1 Corinthians 10:1-11.[8] Some, however, take this Pauline passage merely as a moral exhortation in which the story of ancient Israel functions exclusively as a warning "example" for the moral sanctification of the Corinthian church. It is certainly true that the apostle tries to rectify a basic misunderstanding of the Christian sacraments (baptism and the Lord's Supper) by the Corinthians by means of his warning illustration of Israel's moral failure (1 Corinthians 10:1-5). One would miss, however, the specific teleological thrust and eschatological significance of Paul's admonition to the Corinthian church if the terms *typoi* (1 Corinthians 10:6) and *typikos* (1 Corinthians 10:11) are denied the theological sense which Paul gives to *typos* in his typology of Romans 5:14.[9] Paul presses home his exhortations within the context of the messianic age by using an advance presentation in Israel of some reality to come in Christ Jesus. It was not from an isolated Old testament exegesis that Paul arrived at this forward-looking dimension of Israel's salvation history. From his position as a Christian apostle of the Church, Paul, through the Spirit of prophecy, saw Israel's salvation-historical events as types for the eschatological community of the Messiah, "for us [the Church] on whom the fulfillment of the ages has come" (1 Corinthians 10:11). In fact, to Paul "these things . . . were written down" (1 Corinthians 10:11) specifically for the Church, the last-days' people of God.

The correspondence lies primarily in the essential similarity of God's acts of deliverance and judgment for Israel and the Church. It is the same holy God who redeemed and claimed Israel and the Church. Paul calls Moses and the Israelites simply "our forefathers" (1 Corinthians 10:1). This expresses the theological unity of Israel and the Church. Both participated in the redeeming and sustaining grace of Christ (1 Corinthians 10:4). So, likewise, is God's judgment on Israel a prefiguration of His judgment on Christians who abuse His grace in Christ.[10]

Yet there is more than theological analogy or correspondence in New Testament typology. There is also messianic progress or intensification and eschatological completion beyond the similarity. Paul's moral exhortation to the Corinthian church contains more than the presupposition that the God of Israel is the same moral God of the Church and that He will save and judge the Church in accordance with His acts in ancient Israel (1 Corinthians 10:6). Paul saw Israel's Exodus redemption as a pattern or type which pointed forward "in a remote, concealed, typical sense" (P. Fairbairn)[11] to the cross of Christ. Because Christ was sacrificed as the real Passover Lamb (1 Corinthians 5:7), in the "fullness of time" (Galatians 4:4), all who apply His sacrificial blood to their hearts and lives are the Israel of the new Exodus. Christ gave the new-covenant people of God new sacraments (baptism and the Lord's Supper) and set them on a pilgrimage to the ultimate rest in the New Jerusalem (Hebrews 4).

The Church, as the eschatological Israel, with its new covenant in the blood of Christ, is the fulfillment of God's plan with ancient Israel. The new covenant possesses a glory which far surpasses that of the old covenant (2 Corinthians 3). Since the divine glory left the old temple (Matthew 23:38), the Church of Christ has become the living temple of God on earth (2 Corinthians 3:16-18). Now that "the end(s) of the ages" (1 Corinthians 10:11), the completion of the whole old dispensation, has arrived, the messianic community must follow Christ as the King of Israel and obey His Word (2 Corinthians 7:1). Israel's disobedience during her pilgrimage through the wilderness is, according to Hebrews 4:11, "an illustrative example" (hypodeigma) for the Church on her pilgrimage:

> There remains, then, a Sabbath-rest for the people of God . . .
> Let us, therefore, make every effort to enter that rest, so that

no one will fall by following their example of disobedience (Hebrews 4:9, 11).

Goppelt concludes that "under Paul's influence *typos* became a hermeneutical term in the whole Church."[12] He refers to the later use of the term *antitypon* in 1 Peter 3:21. Peter literally writes that baptism is an "antitype" or "counterpart" of Noah's deliverance from the flood. One may therefore conclude from Peter's typology, "It is only in the light of the antitype, then, that the full significance of the Old Testament type becomes clear. It may be said, therefore, that it is the antitype which determines the identity of the Old Testament type of making clear its deeper, spiritual meaning."[13] In other words, the key to the understanding of the nature and identity of a type in the Old Testament should be sought in the New Testament's interpretation of the Old.

In addition to a horizontal typology, the New Testament develops an explicitly vertical typology, in which Mount Zion, Jerusalem, Israel's tabernacle, and the Levitical priesthood serve as a shadow or reflection of *heavenly* originals (see Hebrews 8:5; Acts 7:44 [cf. Exodus 25:40]; 12:22 [cf. Galatians 4:26]). Hebrews connects Israel's tabernacle directly with Christ's work of salvation in heaven. The main section, Hebrews 8:1-10:18, explains that Christ's present reign as King-Priest at the right hand of God (8:1; 10:12) is the intended eschatological fulfillment of the Old Testament types and shadows of Israel. The clear implication of this progression in salvation history from the old age or dispensation to the messianic age is the *dis*continuity of Levitical priesthood and law, of earthly sacrifices and sanctuary, and of a Davidic kingship on an earthly throne. In the resurrection and ascension of Christ "a better hope is introduced, by which we draw near to God" (Hebrews 7:18). Christ has once and for all fulfilled and "set aside" or "annulled" the whole old regulation of types and shadows (Hebrews 7:18; 10:9). The author of Hebrews refers predominantly to the christological fulfillment of the unique promise to the Davidic King in Psalm 110:1 and 4:

> The LORD says to my Lord:
> "Sit at my right hand
> until I make your enemies
> a footstool for your feet."
> The LORD has sworn

and will not change his mind:
"You are a priest forever,
in the order of Melchizedek."

The context of these Psalm verses indicates that this divine
promise applied first of all to the reign of the Davidic King on
his earthly throne in Jerusalem (verses 2, 3). However, both the
author of Hebrews and the apostle Peter *transfer* the throne of
David from its earthly location in Jerusalem to God's throne in
heaven (Hebrews 1:3, 13; 8:1; 10:12, 13; 12:1; Acts 2:36).
Filled with the Spirit of God on the historic day of Pentecost,
Peter proclaimed to the Jews in Jerusalem:

> Therefore let all Israel be assured of this: *God has made this
> Jesus,* whom you crucified, *both Lord and Christ* (Acts 2:36;
> emphasis added).

The title "Lord" means sovereign ruler, and "Christ"
means Messiah or Anointed One. Christ Jesus, by His ascension
to heaven, *has entered* into His messianic reign, seated at the
right hand of God (Hebrews 1:13; Revelation 3:21). He will
continue to reign until He has put all His enemies under His
feet (1 Corinthians 15:25). New Testament scholars agree that
the heavenly nature of this messianic reign was unforeseen in
the Old Testament. There his reign is from Jerusalem over Israel (Psalm 132:11). But, "In the New Testament his reign is
from heaven and is universal in its scope."[14] It should be clear
that the author of Hebrews understood Psalm 110 in a different and higher sense than had the Old Testament author.[15]
The surprising truth of the christological fulfillment of the
Davidic covenant is the special burden of this epistle. Christ,
ruling from His throne of grace in heaven as the messianic
*King*, in unity with His office as the messianic *High Priest*,
is the message of the vertical typology of Hebrews. The New
Testament application of Psalm 110:1 to Christ's present
rulership is regarded as of fundamental importance for the
apostolic gospel.[16]

Instead of teaching a "postponement" of Christ's Davidic
kingship, or assuming any gap between Psalm 110:1 and 2 as
dispensationalism asserts,[17] Hebrews declares that Christ, by
God's ordination, has begun to fulfill the Davidic covenant by
ruling over the Church and all powers, authorities, and angels.
Reigning from God's throne of grace (Hebrews 4:16) in the

almighty power of God, Christ "is able to save completely those who come to God through him, because he always lives to intercede for them" (Hebrews 7:25). Already in the present age *"God placed all things under his feet . . ."* (Ephesians 1:20-22; emphasis added), because Christ is now seated at God's right hand. Now "angels, authorities and powers [are] in submission to him" (1 Peter 3:22). In a higher sense than the Davidic kings ever could, Christ is reigning now with God on His throne (Revelation 3:21). Separating God's throne from the Davidic throne of Christ[18] is an unwarranted compartmentalizing of the Father and the Son in order to maintain the dogma of a postponement of Christ's kingship to the Millennium. A separation of David's throne and God's throne was already considered a fiction in the Old Testament because the Davidic King was a theocratic King who sat "on the throne of the kingdom of the LORD over Israel" (1 Chronicles 28:5; cf. 29:23; 2 Chronicles 9:8). In the eternal state of glory on earth, Christ's throne is still one with the throne of God (Revelation 22:1,3).

As Abraham recognized one greater than himself in the priest-king Melchizedek, so the descendants of Abraham are called to recognize One who is proclaimed by God as the Priest-King forever, after the order of Melchizedek (Hebrews 5:5-10; 7). This Priest-King meets the needs of Israel and all the Gentiles, because He is holy, blameless, and "exalted above the heavens" (Hebrews 7:26), even "at the right hand of the throne of the Majesty in heaven" (Hebrews 8:1).

The vertical typology of Hebrews does not imply that the inaugurated eschatology of Christ's present priesthood and kingship is the final fulfillment of the Davidic covenant. Constantly the author looks forward to the future, apocalyptic consummation of the kingdom of God, to the coming of a heavenly city, to a better world to come:

> It is not to angels that he has subjected *the world to come,* about which we are speaking (Hebrews 2:5; emphasis added).

> For here we do not have an enduring city, but we are looking for *the city that is to come* (Hebrews 13:14; 11:10; emphasis added).

It is therefore correct to insist on a future consummation of Psalm 110 in connection with the second coming of Christ and the final Judgment. Christ Himself applied the promise of theocratic rulership in Psalm 110 in an apocalyptic sense to the final destruction of God's enemies at His return in glory (see Matthew 25:31-33, 41). When Caiaphas, the high priest, placed Christ under oath to testify whether He was the promised Messiah, Jesus replied:

> Yes, it is as you say. But I say to all of you: In the future you will see the Son of Man sitting at the right hand of the Mighty One and coming on the clouds of heaven (Matthew 26:64; cf. Mark 14:62; Luke 22:69).

In this most solemn moment, Jesus united the apocalyptic Son of Man (of Daniel 7:13-14) and the Davidic Messiah (of Psalm 110) into one Person and applied both to His own coming in glory from heaven to judge the world. At the second coming of Christ, Psalm 110 will therefore receive its final, dramatic, cosmic fulfillment in the salvation of Christ's Church and the destruction of His enemies.

In summary, the typological perspective is fundamental to Christ's own understanding of His messianic mission as well as to the message of the New Testament writers. Christian typology—both in its horizontal and vertical aspects—is characterized by a present *fulfillment* of Old Testament types in Christ's redemptive work, and by hope for the future *consummation* of Christ's kingship in the last Judgment.

The typological approach of the New Testament is motivated by the idea of fulfillment in salvation history.[19] Typology is a theology of the progression of God's acts of salvation through Jesus Christ. It is based on the biblical assumption that God always acts in accordance with the unchangeable principles of His holy nature and will (Numbers 23:19; Malachi 3:6).[20] In the New Testament, typology is characterized by both a *historical* and a *theological* correspondence between type and antitype. The theological correlation consists in the fact that the Old Testament types are all determined theologically by their specific relation *to Yahweh*, the God of Israel, while all the New Testament antitypes are qualified by their relation *to Christ Jesus*, the Son of God. Because the covenantal communion with God is established through Christ only, all typology in the New Testament converges and culminates in Christ. Because Christ fulfills and completes the Old Testament salvation history, New Testament typology originates, centers, and terminates in Christ.[21]

This christological focus and eschatological perspective distinguishes typology from any accidental parallel situation. Wherever historical persons, events, or institutions are understood as foreshadowing some aspect of Christ's ministry, a typological perspective becomes visible. The relation of type-antitype is not simply one of repetition but one of an eschatological completion. The antitype is therefore not a more developed form of the type, but a new and unique work of God, through the Messiah, so that the antitype in some respects can even stand in opposition to the type (e.g., the sacrificial cultus, Adam).

Goppelt has stressed that the typological interpretation of the apostles took place in the freedom of the Holy Spirit and is not a scientific, technical, hermeneutical method like the historical-philological method.[22] New Testament typology does not start with the Old Testament history or symbolic ritual, but with Jesus and His salvation. Beginning with Jesus, who proved Himself to be the Messiah of Israel by His life, death, and resurrection, the apostolic writers looked for Old Testament parallels and then, guided by the Holy Spirit, drew conclusions as to their theological and moral significance for the Church of Christ.

In their constant retrospective[23] to Israel's history in the light of Christ Jesus, the New Testament writers try to disclose *how* God's redemptive act in Christ is related to God's saving acts in the past (see 1 Peter 1:10-12). If one defines exegesis strictly as establishing the true meaning of the original text as the human author intended it, by means of the grammatico-historical method, then typology is not a method of exegesis of the Old Testament.[24] Typology is the theological-christological interpretation of the Old Testament history by the New Testament, which goes beyond mere exegesis. In the words of Francis Foulkes:

> It [typology] takes more than the literal sense of a passage. The New Testament does this when it sees Christ as the theme and fulfillment of all the Old Testament, without limiting this to what is explicitly Messianic prophecy. . . . Typological interpretation shows that the partial and fragmentary revelation in the Old Testament pointed forward to Christ. . . . Typology

reads into Scripture a meaning which is not there in that it reads
in the light of the fulfillment of the history. . . . Nevertheless it
does not read a new principle into the context; it interprets the
dealings of God with men from the literal context, and then
points to the way in which God has so dealt with men in Christ.[25]

The New Testament typological interpretation of the Old Testament thus provides a major key for grasping the theological
unity of the Bible and "helps in avoiding the fragmentation
which is frequently the fruit of purely historical-grammatical
studies."[26]

　Typology does not involve any depreciation of the literal or
historical interpretation of the Old Testament. It is based on the
historical exegesis of the Old Testament in order to grasp the
fuller understanding or fuller sense (the *sensus plenior*) of God's
redemptive-historical acts for the whole human race.[27] One
could also say that the typological sense is the "authentic pro-
longation of the literal sense" of the Old Testament inasmuch as
typological exegesis is a "fundamental perspective" of the New
Testament teaching (J. Daniélou).[28] Thomas Aquinas has presented a perceptive analysis:

> The author of holy Scripture is God, in whose power it is to ex-
> press meaning not only by words—this men also can do—but
> also by means of things. Hence, here, as in all fields of know-
> ledge (*scientia*), words have meanings, but here, in addition, the
> things signified by the words themselves also have a meaning.
> The first meaning whereby words signify things, is their literal or
> historical sense. The meaning whereby the things signified by the
> words signify further things, is said to be their spiritual sense,
> which is based upon the literal and presupposes it.[29]

　We affirm that the genuine typological sense does not
superimpose a different sense on the literal meaning of the
words of Scripture, but pertains to the prophetic meaning of
the things, or events, expressed by the words of Scripture. True
typological interpretation of the Old Testament does not
create a second meaning or allegorization beyond the literal
sense but listens "to how the historical meaning of the text continues to speak in the New Testament situation" (H. W.
Wolff).[30] In an instructive essay Donald A. Hagner states:

> For these men [of the New Testament] typological relationships
> were the results of God's design so that in some sense the type

"prophesied" the antitype, and the latter "fulfilled" the former.
. . . The tracing of typological correspondences is a special instance of detecting the *sensus plenior* of the Old Testament material. That is, the Old Testament is seen to contain a fuller sense than immediately meets the eye, and, indeed, which is discernible only in the light of its New Testament counterpart.[31]

The full theological sense of the Old Testament history of Israel can be grasped only by those who believe that Jesus is the Messiah of Israel, that God's covenant with the twelve tribes of Israel is fulfilled and completed — not postponed — in Christ's covenant with His twelve apostles (2 Corinthians 3; Hebrews 4). We concur with the balanced conclusion of David L. Baker that the "correct understanding and use of the Old Testament depends on the New Testament, and on the other hand, one of the primary uses of the Old Testament is to be the basis for correct understanding and use of the New Testament."[32]

### Limitations of Types

In his *Encyclopedia of Biblical Prophecy* (Harper, 1973), J. Barton Payne teaches that biblical types possess four essential characteristics: (1) a type must have a *divine origin*, e.g., Exodus 25:40; cf. Hebrews 8:5; (2) a type must be *redemptive*, e.g., Zechariah 14:16; cf. John 20:31; (3) a type must be a *symbolic enactment*, e.g., of Levitical priesthood and ritual; (4) a type must be *an acted prophecy*, e.g., Numbers 21:9; cf. John 3:14; Colossians 2:17; Hebrews 10:1 (see pp. 24-26). In short, a type is "a divine enactment of future redemption" (p. 23).

Payne discusses more than fifty biblical types which meet those christological requirements (listed on pp. 671-672 of his *Encyclopedia*), most of which are taken from Israel's sanctuary ritual and cultic festivals. Although their *predictive* design was understood by only few Israelites at that time, such as Moses (Exodus 25:40), their symbolic significance regarding the general substitutionary way of salvation and their function as a symbol of Israel's sanctification to God (Psalm 51:7, 16-17) "seems to have been well understood" by the Old Testament saints.

Helpful is the distinction between a symbol and a type: "A symbol is a fact that teaches a moral truth. A type is a fact that teaches a moral truth and predicts some actual realization of that truth."[33]

The question remains, what are the controls for establishing biblical typology in order to avoid futile speculations and allegorizations?[34] Bernard Ramm stresses that the New Testament focuses its typology on the great facts of Christ and His redemption and on the basic, spiritual, moral truths of Christian experience.[35] New Testament typology does not deal with minutiae and incidentals, nor does it teach a one-to-one correspondence or complete identity between type and antitype. Consequently, a pronounced dissimilarity between type and antitype must be recognized. Ramm therefore concludes: "The typical truth is at the point of similarity. One of the cardinal errors in typology is to make typical the elements of dissimilarity in a type."[36] The Christian's effort to grasp the real essentials of the Old Testament salvation history, and to distinguish them clearly from merely external similarities, demands more than a purely historical exegesis can offer. It requires the enlightenment and guidance of the Holy Spirit to discover the typological pattern between the two Testaments.

The discovery of a new typological pattern in Holy Scripture, through which our hope for the apocalyptic deliverance of the Church of Christ is renewed and strengthened, must be based, however, on clear New Testament authority.[37] God's saving acts in Israel's history must be applied by a New Testament writer to the future redemption of Christ's people by clear literary allusions to the Old Testament and a clear analogy of theological structure with regard to Israel's salvation history.

### Dispensationalism and Typology

In dispensationalism we face the fact that the hermeneutic of literalism accepts Christian typology for some selected historical parts of the Old Testament. But it suddenly rejects each typological application of God's covenant with Israel to Christ's new covenant with His Church, as well as any notion of typology in Israel's prophecy. This seems to be an arbitrary, speculative use of typology within the Old Testament. The dispensationalist Lewis S. Chafer offers this rationale for his acceptance of Christian typology: "It is reasonable to suppose that when an account is given of the marriage of any man of the Old Testament who is himself a type of Christ, that marriage may have typical signification."[38] He then presents many examples of marriage unions in the Old Testament which are typological of Christ's union with the Church in the New Testament, e.g., "Moses is a type of Christ as Deliverer; thus Zipporah his wife, chosen from the Gentiles while he was away from his brethren, is a suggestion of the calling out of the Church during the period between the two advents of Christ."[39]

It is hard to see how Chafer, at the same time, can maintain his thesis that the Church "was wholly unforeseen and is wholly unrelated to any divine purpose which precedes it or which follows it."[40] A type, according to the *New Scofield Reference Bible*, is "a *divinely purposed* illustration of some truth" (p. 6; emphasis added). If Eve, Rebekah, Zipporah, Abigail, Ruth, and the Shulamite, are all recognized as Old Testament types of the New Testament Church, is it then "reasonable" to conclude that the Church of Christ was "unforeseen" and "unrelated" to God's divine purpose with mankind from the beginning? Furthermore, is it not just as reasonable to accept Israel, the covenant people of Yahweh, as a type of the new-covenant people of Christ? But here dispensationalism suddenly remembers its basic hermeneutic of literalism— which principle is not applied to the marriage unions of single persons in the Old Testament: "But no covenant or prophecy brings that nation into heavenly citizenship or into marriage union with Christ."[41]

How can this judgment be justified, if one considers Abraham's hope for a heavenly city and Israel's hope for a better, even a "heavenly" country (Hebrews 11:10, 16)? Christ announces that Abraham, Isaac, and Jacob, together with many gentile believers, will receive heavenly citizenship in the kingdom of God (Luke 13:28-29) or kingdom of heaven (Matthew 8:11; cf. Hebrews 11:39-40).

Chafer's rejection of Israel's marriage union *with Christ* is not justified either. First of all, four Old Testament prophets describe the covenantal relation between Yahweh and Israel in terms of a marriage union: Hosea (2:7, 16, 19-20), Isaiah (54:5-8), Jeremiah (3:8), and Ezekiel (16). The apostle Paul applies the marriage motif to Christ's relation with His Church: "I promised you to one husband, to Christ, so that I might present you as a pure virgin to him" (2 Corinthians 11:2). The *New Scofield Reference Bible*, however, concludes: "Israel will be the LORD's earthly wife (Hos 2:23); the Church, the Lamb's heavenly bride (Rev 19:7)" (p. 920). This view envisions that the Godhead has two different brides in two different places. However, regarding John's apocalyptic vision of the descent of the New Jerusalem from heaven on earth (Revelation 21:2), we read Scofield's comment: "The new Jerusalem is the dwelling place throughout eternity for the saints of all ages and fulfills the hope of Abraham for the heavenly city (Hebrews 11:10-16; cp. Hebrews 12:22-24)" (p. 1375). Does not this comment admit that both the redeemed Israel and the redeemed Church will be gathered into one flock under one Shepherd into one place (compare John 10:14-16 and Isaiah 56:8)? Is not the organic unity of spiritual Israel and spiritual Gentiles in Christ expressed by the combination of the names of the twelve tribes *and* the twelve apostles on the structure of the New Jerusalem (Revelation 21:12, 14)?

Dispensationalism rightfully rejects an unhistorical identification or equation of national Israel with the new-covenant Church. It concludes, however, that both Israel and the Church are basically separated by different purposes and promises. Dispensationalism never considers any typological connection between the Israel of God and the Church. While dispensationalism accepts messianic types in the Old Testament in relation to Christ and the Church,[42] it rejects the old covenant as a type of the new covenant, and Israel as a type of the Church. To interpret the Church as "a new spiritual Israel" is considered by Ryrie an "artificial typological interpretation"[43] because it conflicts with literalism. He declares: "To carry this designation *Israel* over to believers in the Church is not warranted by the New Testament. . . . Believers *as a group* are not called spiritual Israel."[44]

The dispensationalist Charles F. Baker, however, argues strongly, against Scofield and Ryrie, that the Church of Christ and the apostles (without Paul) were *Israel as a New Testament Church* (Matthew 16:18; 18:17; Acts 2:47), which he calls the "Kingdom Church" and completely separates from the "Body Church," created by the apostle Paul (Ephesians 3:9).[45] Baker insists that the Kingdom Church (of Matthew 16:18) already existed on the day of Pentecost in Acts 2, because the thousands of new believers were simply *"added"* to Christ's Church (Acts 2:41, 47). Christ's Kingdom Church was "the Israelitish *ekklesia* of prophecy," because the apostle Peter, filled with the

Holy Spirit, declared "that everything that was happening in connection with that *ekklesia* was in fulfillment of all that the prophets had spoken since the world began (Acts 3:21)."[46] We wholeheartedly agree with Baker's reply to Ryrie. On the other hand, however, Baker creates an untenable sharp distinction of his own when he separates Christ's "Kingdom" Church from Paul's "Body" Church:

> The truth about the Body of Christ was a secret kept from all former ages and generations (Ephesians 3:9), and therefore must of necessity be something different from that which was the subject of all prophetic utterances of old. Thus, the true dispensational distinction which must be made is that between the Israelitish *ekklesia* of prophecy and the Body of Christ *ekklesia* of the mystery, both of which are found in the book called the New Testament.[47]

Such dispensationalist distinctions and dilemmas are the result of unwarranted inferences and a literalism which loses sight of the theological typology between the Israel of God and the Church of Christ in God's single, ongoing plan of salvation for all mankind. Dispensationalism labors under a reduced use of messianic typology in which the christological applications of Old Testament types are accepted but the ecclesiological applications of Israel's mission and mandate are denied and rejected.

The New Testament typology does not create this dichotomy between Christ and the Israel of God. The central thrust of the New Testament gospel and its prophetic hope is that the Church of Christ is appointed to fulfill the divine purpose of Israel's election: to be a saving light for the Gentiles. The apostles Paul and Barnabas saw their gospel mission and mandate expressed in God's call to Israel (Acts 13:47; cf. Isaiah 49:6). The full scope of the New Testament typology can be summarized as follows:

> It is Jesus Christ who provides in the first place the antitype of the Old Testament types; along with him we may mention also the apostolic office in 2 Corinthians 3:7ff., the sacraments in 1 Corinthians 10:1ff., and the experience of grace and judgment by the Christians as the people of the new covenant in 1 Peter 1:5, 9; Revelation 1:6; and 1 Corinthians 10:6. All these cases are not subordinate and insignificant matters, but are central elements in the realization of salvation.[48]

In biblical typology it is not Christ alone who is the antitype but *Christ and His people,* united in an unbreakable, organic unity, in God's saving purpose for the world.[49]

### Typology in Prophetic Eschatology

Typological correspondences were already announced in principle by Israel's prophets, even though they could see only a small portion of the whole salvation history. They wrote their predictive prophecies in the conviction that God's acts of deliverance and judgment in the past would be repeated in essence, because God remains faithful to Himself and His covenant (Deuteronomy 7:9). His acts would be repeated on a larger, universal scale and more gloriously than ever in the past.[50]

The prophets portray the future kingdom of God on earth with motifs and imagery derived from God's perfect creation in Paradise (compare Genesis 2 with Isaiah 11:6-9; 35; 65:23-25; Ezekiel 34:25-30; 36:35). In addition, Isaiah predicts the coming deliverance of Israel from the Assyrian-Babylonian captivity in terms of a new and greater Exodus (Isaiah 43:16-19; 51:10-11; 52; 11:15). Furthermore, Isaiah, Jeremiah, and Ezekiel predict the coming of a Davidic Messiah who would rule Israel and the nations in peace and righteousness. He would be a king like David, but far greater than David (Isaiah 9:1-7; 11:1-9; 55:1-5; Jeremiah 23:5-6; 30:9; 33:14-18; Ezekiel 34:23-31; 37:24-28). There are more examples of Old Testament typological prophecy in the announcements of the coming of a new Melchizedek (Psalm 110), a new Moses (Deuteronomy 18:15-19), a new Elijah (Malachi 4:5), a new temple (Ezekiel 41-48), a new covenant (Jeremiah 31:31-34), and the re-creation of a new people (Isaiah 65:17ff.; 66:22; Ezekiel 36:26; 37:11-14).[51] Constantly, the Old Testament prophets expressed their hope for the future in terms of God's acts in the past, which nevertheless would more gloriously exceed anything experienced in the past. The prophets recall the great acts of God in the past in order to assure Israel of God's great acts in the future. Old Testament prophecies are therefore "at the same time indissolubly memorial and predictive."[52]

In summary, the prophetic future of the Old Testament is characterized by two aspects: (1) God will act in the future according to the principles of His past action; (2) He will do so on an unprecedented, glorious scale through the Messiah in the coming messianic age.

The prophetic portrayal of the future kingdom of God by means of the literary style of a "typical" escalation of God's past actions demonstrates that the dispensational hermeneutic of "absolute literalness" (Scofield) for prophetic interpretation is inadequate and abortive. The problem with dispensational literalism is not its stance on concrete historical and visible fulfillments of Israel's prophecy, but that its literalism comes far short of the surpassing eminence and glorious transformation of the future fulfillment of prophecy in human history. The literal projection into the future of the words of prophecy is only what the human eye has seen already, but "no eye has seen, no ear has heard, no mind has conceived what God has prepared for those who love him" (1 Corinthians 2:9, applying Isaiah 64:4).

Over against all abstract spiritualizations and allegorizations, we affirm a literal, historical fulfillment of the Old Testament prophecy. One should be careful, however, not to be caught on the horns of a false dilemma, as if we should have to choose between two extreme positions: literalism or allegorism. The typological structure is the style of biblical hope and prophecy.[53] In fact, the whole concept of typical thinking, with its historical progress from type to surpassing antitype, "crops up for the first time in (Old Testament) prophetic eschatology" (L. Goppelt).[54] The nascent "typology" in the Old Testament prophecy is not rooted in the widespread cyclic thinking of the surrounding pagan nations which anticipated that the last age in the cosmic course would automatically correspond to the first age. The concept of a literal recurrence of the past in the future age is a pagan motif that has been overcome by the typological approach of the Old Testament prophecy.

Israel's promise of the future renewal is rooted in God's faithfulness to His election of Israel, to bless all the families of the earth who have fallen under the curse (Genesis 12:2-3; Isaiah 42-53; esp. 45:22). Not only will God's purpose be fulfilled in continuity with His redemptive acts in the past; the coming restoration "does not just correspond to what has gone before; it transcends it" (Goppelt).[55] Just as the New Testament antitypes stand on a higher level of glory in Christ than their Old Testament types, so Israel's prophetic typology

forecasts a sacred history into the higher key of a radical newness, of a new creation. The Old Testament prophet is not a
soothsayer with a fixed message which can later be authenticated in terms of a factual correspondence to a predicted set
of facts. As the Lord of history and prophecy, God has the
right to interpret His promises through His fulfillments, "and
the interpretation can be full of surprises even for the prophet
himself" (W. Zimmerli).[56]

The notions of "transcendence" and "transformation" in
the typological fulfillment are basically the same for the category of "newness" in Israel's prophetic eschatology. Typology
and prophecy are twin sisters, both pointing forward to the
great Day of the Lord, the day of the glorious consummation of
all God's covenant promises. Their internal connection can be
explained as follows: "Typology differs from prophecy in the
strict sense of the term only in the means of prediction. Prophecy predicts mainly by means of the word, whereas typology
predicts by institution, act or person."[57]

Bible scholars state that genuine types are "prophetic symbols" (B. Ramm), "acted prophecy" (J. B. Payne), "a species of
predictive prophecy," "every bit as predictive as verbal utterances of predictive prophecy" (S. N. Gundry).[58] Typology
emphasizes the concrete, historical nature of the promised
future. Prophecy, on the other hand, "makes explicit what is
often only implicit and symbolic in typology, and prevents the
sense of 'repetition' from relapsing into pagan, history-
escaping cyclicism."[59] The prophet, looking in faith to the
future, was a "typologist," says Lampe,[60] because he based his
faith on the past acts of God (e.g., the exodus deliverance).[61]

Prophecy correlates prediction and fulfillment. Addition-
ally, typology expresses its restless progress from initial realization to greater fulfillment. The typological correlation of type
and antitype is therefore considered a part of Old Testament
eschatology. "Typology belongs in principle to prophecy; it is
extremely closely connected with the eschatological hope and
must be explained from the same fundamental forces as the
latter."[62] Trying to interpret the prophetic portrayals of the
messianic age by the rationalistic principle of "absolute
literalness," as if such pictures were parts of a jigsaw puzzle[63] or
photographic snapshot in advance, is just as inadequate as to
construe in detail the glories of the antitype (e.g., the Messiah,

the apostolic remnant, the final gathering of Israel) from its Old Testament type alone, or the reality from its shadow.

Divine fulfillments of Israel's fragmentary types and prophecies have always been full of surprise and the unexpected, because Yahweh remains the Lord over the way in which His will is to be realized. This surprisingly new way is revealed in the New Testament. The recognition of this directedness of the Old Testament to the messianic history of the New Testament distinguishes *Christian* exegesis from the literalistic exegesis of the Old Testament. The Christian listens to the Bible "stereophonically,"—that is, to both Testaments of Holy Scripture— because God's revelation in both Testaments is basically one and consistent. Christian typology is the expression of the conviction that history is under God's control and moves forward to the glorious consummation of God's promises through Jesus Christ.

Biblical typology is not confined to the period of this age but concerns also the Kingdom of God in the age to come and the renewal of the whole creation. In other words, typology has also a definite apocalyptic dimension and fulfillment in connection with the glorious second advent of Christ.[64]

### Notes on Chapter 4

[1]See H. D. Preuss, *Jahweglaube und Zukunftserwartung*, BWANT 7 (Stuttgart: Kohlhammer Verlag, 1964), especially pp. 205-214. W. C. Kaiser, Jr., *Toward an Old Testament Theology* (Grand Rapids, Mich.: Zondervan, 1978), has shown that the whole Old Testament centers around the ever-expanding but constant core: the promise of God.

[2]C. T. Fritsch, "Principles of Biblical Typology," *BSac* 104 (1947):214.

[3]Ibid., p. 230.

[4]Ibid., p. 215.

[5]Cf. L. Goppelt, *Typos. Die Typologische Deutung des Alten Testaments im Neuen* (Darmstadt: Wissensch. Buchg., 1969; reprint of 1939), pp. 286, 240. R. T. France, *Jesus and the Old Testament* (London: Tyndale, 1971), chapter 3.

[6]See Goppelt, *Typos*, especially pp. 239-249.

[7]Ibid., p. 239 (my translation).

[8]Ryrie, *The Basis of the Premillennial Faith*, p. 43, acknowledged "that Israel typifies the Church."

[9]See C. T. Fritsch, "Biblical Typology: Typological Interpretation in the New Testament," *BSac* 104 (1946):87-100.

[10]H. Mueller in *NIDNTT*, vol. 3, p. 905. E. E. Ellis, *Prophecy and Hermeneutics in Early Christianity* (Grand Rapids, Mich.: Wm. B. Eerdmans Pub. Co., 1978), p. 168, refers to a larger "judgment typology" in the New Testament.

[11]P. Fairbairn, *The Typology of Scripture*, vol. 2 (Grand Rapids, Mich.: Baker Book House, 1975; reprint of 1900), p. 65. E. E. Ellis (*Prophecy and Hermeneutics in Early Christianity*, p. 166) states: "Covenant typology approaches the whole of Old Testament as prophecy."

[12]*TDNT*, vol. 8, p. 253.

[13]C. T. Fritsch, "To 'Antitypon'," in *Studia Biblica et Semitica*, Festschrift for Th. C. Vriezen; W. C. van Unnik, ed. (Wageningen: H. Veenman, 1966), p. 101.

[14]Ladd, *The Last Things*, p. 18. Also F. F. Bruce, *New Testament Developments of Old Testament Themes* (Grand Rapids, Mich.: Wm. B. Eerdmans Pub. Co., 1970), p. 79.

[15]Cf. S. Kistemaker, *The Psalm Citations in the Epistle to the Hebrews* (Amsterdam: G. van Soest, 1961), p. 132. Also H.-J. Kraus, *Psalmen*, BKAT XV/2 (Neukirchen-Vluyn: Neukirchener Verlag, 1972), pp. 752-764.

[16]See C. H. Dodd, *According to the Scriptures: The Substructure of New Testament Theology* (London: Nisbet, 1952), p. 35. Cf. the index of quotations of Psalm 110 in *The Greek New Testament*, K. Aland, et al., eds. (London: United Bible Society, 1966), p. 908.

[17]J. F. Walvoord quotes H. A. Ironside for a number of so-called gaps or intervals "in God's program," among which would be "a great parenthesis between Psalm 110:1 and 110:2" (in *BSac* 101 [1944]:47).

[18]The *New Scofield Reference Bible* comments on Revelation 3:21 that this passage "is conclusive that Christ is not now seated upon His own throne" (p. 1355), so that the Davidic Covenant and "the Messianic kingdom await fulfillment" (pp. 1355-56).

[19]Cf. Goppelt, *TDNT*, vol. 8, p. 259.

[20]See F. Foulkes, *The Acts of God: A Study of the Basis of Typology in the Old Testament* (London: Tyndale, 1955).

[21]France, *Jesus and the Old Testament*, p. 43.

²²Goppelt, *Typos*, pp. 244, 277f.

²³The major conclusion of S. Kistemaker's dissertation, *The Psalm Citations in the Epistle to the Hebrews* (Free University, Amsterdam, 1961; published by G. van Soest [Amsterdam], 1961), confirms this retrospective flow in typology: "The author to the Hebrews interpreted the Scripture passages only in the light of the fulfillment of the Old Testament" (p. 90).

²⁴Bright, *The Authority of the Old Testament*, p. 92. France, *Jesus and the Old Testament*, pp. 41-42. Foulkes, *The Acts of God*, pp. 38-40.

²⁵Foulkes, *The Acts of God*, pp. 38, 39.

²⁶R. C. Dentan, "Typology — Its Use and Abuse," *Anglican Theological Review* 34 (1952):211-217; quotation from p. 215.

²⁷G. W. H. Lampe, "Typological Exegesis," *Theology* 16 (1953): 201-208.

²⁸Jean Daniélou, *Sacramentum Futuri. Études sur les Origines de la Typologie Biblique* (Paris: Beauchesne, 1950), pp. 52, 143.

²⁹Thomas Aquinas, *Summa Theologica*, trans. Fathers of the English Dom. Prov. (New York: Benziger Brothers, 1947), Ia, q, 1, art. 10. Cf. Robert A. Markus, "Presuppositions of the Typological Approach to Scripture," *Church Quarterly Review* 158 (1957): 442-451. Also Jean Daniélou, *Dieu Vivant*, p. 151, as quoted by W. Eichrodt, "Is Typological Exegesis an Appropriate Method?", in *EOTH*, p. 242. E. C. Blackman, "Return of Typology?", *Congressional Quarterly* 32 (1954):53-59. Oscar Cullmann, *Salvation in History* (New York: Harper, 1967), p. 133.

³⁰H. W. Wolff, "The Hermeneutics of the Old Testament," in *EOTH*, p. 189.

³¹D. A. Hagner, "The Old Testament in the New Testament," in *Interpreting the Word of God*, ed. S. J. Schultz and M. B. Inch (Chicago: Moody Press, 1976), p. 94.

³²D. L. Baker, "Typology and the Christian Use of the Old Testament," *Scottish Journal of Theology* 29 (1976):137-157; quotation from p. 155.

³³Davidson, *Old Testament Prophecy*, p. 229.

³⁴Like those of the Letter of Barnabus (see Goppelt, *Typos*, pp. 245-248), and of the Cocceian School (see Fairbairn, *The Typology of Scripture*, vol. 1, pp. 1-14).

³⁵Ramm, *Protestant Biblical Interpretation*, pp. 229f.

³⁶Ibid.

[37]Gerhard F. Hasel, *New Testament Theology: Basic Issues in Debate* (Grand Rapids, Mich.: Eerdmans, 1978), pp. 190-193.

[38]Chafer, *Systematic Theology*, vol. 4, p. 137.

[39]Ibid.

[40]Ibid., vol. 5, p. 348.

[41]Ibid., vol. 4, p. 142.

[42]The *NSRB* even states, "Aaron and his sons typify Christ and believers of the Church age (Rev 1:6; cp. 1 Pet 2:9)," pp. 106, 107.

[43]Ryrie, *Dispensationalism Today*, pp. 149, 154, 190.

[44]Ibid., pp. 144, 150.

[45]Charles F. Baker, *A Dispensational Theology* (Grand Rapids, Mich.: Grace Bible College Pub., 1972), pp. 470f., 500, 508, 527, 655. He maintains that the spiritual Israelites among ethnic Israel were also a "church" in the Old Testament, "the Israelitish Church."

[46]Ibid., pp. 471, 497-500.

[47]Ibid., p. 471.

[48]W. Eichrodt, "Is Typological Exegesis an Appropriate Method?", in *EOTH*, p. 226.

[49]See H. W. Wolff, "The Old Testament in Controversy: Interpretive Principles and Illustration," *Interpretation* 12 (1958):281-91.

[50]See Foulkes, *The Acts of God.* Daniélou, *Sacramentum Futuri;* English translation, *From Shadows to Reality* (Westminster, Md.: Newman, 1960). S. Amsler, "Prophetie et Typologie," *Revue de Theol. et de Phil.* 3 (1953):139-148.

[51]Foulkes, *The Acts of God*, pp. 23-33. Goppelt, *TDNT*, vol. 8, p. 254. Fritsch, "Biblical Typology," pp. 91-100.

[52]Daniélou, *Sacramentum Futuri*, p. 4.

[53]Cf. Markus, "Presuppositions of the Typological Approach to Scripture," pp. 442-451. S. Amsler, "Prophetie et Typologie," pp. 139-148.

[54]Goppelt, *TDNT*, vol. 8, p. 254.

[55]Ibid. Cf. Foulkes, *The Acts of God*, pp. 22, 32. G. W. H. Lampe, "Hermeneutics and Typology," *London Quarterly and Holburn Review* 190 (1965):17-23.

[56]W. Zimmerli, "Promise and Fulfillment," in *EOTH*, pp. 106-107.

[57]Fritsch, "Principles of Biblical Typology," *BSac* 104 (1947): 215. Cf. Art Moorehead, "Type," in *ISBE*, vol. 5.

[58]S. N. Gundry, "Typology as a Means of Interpretation: Past and Present," *JETS* 12 (1969):233-240; quotation from p. 237. Cf. Fritsch, "Biblical Typology," p. 90. Terry, *Biblical Hermeneutics*, p. 248. Berkhof, *Principles of Biblical Interpretation*, pp. 144-145.

[59]H. D. Hummel, "The Old Testament Basis of Typological Interpretation," *Biblical Research* 9 (1964):38-50; quotation from p. 49.

[60]Lampe, "Hermeneutics and Typology," p. 24.

[61]See B. W. Anderson, "Exodus Typology in Second Isaiah," in *Israel's Prophetic Heritage*, ed. B. W. Anderson and W. Harrelson (New York: Harper, 1962), chapter 12.

[62]Eichrodt, "Is Typological Exegesis an Appropriate Method?", in *EOTH*, p. 234. Cf. Ramm, *Protestant Biblical Interpretation*, p. 239.

[63]See T. Boersma, *Is the Bible a Jigsaw Puzzle? An Evaluation of Hal Lindsey's Writings* (St. Catherines, Ontario, Canada: Paideia Press, 1978).

[64]Goppelt, *Typos*, p. 248. Cf. his "Apokalyptik und Typologie bei Paulus," *ThLZ* 89 (1964):321-344; also his *Typos*, pp. 259-299. Ellis, *Prophecy and Hermeneutics in Early Christianity*, pp. 168-169. R. H. Smith, "Exodus Typology in the Fourth Gospel," *JBL* 81 (1962):324-342. M. D. Goulder, *Type and History in Acts* (London: S.P.C.K., 1964), chapter 1, "The Typological Method." R. E. Nixon, *The Exodus in the New Testament* (London: Tyndale, 1962), pp. 29-32. See also the important study of R. M. Davidson, *Typology in Scripture*, Andrews University Seminary Doctoral Dissertation Series, Vol. 2 (Berrien Springs, Mich.: Andrews University Press, 1981), especially pp. 396-408.

# 5

## The Christological

## Interpretation

In the realm of prophetic interpretation the study of the proper method has often been neglected or not given its necessary care. We have learned that Christ and the New Testament are the Christian's final authority and highest norm for the theological understanding of Israel's history, prophecy, wisdom, and sacred poetry. We have established that verbal prophecy and typology—as indirect prophecy—are not unrelated strands in the Old Testament with inherently different hermeneutical principles. Predictive prophecy and typological thought patterns form a natural, integral unity. To the central core of the Old Testament hope belong the messianic prophecies. In these, all covenant promises of Israel converge, and from them Israel's universal mission emerges. Even the specific apocalyptic prophecies with their highly developed symbolism are often Messiah-centered (Daniel 7-12).

### Messianic Prophecies

In the light of the New Testament, three categories of messianic prophecies can be distinguished in the Old Testament. First, there are the direct or rectilinear prophecies such as those which predicted the Messiah's birthplace, Micah 5:2 (see Matthew 2:5-6); His substitutionary atonement, Isaiah 53 (see Luke 22:37; Romans 5:19; 1 Peter 2:24); His being "cut off" and His "putting an end to sacrifice and offering," Daniel 9:26, 27 (see Matthew 27:51; Hebrews 10:8-9); His resurrection, Psalm 16:10 (see Acts 2:27, 31); His triumphal entry into Jerusalem, Zechariah 9:9 (see Matthew 21:12, 23); and His reign of everlasting world peace, Isaiah 9:5-7 (see Luke 1:32-33; Revelation 11:15). Predictions such as these have been or will be fulfilled directly and exclusively in Christ Jesus and therefore represent the simple scheme of prediction and fulfilling event or verification.

The fulfillment of such predictions magnifies God's foreknowledge and sovereign providence. His predictions are not disconnected fragments but constitute parts of one single, ongoing plan or promise of salvation.

Secondly, there are the typological messianic prophecies which have already found their initial and partial fulfillments in the succession of prophets since Moses (Deuteronomy 18:15, 18-19),[1] and in the succession of kings in Jerusalem (2 Samuel 7:12-16),[2] until both lines would culminate in the one and only Messiah. Although the immediate fulfillment of the promised *prophet* came in Moses' successor Joshua (Numbers 27:18-23; Deuteronomy 34:9) and the immediate fulfillment of the promised *king* came in David's son Solomon (2 Samuel 7:14; Psalm 132:12), only the Messiah Himself would be the greatest Prophet and the eternal King, according to the New Testament (Acts 3:22-26; Luke 1:32-33). To the category of typological promises belong the majority of messianic prophecies, especially the Royal Psalms: 2:7ff.; 18:43ff.; 22; 45:6-8; 72:8; 89:26ff.; 110:1, 4; 118:22-23; 132:11-18.

The New Testament seems to take it for granted that the Davidic psalms possess an added messianic dimension. In the Epistle to the Hebrews, for instance, four Psalm passages are quoted, exegeted, and applied eschatologically as having found their fulfillment in Christ Jesus: Psalm 8:4-6 (man's perfect humanity); 95:7-11 (his perfect rest); 110:4 (the perfect Mediator); 40:6-8 (His perfect self-sacrifice); respectively in Hebrews 2:12, 13; 3:7-11; 5:6; 10:5-7. The author of Hebrews added his interpretation of the psalm citations to the historical meaning these words had originally. As S. Kistemaker concludes in his dissertation regarding these four psalm quotations in Hebrews: "The author linked prophecy in its original setting to its fulfillment realized in the time when he wrote the Epistle. Therefore those Scripture passages which are taken up in his *Midrash pesher* [Jewish eschatological interpretation] type of interpretation sparkle with historical perspectives directed towards fulfillment in Jesus Christ."[3] In these historical perspectives a prophet or priest or a Davidic king functioned in his holy office as a representative of the victorious Redeemer, as a type of the greater antitype to come.

This kind of typological prophecy provides room for a basically dual application, with an initial and partial fulfillment of the messianic promise, without having a "double" or ambiguous sense.[4] The one intended sense of an immediate historical application or partial realization of the promise is to serve as a historical type, or acted prophecy, which reaffirms the promise and intensifies the hope for the future fulfillment. One Lutheran scholar explains: "A prophecy that is Messianic by type is in no wise Messianic in an inferior sense, since the type is not an accidental but a divinely ordained type and is described to us by the Spirit of prophecy."[5] The *Seventh-day Adventist Bible Commentary* explains more fully (on Deuteronomy 18:15):

> The force of a prophecy regarding Christ is in no way weakened because the prophet's words apply first to a more immediate historical situation. Often the first and more immediate fulfillment serves not only to confirm and to clarify the second but may even be requisite to it. When a NT writer applies the statement of an OT prophet to NT or subsequent times, to deny the validity of such an application is to deny the inspiration of the NT writer. But when the context of an OT statement makes evident that it applies also to an immediate historical situation, to deny this application would be to violate a primary rule of interpretation; namely, that an examination of context and historical setting is fundamental to a correct understanding of any passage.

We need to realize that the messianic prophecies are not detached and scattered predictions, but all make up one continuous plan of God. This plan started with the first promise after the fall in the garden of Eden, when the Redeemer was promised from the "seed of the woman" (Genesis 3:15). In order to fulfill this original "mother" promise, God chose to call Abram and gave him the promise of the Redeemer from the "seed of Abraham" (Genesis 12:2-3; 22:17-18; 28:13-14). God confined His promise of a royal Redeemer specifically to the tribe of Judah (Genesis 49:10; cf. Numbers 24:17). Finally, God restricted the promise of the Redeemer King, whose reign would be eternal and universal, to the house of David (2 Samuel 7:12-15). This line of repeated and progressive revelations of the Redeemer-King is essential for the proper perspective of the numerous messianic predictions within the one great Promise which only comes to rest in the realization of a new heaven and a new earth, the home of righteousness (2 Peter 3:13).

One Old Testament scholar stresses the "breathtaking sweep" of this messianic perspective: "Each prediction is added to the continuous promise of God that was announced first to prepatriarchal peoples, then enlarged and continuously supplemented from the patriarchs down to the postexilic era of Haggai, Zechariah, and Malachi. But it remained God's single, cumulative promise."[6]

There remain, however, a number of nonpredictive historical passages which are applied in the New Testament as being "fulfilled" in Christ, but which in their original context contain no apparent predictive intention. Such passages can be historical narratives or occurrences, experiences of suffering, lamentation, supplication, or thanksgiving by a psalmist, or descriptive assertions in the prophetic books.

A few examples may illustrate this particular New Testament pattern of promise-fulfillment. Christ quotes the experience of Jonah's being in a huge fish for "three days and three nights" (Jonah 1:17) as His own sign of appeal to the unbelieving scribes and Pharisees (Matthew 12:40; Luke 11:29-30, 32). Although Jonah's narrative is a purely historical description of his experience of virtual death and miraculous deliverance, which led to the repentance of the Gentiles in Nineveh, Jesus applies Jonah's experience as a messianic sign, that is, as a prophetic type of His own death and supernatural resurrection. The implication seems to be: as Jonah was authorized by his sign to preach repentance to the Ninevites, so Jesus as Messiah will likewise be authorized in His message to the Jewish people. As Christ is greater than Jonah, failure to repent on Christ's message will incur, therefore, a greater condemnation by God than that which the Ninevites acquired, but averted by their repentance.

Likewise, Jesus' appeals to Solomon's wisdom (Matthew 12:42; Luke 11:31) and to David's authority to keep the Sabbath free from certain ceremonial restrictions (Mark 2:25-26;

Matthew 12:3-4, 5-6; Luke 6:3-4) belong basically to the same category of messianic typology as His appeal to the sign of Jonah. Because the messianic hope was exemplified in Israel's three types of mediators between God and His covenant people—the prophet, the priest, and the king—it had profound significance when Jesus claimed these three sacred offices as types of His own mission for Israel and the world.[7]

It is therefore very meaningful to study the messianic types in Israel's religious, cultic, and political life. They are essential to a better and more adequate understanding of Jesus' work and mission. The Old Testament remains valid and necessary for the Christian in order to know what the mission of Christ, the Anointed One, implies. A fuller understanding may be gained, furthermore, by considering how Jesus applied Israel's early history in a unique way to Himself. As the appointed Representative of Israel, Jesus recapitulated—that is, He repeated and consummated—God's plan with Israel and, through Israel, with man.[8] He deliberately went over the same ground in order to conquer where Israel had failed. Christ consciously knew that He was called to become the predicted "Servant of the LORD" of Isaiah 42-53, especially since His Father's voice had identified Christ as His Son and beloved Servant (Matthew 3:17) and endowed Him publicly with the Spirit of God (Matthew 3:16; cf. Isaiah 42:1). As Messiah, Jesus was not only solidary with Israel but the embodiment of Israel, likewise called God's "firstborn Son" (Exodus 4:22). Through this Servant "the will of the LORD will prosper" (Isaiah 53:10).

The gospel writers stress that Jesus, after His baptism, was led immediately "by the Spirit into the desert to be tempted by the devil" (Matthew 4:1; cf. Mark 1:12; Luke 4:1). Ancient Israel, after its exodus from Egypt and "baptism" in the Red Sea, was tested by God for *forty years* in the wilderness before it could enter the promised land (Deuteronomy 8:2). So Christ was led into the desert for *forty days* to be tempted by the devil concerning His messianic trust in God's sovereign will, before beginning His unique commission. In his deliberate fasting for exactly forty days, Jesus reenacted the experience of Israel, but manifested ultimate obedience to God by His appeal to the revealed word of God to Israel (three times: Matthew 4:4, 7, 10; quoting, respectively, Deuteronomy 6:13, 16; 8:3). The remarkable fact is that Christ, as His answer to the three temptations, each time quoted a passage from the book of Deuteronomy, chapters 6-8, when other passages were also available. Robert T. France suggests:

> Was it not because He saw in these chapters, with their vivid reminders of the lessons learned by Israel in their forty years of wandering in the desert, a pattern for His own time of testing? God had tested the obedience of Israel (Deut 8:2), His 'sons' (Deut 8:5; cf. Exod 4:22), in the desert for forty years, prior to their mission of the conquest of the promised land. Now He was testing His Son Jesus in the desert for forty days, prior to His great mission of deliverance.[9]

In the light of a more detailed study of the linguistic and theological context of Deuteronomy 8, which several scholars have undertaken,[10] it becomes clear that Jesus saw Himself in typological terms as the new Israel. Both times a "son of God" was tested (Exodus 4:22; Deuteronomy 8:5); both times the testing occurred just after their baptism (Matthew 3:16; 1 Corinthians 10:2); and each time there is the temptation to test God whether He will perform a miracle to fulfill His promises (Deuteronomy 6:16; Exodus 17:2-7; Matthew 4:3-7), as well as the test whether Israel will worship God alone (Deuteronomy 6:13-15; Matthew 4:10). Israel had failed the test, but Jesus did pass the test in triumph on behalf of Israel and mankind. In this way Israel's history is repeated and carried to a successful fulfillment in Christ before God. The truth of Christ's inclusive representation is the reason why the New Testament does not only affirm that direct and typological messianic prophecies are "fulfilled" in Christ, but also that certain historical experiences in the lives of the Old Testament Israelites — mostly of Davidic kings — are also "fulfilled" in Christ's life. It seems as if the New Testament takes Israel's history and prophecy as "typical" of the infinitely greater history of the Messiah of Israel, who will suffer and be exalted in an infinitely deeper sense.

The New Testament truth that Jesus Christ incorporates the Israel of God as a whole and thus brings the essential fulfillment of Israel's history and prophecy in His own life, is crucial to the Christian understanding of Israel's eschatology.[11] On the basis of the Old Testament concept that the Messiah includes in Himself the whole people of God, or redeemed humanity, Christ's sufferings, death, and resurrection mean more than the isolated experience of a righteous individual. They fulfill God's eternal purpose with Israel for mankind.

The earliest Christian confession of faith in the New Testament reflects this christological interpretation of Israel:

> Christ died for our sins *according to the Scriptures,* he was buried, he was raised on the third day *according to the Scriptures* (1 Corinthians 15:3-4; emphasis added).

To which passages in the Old Testament does this religious confession refer? How do Christ and the New Testament writers refer to the Old Testament for their christological interpretation?

According to C. H. Dodd,[12] the New Testament writers do not argue with detached proof texts from the Old Testament, but quote single phrases or sentences only as a pointer to a whole context in the Old Testament. That larger context unfolds the "plot" within Israel's history and provides the key for the unique significance of Jesus' life, death, and resurrection, and of His Church. What happened with Jesus of Nazareth and His people was not a tragic frustration or postponement of God's plan and prophecies. On the contrary, according to the apostle Peter on the day of Pentecost, all these events took place "by God's set purpose" (Acts 2:23; cf. 4:28) as revealed in the Old Testament. How, then, was God's "set purpose" revealed? Our particular concern here focuses on the much-neglected and overlooked style in which Christ and the New Testament writers looked at some historical experiences of collective Israel as typological of the Messiah's experiences (exodus, baptism, desert experiences with temptations). They saw a deeper, fuller sense in the prophecies concerning Israel's national restoration after the Assyrian-Babylonian exile.

### Resurrection of Christ "on the Third Day" in the Old Testament

Christ announced several times that His resurrection from the dead would take place "after three days" (Mark 8:31; 9:31; 10:34), or, "on the third day" (Matthew 16:21; 17:23; 20:19; Luke 9:22; 18:33; 24:7, 46). He stated that not only His suffering and death but also His resurrection "on the third day" was predicted in the Old Testament (Luke 18:31-33; 24:46).

Which Old Testament passages, however, suggest this particular messianic prediction? While the apostles appealed

to three Psalms (2:7; 16:10; 118:22) to substantiate their conviction that God's promises to the fathers had been fulfilled in
the resurrection of Jesus (Psalm 2:7 in Acts 13:33; Psalm 16:10
in Acts 2:31 and 13:35; Psalm 118:22 in Acts 4:11), not one of
these quotations suggests any resurrection "after three days"
and therefore cannot be regarded as the particular source of
Jesus' predicted time element. However, two other Old Testament passages may be recognized as the specific source of Jesus'
announcement: Jonah 1:17 and Hosea 6:2.

It is evident that Jesus saw in Jonah's experience of im-
prisonment in the fish for "three days and three nights" a messianic type of His own stay in the grave. Hosea's remarkable
prediction—made before 722 B.C.—that Israel as God's covenant people would be revived and restored after the Assyrian
captivity, is extremely instructive for understanding Christ's
messianic application of Israel's prophecy. Within the setting
of the impending judgment of God on the nation of the Ten
Tribes by means of the Assyrian exile, Hosea portrays a repentant Israel which will show a real change of heart, by saying:

> Come, let us return to the LORD. He has torn us to pieces but
> he will heal us; he has injured us but he will bind up our
> wounds. *After two days* he will revive us; *on the third day* he
> will restore us, that we may live in his presence (Hosea 6:1-2;
> emphasis added).

One scholar remarks on Hosea 6:2, "Verbally, this verse is
the nearest parallel the Old Testament offers to Jesus' predictions of his resurrection, and its influence on them is widely accepted."[13] Another one calls Hosea 6:2 the "fundamental" text
for Christ's resurrection.[14] Applied to Israel in Assyrian exile,
Hosea's promise of revival and restoration of a repentant Israel
"after two days" and "on the third day," could mean only the
restoration of Israel in the near future. Hosea's prophecy concerning the "two days" and "the third day" clearly referred to
Israel's return from the Assyrian exile. This exile began in 722
B.C. and did not terminate until after the fall of Babylon in 539
B.C. After the exile the rabbis applied Hosea's promise in a
new, eschatological way to the resurrection of Israelites from
the dead, a fact that causes Matthew Black to remark: "The
interpretation of Hosea vi. 2, however, of resurrection is not a
Christian invention. It is a very old Jewish traditional exegesis

of Hosea vi. 2."[15] Jewish exegesis also combined Hosea 6:2 with Jonah 1:17, in order to strengthen Israel's hope for the resurrection from the dead.[16] We conclude, therefore, that Jesus' scriptural source for His conviction that He would be raised from the dead "on the third day" was His combination of the passages Hosea 6:2 and Jonah 1:17.[17]

Jesus applied the symbolic expression of Hosea's prophecy concerning Israel's restoration after "two days" and "on the third day" literally to Himself, to His substitutionary death and resurrection. In other words, Jesus applied a prophecy which originally pertained to the national restoration of a faithful remnant of Israel, to Himself as the Messiah of Israel and to His own speedy resurrection from the dead. While the rabbis made an eschatological application of Hosea's prophecy (6:2), referring to Israel's resurrection from the dead, Jesus made a new and unique messianic application of Israel's restoration to His own resurrection. This was the deeper sense of Hosea's prophecy in Jesus' view. The implication of Jesus' principle of prophetic interpretation is revealing: Jesus *is* Israel, and in His resurrection Israel's restoration is accomplished. C. H. Dodd even says, "The resurrection of Christ *is* the resurrection of Israel of which the prophet spoke."[18]

If Jesus' resurrection is the deeper sense and fulfillment of the prophecy of Hosea 6:2, then the terms "Israel" and her "restoration" should always be understood messianically—that is, christologically—in its eschatological application. The literal prophetic fulfillment in eschatology goes through the cross of Christ and is transformed into Christ's resurrection. Israel's mission and destiny have found completion in Jesus Christ. In His resurrection Israel's hope of restoration has been realized. This messianic style of interpreting Hosea's prophecy concerning Israel's restoration has profound and far-reaching implications for the Christian understanding of Old Testament prophecy. It is reflected in the many New Testament applications to Christ Jesus of Old Testament events that pertain to Israel or representative Israelites.

### Jesus' Messianic Applications
### of Israel's Cultic Songs

Four psalms to which Jesus appealed specifically as prefigurations of His messianic experience (Psalms 22, 41, 69, and 118) deserve our closer attention in order to establish firmly Christ's own principle of messianic interpretation.

Psalms 22, 41, and 69 belong to the recognized class of cultic Lamentations which applied to both the individual Israelite and Israel collectively in times of crisis and suffering. Yet, confidence and thanksgiving to God for His redemptive intervention can also be heard in the Lamentations. The relation between the individual and the people as a whole was very close in Israel, especially when the individual in a song of Israel's communal worship was the king or some other representative leader of the people.

In His moment of deepest agony at the cross, Christ cried out, "My God, my God, why have you forsaken me?" (Matthew 27:46; Mark 15:34). He was quoting the very words of Psalm 22:1 which David had cried out much earlier, in the context of his own despair while being surrounded by bloodthirsty enemies. Because the psalm as a whole is a unit, consisting of an extended lamentation about intense suffering and taunt (verses 1-21), Christ saw in David's bitter experience a clear correspondence or even a type of His own, infinitely deeper agony. David's historic lamentation in Psalm 22 is not a direct messianic prophecy, yet Christ and the New Testament writers apply many aspects of Psalm 22 typologically to the cross and the glory which followed. Psalm 22 is one of the psalms most referred to in the New Testament as having found a deeper fulfillment in Christ. David's rejection in Psalm 22:18, concerning the casting of lots for the condemned one's clothes, is quoted in John 19:24 as "fulfilled" in Christ. David's thanksgiving in Psalm 22:22 is quoted in Hebrews 2:12 as being fulfilled in Christ's glorification.

In Psalm 41 the king of Israel expressed his need in time of severe illness (verses 3, 4) and how his enemies were closing in on him, seeking his death with false accusations (verses 5-8). At the center of this lamentation stands the complaint that even a close friend, who was accustomed to eat at the royal table, had betrayed him:

> Even my close friend, whom I trusted,
> he who shared my bread,
> has lifted up his heel against me.
> —Psalm 41:9

It is possible to see here a reference to Ahithophel, David's trusted counselor (2 Samuel 15:12, 31).

Jesus apparently referred to this experience of David when He said to the Twelve, "I tell you the truth, one of you will betray me—one who is eating with me" . . . "The Son of Man will go just as it is written about him . . ." (Mark 14:18, 21; cf. Luke 22:22). And He added, "This is to *fulfill* the Scripture 'He who shares my bread has lifted up his heel against me'" (John 13:18, emphasis added; cf. 17:12).

King David's shocking betrayal by a close friend (Psalm 41:9) was not a prediction or direct messianic prophecy. Nevertheless, Jesus applied this historic experience and cultic lamentation to Himself, and thereby elevated David's unfortunate betrayal to a type which was "fulfilled" in Christ. Thus He unfolded Psalm 41:9 in a deeper, christological sense.

Psalm 69 contains a desperate lamentation of Judah's King, because he is falsely accused and bitterly persecuted. Nevertheless it concludes with a thanksgiving song and a call for universal praise of God (verses 34-36; cf. Psalm 22:22ff.; 41:13). This leader is compelled by a consuming zeal, a passionate love for God's house, the temple. Accused of robbery, he suffers innocently in this respect (verses 4, 9). He sees himself in his sufferings as a representative and exemplary of others who share a similar plight (verse 6).[19] He stands alone, as God's servant, for the cause of God (verses 8-9, 17), but in spite of his extreme anguish he continues to hope in God (verse 6). Divine intervention brought about a sudden change for the king so that a call for praise and thanksgiving from all Israel concludes this moving song (verses 30-36).

Several quotations from Psalm 69 in the New Testament reveal the messianic significance of this lamentation and doxology.

> Those who hate me without reason . . . (verse 4).
>
> . . . for zeal for your house consumes me
> and the insults of those who insult you f    on me (verse 9).
>
> They put gall in my food
> and gave me vinegar for my thirst (verse 21).

When Christ noticed that the Jews began to reject Him and started to persecute His disciples, He said, "He who hates me hates my Father as well. If I had not done among them what no one else did, they would not be guilty of sin. But now they have seen these miracles, and yet they have hated both me and my

Father. But this is *to fulfill* what is written in their Law: 'They have hated me without reason'" (John 15:23-25; emphasis added). The New Testament connects a particular situation of David's life with a similar situation in Christ's life. More than that, it calls Israel's rejection of Christ a "fulfillment" of what was written in Psalm 69. This connection is justified according to the principle of messianic typology.

Shortly after the incident of Jesus' cleansing of Jerusalem's temple from cattle sellers and money changers, the disciples remembered the words of Psalm 69:9, "Zeal for your house will consume me" (John 2:17). The change from the original present tense in Psalm 69:9 to the future tense in John 2:17 seems to indicate the recognition of a prophetic dimension in Psalm 69. The apostle Paul also applies other words of Psalm 69:9, which pertained originally to David, to Christ's experience (see Romans 15:3). In addition, the description in the synoptic gospels that Jesus was offered wine vinegar while He was hanging on the cross (Matthew 27:48; Mark 15:36; Luke 23:36) corresponds to the experience of the psalmist in Psalm 69:21. The Gospel of John explicitly states that Jesus said on the cross, "I am thirsty," *"so that the Scripture would be fulfilled"* (John 19:28; emphasis added). This "Scripture" is found in Psalm 69:21: "They . . . gave me vinegar for my thirst."

The judgment which David had called down on his own persecutors in Psalm 69:25 is furthermore fulfilled in the fate of Judas, the betrayer of Christ, according to Acts 1:20. Hans J. Kraus observes perceptively:

> Through the sufferings of Jesus, the Servant of God, the mysterious message of Psalm 69 is finally brought to light. From now on the essential message of this psalm will be accessible in no other way. The fulfillment "fills up" the kerugma of the Old Testament psalm, transcending each individuality; it penetrates into the inexhaustible depth of suffering expressed in a song which, in its majestic proclamation, stands beside Is 53, Ps 22, and Ps 118.[20]

Psalm 118 is considered to be part of a thanksgiving liturgy in the temple. It contains responsive acclamations of praise by the worshiping community. An individual worshiper who belonged to the "righteous ones" (verse 20), possibly the king, has experienced a miraculous deliverance from death (verse 17). He feels urged to thank God in the midst of Israel and to recount the act of Yahweh's deliverance (verse 17) as the answer to his supplications (verse 21). His fellow worshipers in the temple express their amazement about the redemption of this oppressed one and the wondrous turn of events for him. He was like a stone which the builders had rejected, which proved to be nevertheless of fundamental importance:

> The stone the builders rejected
>   has become the capstone;
> the LORD has done this,
>   and it is marvelous in our eyes.
>       —Psalm 118:22, 23

The basic idea of this proverbial saying is that a despised one has risen to esteem and honor; one who was doomed to death has received a new life (verses 17-18). All Israel is called to rejoice in his salvation (verses 24-29). Psalm 118 shows how the individual and the collective experience in Israel are interwoven. The gospel writers applied Psalm 118:22 prophetically to the Messiah's suffering and resurrection from the dead (Matthew 21:42, cf. verses 14-15). According to Luke, Jesus asked the rabbis and chief priests who were bent on His destruction, "Then *what is the meaning of that which is written:* 'The stone the builders rejected has become the capstone'?" (Luke 20:17; emphasis added). Apparently Jesus saw in the traditional thanksgiving song of Psalm 118 a messianic meaning which went beyond a purely historical exegesis. Christ penetrated to the hidden meaning of this thanksgiving song through the typological mode of application. The christological interpretation unlocked the significance of this psalm.

Peter's application of Psalm 118 stresses the resurrection of Christ as God's marvelous act. This seemingly nonpredictive psalm has found its fulfillment in Christ. Peter specifically identified Jerusalem's rulers and teachers as "you builders" (Acts 4:11). The Jewish Targum had explained Psalm 118:22 as referring only to David, who had been rejected before he was chosen as the anointed one.[21] But Peter develops with apostolic conviction the eschatological, christological fulfillment of Psalm 118 (see 1 Peter 2:4, 7).

Both Peter and Paul, furthermore, apply "the stone" of Psalm 118 also in a collective or corporate sense to the Church of the apostles (1 Peter 2:4-5; Ephesians 2:20). Christian believers are like living stones "built on the foundation of the apostles and prophets, with Christ Jesus himself as the chief cornerstone" (Ephesians 2:20; 1 Peter 2:5). Consequently, the building of the true temple of God on earth has not been halted or postponed, but was rather advanced and accelerated since Pentecost by the risen Christ Himself.

In summary, the psalms of Israel which have met their fulfillment in Christ Jesus (Psalms 22, 41, 69, 118) were not direct messianic predictions. They are prayers and thanksgivings of Israel which applied directly to the time of the psalm poet or of the Davidic king himself. In the footsteps of Jesus, the New Testament writers proclaimed that Christ's mission, His progression from suffering and rejection to resurrection and exaltation as Lord, was the "fulfillment" of some of the most dramatic experiences of Israel described in the cultic songs of Israel. Thus the New Testament teaches the typological interpretation of Israel's psalms and prayers.[22] This surprising pattern of typology in the Book of Psalms, which came to light only through Jesus Christ and the New Testament, justifies the classification of such psalms as indirect messianic prophecies. The hermeneutical principle that underlies their christological application seems to be that Christ must repeat the experience of Israel in a much fuller sense in order to *fulfill* God's purpose for Israel and the world.[23]

The purpose of these New Testament quotations is not simply to show how hidden messianic predictions were accurately verified in Jesus' life, but rather to proclaim Jesus as the goal of Israel's history and the perfect realization of God's covenant with Israel. Jesus is treasured in the New Testament as infinitely higher than the verifier of verbal predictions. On Him are bestowed at once messianic titles — Messiah, Chosen One, Beloved, Son of David — and Israel-titles — Servant of Yahweh, rejected-but-vindicated stone, cornerstone, temple. In short, the New Testament exalts Christ Jesus as "the perfecter of our faith" (Hebrews 12:2), as "the climax of the pattern of true covenant-relationship."[24]

### Christological Interpretation
### of Historical Descriptions
### in the Prophetic Books

The Gospel writers often declare that certain historical occurrences in Israel's past were "fulfilled" in Christ's own life.

Matthew quotes a historical reference in the book of the prophet Hosea, "Out of Egypt I called my son" (11:1), a statement which reminded Israel of its historic exodus from Egypt. He applies these words to the flight of Joseph and Mary to Egypt until the death of Herod: "And so was fulfilled what the Lord had said through the prophet: 'Out of Egypt I called my son'" (Matthew 2:15). The point of Matthew's quotation is that Hosea's Scripture was "fulfilled" in the little Jesus. Hosea's words, however, were not a prophecy but a meaningful reminder of Israel's historical experience as God's "son" (cf. Exodus 4:22). How, then, can Matthew state that Hosea 11:1 was "fulfilled" in Jesus? By the same rationale which justified the messianic interpretation of David's experiences (see the previous section). As *the* Son of God, Christ not only represents Israel before God, but He also represents Israel's history and destiny in His own life. Matthew tries to teach that the meaning of Israel's history is fully revealed in the life and mission of Jesus Christ.

Matthew goes on to describe the murder of all baby boys two years old and under in Bethlehem by Herod. Now he refers to an event in Israel's history, described in the book of the prophet Jeremiah, as being "fulfilled" in the shocking events in Bethlehem.

> Then what was said through the prophet Jeremiah was fulfilled:
> A voice is heard in Ramah,
>    weeping and great mourning,
> Rachel weeping for her children
>    and refusing to be comforted,
>    because they are no more.
> —Matthew 2:17-18; cf. Jeremiah 31:15

These words refer to the deportation of the Jews from Jerusalem — via Ramah — to Babylon, which Jeremiah witnessed himself. Symbolically, Rachel, as the mother of Israel, was weeping then. According to Matthew this weeping has been "fulfilled," however, in the wailing of the Bethlehemites because of the massacre decreed by Herod in order to kill Jesus. Matthew interprets many crucial events in Israel's history as a foreshadowing of messianic fulfillments. In the life of Christ the fuller meaning of Israel's sacred history is brought to light.[25] In this way Matthew tries to confirm the Christian faith that Jesus is the Messiah of Israel and that God has achieved His goal in His salvation-history with Israel.

Bible scholars begin to accept the theological term *sensus plenior*, or "fuller meaning", in order to acknowledge that Israel's Old Testament history has a deeper meaning than a purely historical-grammatical exegesis can bring to light.[26] Guided by the proper controls,[27] the concept of "fuller meaning" or "deeper sense" is valid and indispensable to recognize how the Gospel writers—and the Apocalypse—interpret the Old Testament. The "fuller" meaning of Scripture stands, by definition, for God's intended meaning in Scripture, which may or may not have been discerned by the human author, but which is made clear by the subsequent revelation of the Holy Spirit. As one scholar clarifies, "In either event, the author does not intentionally convey the *sensus plenior* to his hearers. But at a later date, in the light of further revelation, the fuller meaning becomes clear to readers under the influence of the Spirit who inspired the original author."[28]

Some examples from John's Gospel are instructive in learning how the apostles understood the significance of Israel's history in the Old Testament. John interprets the Jewish disbelief of Jesus as the Messiah as a fulfillment of Jerusalem's disbelief of Isaiah's message.

> Even after Jesus had done all these miraculous signs in their presence, they still would not believe in him. *This was to fulfill the word of Isaiah* the prophet: "Lord, who has believed our message and to whom has the arm of the Lord been revealed?" (John 12:37-38, emphasis added; cf. Isaiah 53:1).

While ancient Israel disbelieved the prophetic message of Isaiah concerning the coming Servant of Yahweh (Isaiah 53), the Jews in Jesus' days disbelieved in a deeper sense, because they saw the fulfillment of Isaiah's prophecy before their eyes and still would not believe in Him. John proceeds to clarify the theological implication of the Jewish rejection of Christ Jesus, appealing to Isaiah 6:9-10 in a literary form which conforms neither to the Hebrew text nor to that of the Septuagint. John introduces Jesus as actually doing what Isaiah originally had been commanded to do by Yahweh. According to Isaiah, God commanded him to tell Jerusalem:

> 'Be ever hearing, but never understanding;
> be ever seeing, but never perceiving.'
> Make the heart of this people calloused;

> make their ears dull and close their eyes.
> —Isaiah 6:9, 10

John quotes Isaiah, however, as saying, "He [the Lord] *has* blinded their eyes and deadened their hearts, so they can neither see with their eyes, nor understand with their hearts . . ." (John 12:40, emphasis added). John, therefore, turns God's commission to the prophet Isaiah into a task fulfilled by Jesus Christ. He adds significantly, "Isaiah said this because he saw Jesus' glory and spoke about him" (John 12:41).

This impressive statement declares nothing less than that Isaiah—in his vision of the awesome holiness of Yahweh in the heavenly temple and of Isaiah's prophetic calling to the people of Israel (Isaiah 6:1-8)—had in reality seen the glory of Christ in His pre-incarnate glory and had spoken about Christ Jesus. For John, the person of Jesus manifests a merger of the glory of Yahweh and of the prophetic mission of Isaiah[29] (cf. John 1:14; 17:4-5). In this surprising way, the apostle John unfolds the fuller meaning of Isaiah's prophetic mission and the subsequent blinding of Israel.

Jesus even read Isaiah's description of the hypocrisy of Jerusalem's worshipers—in the eighth century B.C.—as a prophecy of the hypocrisy of the Pharisees and rabbis of his own day:

> You hypocrites! Isaiah was right when *he prophesied about you:*
>> "These people honor me with their lips,
>> but their hearts are far from me.
>> They worship me in vain; their teachings
>> are but rules taught by men."
> —Matthew 15:7-9, emphasis added; cf. Isaiah 29:13

A literary comparison of Isaiah 6:9-10—both in the Masoretic text and in the Septuagint—and John 12:40 shows that John does not conscientiously stick to the letter of the Old Testament when he quotes it. While preserving the original meaning of the Hebrew text, John feels free to modify the original text—or its Greek version—in order to present the christological meaning more appropriately.[30] For John, as well as for other New Testament authors,[31] the christological meaning of the original text was of primary importance for their Christian understanding of the Old Testament. Henry M. Shires concludes from his study of John's Gospel, "The Evangelist is primarily influenced by his theological conviction [that Jesus is the Messiah of Israel], and he sees the O.T. as a resource that he may use in the effective formulation of his views. But for Christians the meaning of the O.T. is prophetic."[32]

In summary, the New Testament reveals a multiplex, Christ-centered approach to the Old Testament, which is theologically richer and more comprehensive than the hermeneutic of literalism. A consideration of several examples of the New Testament interpretation of messianic prophecies in the Old Testament has disclosed some fascinating patterns of promise and fulfillment within the larger framework of God's ongoing salvation history. Based on the underlying presupposition of God's sovereignty in Israel's history, the New Testament recognizes some *direct* messianic prophecies in the Old Testament which have found their fulfillment in Christ Jesus. More often, however, the New Testament recognizes many *indirect* messianic prophecies which have been confirmed in their fuller meaning (*sensus plenior*) in Christ through a typological fulfillment, especially in the pattern of suffering followed by exaltation in the Royal Psalms. Finally, the New Testament innovated a messianic interpretation of *nonpredictive* historical passages of Israel's experience in the Old Testament, again in terms of typological correlations. In these various ways the New Testament teaches that the events in Christ's life—His birth in Bethlehem, His humiliating death, but also His resurrection and exaltation at the right hand of God—were not unforeseen, accidental events. They were the design of God's predetermined purpose in His formation and calling of Israel. While the direct messianic prophecies have a definite apologetic usefulness for the gospel proclamation to non-Christians, the promise-fulfillment pattern in the typological prophecies and in the history of Israel seem valid and cogent only for Christians who already believe that Jesus is the Messiah of Israel's prophecy.

This faith in Christ Jesus is ultimately based on the objective historical facts of Christ's life and resurrection from the dead. Such faith opens the eyes to see Christ in the entire Old Testament,[33] so that messianic prophecies are no longer isolated and limited to a particular group of predictive prophecies or to some sections of the Scriptures (see John 5:39, 46; Luke 24:27, 44-47). This view of Christ as the embodiment of Israel and the representative of mankind we owe to Jesus Himself, because He understood the Old Testament, as a whole, typologically. For this reason the Old Testament cannot be exhausted or antiquated, even by the literal fulfillment of its predictions and prefigurations. "The conviction grows that the New Testament writers used the Scriptures with knowledge and spiritual understanding, fully knowing what they were doing. To them the Old Testament as a whole and in all its parts was a witness to Christ."[34] Through the Spirit of Christ, the believer becomes excited in the joy of discovery to discern new veins of truth in Scripture which confirm the spiritual unity of the Old and New Testaments. The Old Testament becomes to him a Christian book just as much as the New Testament, because "the entirety of the Old Testament points as one great arrow to the fulfillment which the New Testament records."[35]

### Notes on Chapter 5

[1]See W. C. Kaiser, Jr., "Messianic Prophecies in the Old Testament," in *Handbook of Biblical Prophecy*, ed. C. E. Amerding and W. W. Gasque (Grand Rapids, Mich.: Baker Book House, 1978), p. 84. Also his *Toward an Old Testament Theology*, p. 141. Cf. *SDABC*, vol. 1, pp. 1017-19 (on Deuteronomy 18:15).

[2]See Kaiser, *Toward an Old Testament Theology*, pp. 149-157 (on 2 Samuel 7); pp. 159-166 (on the Royal Psalms); pp. 208-210 (on Isaiah 7:14). On Isaiah 7:14, see *Problems in Bible Translation*, ed. a committee of the General Conference of Seventh-day Adventists (Washington, D.C.: Review and Herald Pub. Assn., 1954), p. 151-169.

[3]Kistemaker, *The Psalm Citations in the Epistle to the Hebrews*, pp. 145-146.

[4]W. J. Beecher, *The Prophets and the Promise* (Grand Rapids, Mich.: Baker Book House, 1975; reprint of 1905), pp. 129-131.

[5]Paul Peters, quoted in W. J. Hassold, "Rectilinear or Typological Interpretation of Messianic Prophecy," *Concordia* 38 (1967): 155-167; quotation on p. 155. This article presents an instructive report of the debate in Lutheranism about direct *or* typological messianic prophecy.

[6]Kaiser, "Messianic Prophecies in the Old Testament," in *Handbook of Biblical Prophecy*, p. 77.

[7]See France, *Jesus and the Old Testament*, pp. 43-49.

[8]K. J. Woollcombe (*Essays on Typology*, ed. Lampe and Woollcombe [Napierville, Ill.: A. R. Allenson, 1957], pp. 43-44) finds the concept of *recapitulation* entrenched in the Old Testament eschatological prophecies, e.g., Ezekiel's temple vision, in view of Solomon's temple and Israel's tabernacle.

[9]R. T. France, "'In All the Scriptures' — A Study of Jesus' Typology," *TSF Bulletin* (1970), p. 14.

[10]France, *Jesus and the Old Testament*, pp. 50-53. B. Gerhardsson, *The Testing of God's Son* (Lund: CWK Gleerup, 1966), chapters 1-4, especially pp. 19-35.

[11]Dodd, *The Old Testament in the New*, p. 29. Cf. H. Wheeler Robinson, *Corporate Personality in Ancient Israel* (Philadelphia: Fortress Press, 1967).

[12]Dodd, *According to the Scriptures*. Also his *The Old Testament in the New*; H. M. Shires, *Finding the Old Testament in the New* (Philadelphia: Westminster Press, 1974); Bruce, *New Testament Development of Old Testament Themes*.

[13]France, *Jesus and the Old Testament*, p. 54. Cf. Dodd, *The Old Testament in the New*, p. 30; C. Westermann, *The Old Testament and Jesus Christ*, tr. Omar Kaste (Minneapolis: Augsburg Publ., 1971).

[14]H. E. Tödt, *The Son of Man in the Synoptic Tradition*, tr. Dorothea M. Barton (Philadelphia: Westminster Press), p. 185.

[15]See M. Black, "The Christological Use of the OT in the NT," *NTS* 18 (1972):1-14; quotation from p. 6.

[16]J. W. Doeve, *Jewish Hermeneutics in the Synoptic Gospels and Acts* (Assen: Van Gorcum, 1954), p. 149, who refers to *Ber. Rabba* LVI:1; XCL:7 (end).

[17]See France, *Jesus and the Old Testament*, p. 55.

[18]Dodd, *According to the Scriptures*, p. 103. Cf. also France, *Jesus and the Old Testament*, p. 55.

[19]See Kraus, *Psalmen*, p. 482 (on Psalm 69:7).

[20]Kraus, *Psalmen*, p. 485 (my translation).

[21]Black, "The Christological Use of the OT in the NT," pp. 12-13.

[22]Mowinckel, *He That Cometh*, p. 12.

[23]France, *Jesus and the Old Testament*, p. 59.

[24]C. F. D. Moule, "Fulfillment-Words in the New Testament: Use and Abuse," *NTS* 14 (1968):293-320; especially 298-302.

[25]For a fuller treatment, D. A. Hagner, "The Old Testament in

the New Testament," pp. 90-104. J. C. K. Von Hofmann, *Interpreting the Bible* (Minneapolis: Augsburg Publ., 1972), pp. 169-204.

[26]D. A. Hagner, in *Handbook of Biblical Prophecy*, ed. C. E. Amerding and W. W. Gasque (Grand Rapids, Mich.: Baker Book House, 1978), p. 91. W. S. LaSor, "Interpretation of Prophecy," in *Hermeneutics*, ed. B. Ramm, et al. (Grand Rapids, Mich.: Baker Book House, 1971), pp. 106-108. See the Roman Catholic scholar R. E. Brown, *The Sensus Plenior of Sacred Scripture* (Baltimore: St. Mary's University, 1955), p. 92.

[27]See Hagner, in *Handbook of Biblical Prophecy*, p. 93f.; LaSor, "Interpretation of Prophecy," in *Hermeneutics*, p. 116.

[28]LaSor, "Interpretation of Prophecy," in *Hermeneutics*, p. 108.

[29]Cf. Von Hofmann, *Interpreting the Bible*, pp. 202-204.

[30]Cf. *Old Testament Quotations in the New Testament*, ed. R. G. Bratcher (London: United Bible Societies, 1967), p. 24. For the version of Isaiah 6:9-10 in Mark 4:12 according to the version found in the Targum of Jonathan, see Hagner, "The Old Testament in the New Testament," in *Interpreting the Word of God*, pp. 87-88. The quotation in Matthew 13:14-15 agrees with the Septuagint of Isaiah 6:9-10.

[31]Another example of remarkable freedom in deviating from the original text is found in the "quotation" in Hebrews 10:37-38 of Habakkuk 2:3-4. See T. W. Manson, "The Argument From Prophecy," *JTS* 46 (1945):129-136.

[32]Shires, *Finding the Old Testament in the New*, p. 60.

[33]See Westermann, *The Old Testament and Jesus Christ*; J. A. Borland, *Christ in the Old Testament: A Comprehensive Study of OT Appearance of Christ in Human Form* (Chicago: Moody Press, 1978); Wenham, *Christ and the Bible*.

[34]Wenham, *Christ and the Bible*, p. 108.

[35]Hagner, "The Old Testament in the New Testament," in *Interpreting the Word of God*, p. 103. Cf. H. L. Ellison, *The Centrality of the Messianic Idea for the Old Testament* (Leicester: Theological Students Fellowship, 1977), p. 6: "The whole Old Testament, and not merely an anthology of proof passages, was looked on as referring to Christ Jesus."

# 6

## The Theological Significance
## and Mission of Israel

In his *Studies in the Name 'Israel' in the Old Testament*
(Uppsala, 1946), the Swedish scholar Gustaf A. Danell concludes that the name "Israel," besides being used as the name of
a person, can designate three related groups: (1) the union of
the twelve tribes before the division of the kingdom; (2) the ten
tribes of northern Israel; (3) Judah, after the fall of the northern
kingdom, as the remnant of Israel (p. 9). Our primary interest
seeks to penetrate beyond these external designations to the religious nature and the theological meaning of the name "Israel"
as presented in the Old and New Testaments. In this respect the
Dutch Old Testament scholar A. R. Hulst has demonstrated
that the name "Israel" has a twofold meaning from the outset:
"people" or "nation" and "people of Yahweh" or "religious congregation."[1] Let us briefly consider the religious-theological use
of the name "Israel" in the Old Testament.

### Israel in the Old Testament

The very first use of the name "Israel" in the Bible, in
Genesis 32, presents an explanation of the origin and meaning
of this new name. About to enter the land of Canaan, the guilt-
ridden patriarch Jacob, out of fear for his life, began to wrestle
one night with an unknown "Man" who appeared to possess
superhuman strength. Jacob persistently entreated this Man
for his blessing. The reply was then given, "Your name will no
longer be Jacob, but Israel, because you have struggled with
God and with men and have overcome" (Genesis 32:28; cf.
35:9-10). Later the prophet Hosea interpreted Jacob's struggle

as a struggle "with God," "with the angel" (Hosea 12:3,4). The new name "Israel" is thus revealed to be of divine origin. It symbolizes Jacob's new spiritual relation to Yahweh and stands for the reconciled Jacob through God's forgiving grace.

It has been stressed that Jacob's struggle was initiated by God and that Jacob's victory was his progress "from resisting to clinging," meaning that Jacob abandoned his own self-sufficiency and self-defense by clinging in trust to the Angel of God in order to receive the divine assurance of acceptance.[2] E. G. White explains Jacob's change of name as follows: "As an evidence that he had been forgiven, his name was changed from one that was a reminder of his sin, to one that commemorated his victory."[3]

In other words, the name "Israel" from the beginning symbolizes a personal relation of reconciliation with God. The rest of Holy Scripture never loses sight of this sacred root of the name. In fact, God wants to repeat His initiative of wrestling with man to all Israelites who have descended from Jacob. Through the prophet Hosea, God presents Jacob's struggle and total trust in Yahweh as an example that needed to be imitated by the apostate tribes of Israel, who were trusting more in the war-horses of Assyria and Egypt (Hosea 12:3-6; 14:1-3). In other words, Jacob's struggle with God is set forth by Hosea as a prototype of the true Israel, as the normative pattern for the house of Israel in order to become the Israel of God.

God's purpose for the people of Israel was indicated by Moses when he said to Pharaoh, "This is what the LORD says: Israel is my firstborn son, and I told you, 'Let my son go, so he may worship me'" (Exodus 4:22). The tribes of Israel are called to worship the Lord, the Holy One, according to His revealed will. They are "His people Israel" (Exodus 18:1), "the LORD's community" (Numbers 20:4).

Israel is different from all other nations, not because of any ethnic, moral, or political quality, but solely because Israel was chosen by the Lord to receive His promises made to the patriarchs (Deuteronomy 7:6-9). God redeemed Israel from its bondage to Egypt in order to bind Israel exclusively to Himself:

> You yourselves have seen what I did to Egypt, and how I carried you on eagles' wings and brought you to myself. Now if you obey me fully and keep my covenant, then out of all nations you will be my treasured possession. Although the whole earth

is mine, you will be for me a kingdom of priests and a holy nation (Exodus 19:4-6).

We may distinguish two aspects of God's covenant with Israel. First, Israel as an ethnic unity was chosen to be God's own people in order to worship Him because of His redeeming grace and love (cf. Ezekiel 16); secondly, Israel would only remain God's treasured possession and holy nation if Israel would obey God and keep His covenant (Exodus 20-24). This is a clearly conditional aspect regarding Israel's future status in God's covenant.

Basic is the revelation that Israel's national unity was from the outset based on God's redeeming act for Israel and His claim on Israel's worship and allegiance. The ethnic and the religious concepts are kept together through the Old Testament concept of a faithful remnant.[4] G. E. Ladd explains:

> The prophets saw Israel as a whole as rebellious and disobedient and therefore destined to suffer the divine judgment. Still there remained within the faithless nation a remnant of believers who were the object of God's care. Here in the believing remnant was the true people of God.[5]

God's covenant with Israel will therefore always continue through the remnant, even when the covenant curses would disperse Israel as an ethnic group among all the other nations of the world (see Deuteronomy 27-28) and the temple would be destroyed (see Leviticus 26). The divine promise is given that, in spite of Israel's disobedience and rebellion against God, "I will not reject them or abhor them so as to destroy them completely, breaking my covenant with them. I am the LORD their God" (Leviticus 26:44). God's plan for Israel on behalf of the nations will be fulfilled, but in God's own, surprising way.

The book of Deuteronomy stresses the objective of Israel's election as a deeply religious mission. Israel is characterized as "the children of the LORD your God" (Deuteronomy 14:1), as "a people holy to the LORD your God," "chosen to be his treasured possession" (Deuteronomy 14:2). Israel is called to respond to her Redeemer by worshiping Yahweh (Deuteronomy 13:6-10) and thus to be religiously "blameless" before God (Deuteronomy 18:9-13).

On all Israelites God had placed a sacred obligation:

> I am the LORD your God, who brought you out of Egypt,

out of the land of slavery.
You shall have no other gods before me . . .

—Exodus 20:2

Hear, O Israel: the LORD our God, the LORD is one.
Love the LORD your God with all your heart and with all your
soul and with all your strength.

—Deuteronomy 6:4-5

And again:

Be silent, O Israel, and listen!
You have now become the people of the LORD your God.
Obey the LORD your God and follow his commands and
decrees that I give you today.

—Deuteronomy 27:9-10

At Mount Sinai the tribes of Israel were officially constituted as Israel, the people of the Lord. God's own word and
act elevated Israel into a worshiping congregation or assembly
(qahal), in order to be a priestly light for the rest of humanity.
Significant is the conclusion of A. Hulst regarding the meaning
of the name "Israel" in Deuteronomy:

Its concern is not with a conglomerate of different tribes and
groups, not with a sum total of individuals, not — and this must
be stressed — with a people as an ethnic entity beside other peoples, but rather with the "assembly," the religious community
which finds its unity in the word and law of Yahweh, and thereby ultimately in Yahweh Himself.

The name "Israel" in Deuteronomy signifies, therefore, the
people in their relation to Yahweh. In focus is not the people in
their national aspect, not first of all as an ethnic group, but the
people as a religious unit. It pertains to the purity of life in its
social, religious and cultic spheres.[6]

In the book of Deuteronomy the term "Israelites" (literally: sons of Israel) (1:1; 4:44-46; 10:6; 28:69; 33:1; 34:8, 9;
etc.) seems to designate more the physical descendents of
Jacob, while the name "Israel" indicates the religious unity of
the covenant people of God. Of course, blood relationship is
not necessarily identical with faith relationship. Deuteronomy
shows a distinction between the *worshiping* community and
*ethnic* bonds.

The religious law of Deuteronomy 23 allows Egyptian and
Edomite families who had lived for three generations among

Israel to participate in the worship of "the assembly of the LORD" (*qahal*; Deuteronomy 23:7-8). The blessing of prosperity in the promised land in Deuteronomy is never unconditional, but always depends on whether Israel keeps the Lord's commandments and Torah (see Deuteronomy 26:16-19; 27:9-10). Joshua, the successor of Moses, reports how at Shechem Israel accepted the worship of the Lord alone as the basis of its common life (Joshua 24:16-18). Israel continually renewed her covenant with God in the sacred liturgy of her yearly festivals:

> At the central sanctuary the confederation of the twelve tribes was ever and again called back to its covenant relationship with the Lord, and pledged anew to the service of God through obedience to His law. So those things which happened at Sinai are not simply a series of historical happenings in the past; in the solemn worship of the twelve tribes they become again a present and contemporary reality . . . The word of proclamation makes visible the basis of Israel's being. Unless this word is spoken, the fellowship of the twelve tribes is in danger of falling away into the error of self-assertion and self-determination.[7]

In the book of Psalms, which contains the name "Israel" fifty-nine times, "Israel" denotes the people as an assembly which worships Yahweh in the temple at Jerusalem.[8] The name "Judah" is practically never used to designate the worshiping community.

The prophets of Israel began to indicate that Israel as a nation, because of her religious apostasy from Yahweh and her social injustice, would, like other nations, fall under the Lord's punishing justice (Amos 3:2). Nevertheless, a remnant, a "holy seed," would remain (1 Kings 19:18; Isaiah 6:13; 8:17-18; 10:20-22). Amos was the first prophet who rejected the popular idea that Israel as a nation would be saved in the Day of Yahweh's judgment of the world (Amos 3:2; 9:1-4, 9, 10). He stressed the condition of Israel's *religious* response to the promise of salvation:

> Seek the LORD and live, or he will sweep through the house of Joseph like a fire (Amos 5:6).

Only a remnant from the nation of Israel would survive God's future judgment (Amos 3:12; 5:15). This remnant would be sifted out through faithfulness to the covenant on the Day of Yahweh (5:15), just as God chose His remnant in the days of

Elijah (1 Kings 19:18). Surprisingly, Amos revealed another vital aspect of Israel's restoration promise: also non-Israelites will be drawn into the circle of the eschatological remnant of Israel and the house of David:

> In that day I will restore David's fallen tent. I will repair its broken places, restore its ruins, and build it as it used to be, so that they may possess the remnant of Edom and all the nations that bear my name, declares the LORD, who will do these things (Amos 9:11-12).

Amos' prophecy announces that the eschatological remnant of Israel is "largely an entity of religious instead of national destination."[9]

The remnant motif becomes a leading element in Isaiah's proclamation of judgment and salvation. The combination of doom and salvation is inherent in the concept of the holiness of Yahweh. The prophet Isaiah felt totally lost, yet was graciously reconciled, purified, and called to be God's ambassador (6:1-8). G. F. Hasel explains, "So the prophet himself may be considered the proleptic representative of the future remnant because he was confronted by Yahweh's 'holiness' and emerged as a cleansed and purified individual."[10]

The destructive judgment on the house of Israel and the house of David would not annihilate all life in Israel. "But as the terebinth and oak leave stumps when they are cut down, so the holy seed will be the stump in the land" (Isaiah 6:13). This "stump" or root stock represents both the destruction of the nation of Israel and the preserved life which would continue in the remnant. But this remnant of Israel wil be holy only because it has, like Isaiah, experienced God's cleansing judgment. And "because of this experience it will stand in the right relationship of faith and trust and obedience to Yahweh. It will then be the carrier of election."[11]

Isaiah uses the name "Israel" also for the house of Judah (Isaiah 1:1-3; 8:14). He announces the destruction of Israel as a nation (Isaiah 6:11-13) so that only God's faithful remnant will inherit the covenant promises. God's purpose with Israel as a "holy" nation (Exodus 19:6) or "holy" people (Deuteronomy 7:6) was that "the whole earth" may be full of God's glory (Isaiah 6:3). This aim had been thwarted by Israel's unfaithfulness. Yet God's eternal purpose will stand and be fulfilled through the holy remnant of Israel (Isaiah 4:2-6; 6:13). This concept of a holy remnant belongs to the core of Isaiah's eschatology (cf. Isaiah 1:24-26).

During the Syro-Ephraimitic crisis in Jerusalem (734-733 B.C.), Isaiah revealed that a trusting faith in Yahweh is the distinctive criterion of the holy remnant (Isaiah 7:9; cf. 30:15-18). Isaiah, and his children and disciples, were "signs and symbols in Israel from the LORD Almighty" pointing forward to the future remnant (Isaiah 8:18). This fact shows that Isaiah uses the remnant motif not only for the eschatological judgment of God, but applies it also to the political crisis of his own time (cf. Isaiah 1:4-9; 11:11, 16). Isaiah's hope is that the contemporary remnant of Israel will provide the condition for the emergence of the holy remnant of the future. Isaiah "does not know the distinction of a 'secular-profane' and a 'theological' remnant motif."[12] He uses his remnant motif only in a religious-theological sense, both for his own time and for the future.

More than any other prophet's words, Isaiah's predictive prophecies of chapters 40-66 stand out as the great promises of Israel's restoration after the Assyrian-Babylonian exile. In these accumulating assurances of Israel's gathering out of the great dispersion, the prophetic focus is not exclusively on the physical descendants of Jacob who are committed to worship Yahweh. Isaiah envisions that among post-exilic Israel, many non-Israelites would be gathered who have chosen to worship the God of Israel. Two classes of people, foreigners and eunuchs (castrated males), who were forbidden entrance into the worshiping assembly of Yahweh according to the law of Moses (Deuteronomy 23:1-3), are now welcome to worship in the new temple on Mount Zion on the condition that they accept the Sabbath of the Lord and hold fast to God's covenant.

> These I will bring to my holy mountain and give them joy in my house of prayer. Their burnt offerings and sacrifices will be accepted on my altar; *for my house will be called a house of prayer for all nations.* The sovereign LORD declares—he who gathers the exiles of Israel: I will gather still others to them besides those already gathered (Isaiah 56:7-8, emphasis added; cf. 45:20-25).

When Gentiles join themselves in faith and obedience to the Lord (Isaiah 56:3), the God of Israel will give those foreigners within Israel "a memorial and a name better than sons and daughters . . . an everlasting name" (Isaiah 56:5). In this way Isaiah unfolds how God's universal outreach to the world, as indicated in his covenant with Abraham (Genesis 12:2, 3) and Israel (Exodus 19:6), will be ultimately fulfilled through a new Israel. The essential characteristic of this new Israel is not ethnic descent from Abraham, but the faith of Abraham, the worship of Yahweh. Believing Gentiles will enjoy the same rights and hopes of the covenant promises as believing Israelites. Claus Westermann observes in Isaiah 56:

> Here . . . the physical and the spiritual have ceased to be necessarily united in this way. The name [Israel] may live on without descendents born of one's body. . . . The new community is on the way to a new form of association which is no longer identical with the old concepts of the chosen people. As early as here [Isaiah 56] we find important elements of the New Testament's concept of community. . . . He 'gathers' Israel also from those who hitherto have not been able to belong to her.[13]

Westermann concludes that Isaiah views Israel, not primarily as an ethnic or political entity, but rather as a religious congregation or "church," as the people of God.

The prophet Micah unites the promise of a "remnant of Israel" (2:12), the new people of God, with the promise of the Messiah who would come out of Bethlehem (5:2). He will gather the remnant of Israel "like sheep in a pen, like a flock in its pasture" (2:12). "He will stand and shepherd his flock in the strength of the LORD" (5:4).

The prophet Jeremiah, who served God during the last forty years of the kingdom of Judah (625–586 B.C.), uses the name "Israel" in various ways depending on each immediate context. It becomes clear, however, that Jeremiah does not focus his promises and predictions on the restoration of Israel as an independent political state, but on Israel as a restored spiritual people of God gathered from all twelve tribes. The new covenant which Yahweh shall make with the house of Israel and the house of Judah after the Babylonian exile will be explicitly different from the Sinaitic covenant (31:31-34). The restored Israel shall be a praying, worshiping remnant from all the twelve tribes, in which each Israelite, individually, has the experience of a saving relationship with God and obeys

His holy law with an undivided heart (31:6; 32:38-40).

Although Jeremiah does not explicitly include non-Israelites in his prophecy of God's new covenant with Israel, nevertheless all believers in Yahweh from all nations are included in principle. The privilege of belonging to the new covenant community is made contingent, not on ethnic or political conditions, but on a personal, spiritual connection with God, "or better, on God's attitude to man."[14] God's purpose, according to Jeremiah, is not a Jewish state as such, "but a people that obeys Yahweh, a community which serves Him and is wholly oriented toward Him."[15] This conclusion is underscored by Jeremiah's prediction that even the ark of the covenant of the Lord, the visible symbol of God's presence in the temple of Jerusalem, shall no longer be remembered or needed (Jeremiah 3:16).

The prophet Ezekiel, who was himself deported to Babylon in 597 B.C., also predicted that a new, spiritual Israel shall return from exile in all nations to their homeland:

> They will return to it and remove all its vile images and detestable idols. I will give them an undivided heart and put a new spirit in them; I will remove from them their heart of stone and give them a heart of flesh. Then they will follow my decrees and be careful to keep my laws. They will be my people, and I will be their God. But as for those whose hearts are devoted to their vile images and detestable idols, I will bring down on their own heads what they have done, declares the Sovereign LORD (Ezekiel 11:18-21).

These and similar predictions (cf. 36:24-33; 37:22-26) stress that God's central concern with Israel is her restoration, not as a secular, political state, but as a united theocracy, a spiritually cleansed and truly worshiping people of God. Ezekiel's focus in his restoration promises is not primarily on Israel's return to her homeland, but on her return to Yahweh. He states that God shall purge the exiled Israelites in "the desert of the nations" from their defiling idolatry and spirit of secularization so that only a repentant and cleansed Israel would return to the land of Israel (Ezekiel 20:32-36).[16]

The post-exilic Israel was a religious community centered around the rebuilt temple, not around a royal throne. Although the majority of the returned exiles were from the tribes of Judah and Levi, this spiritual remnant regarded itself as the continuation and representation of the Israel of God (Ezra 2:2, 70; 3:1, 11; 4:3; 6:16-17, 21; Nehemiah 1:6; 2:10; 8:1, 17; 10:39; 12:47; Malachi 1:1, 5; 2:11).

The prophet Zechariah predicted that in Israel the difference between ritual holiness and the ordinary life will ultimately be abolished and that no idolater shall remain in Israel:

> Every pot in Jerusalem and Judah will be holy to the LORD Almighty, and all who come to sacrifice will take some of the pots and cook in them. And on that day there will no longer be a Canaanite in the house of the LORD Almighty (Zechariah 14:21).

The last prophet, Malachi, stressed that those Israelites who "fear Yahweh" are the people of God, and that only those "who serve God" are recognized as God's own treasured possession in the last Judgment Day (Malachi 3:16-4:3). Judah is regarded as the sons of Jacob and the inheritor of God's covenant with Israel (1:1; 2:11; 3:6; 4:4).

In summary, the Old Testament uses the name "Israel" in more than one way. First and foremost, it stands for the religious covenant community, the people who worship Yahweh in truth and Spirit. Secondarily, it denotes a distinct ethnic group or nation which is called to become spiritual Israel. Decisive for the Old Testament prophets and their prophecies is the theological quality of "people of God," not their ethnic and political characteristics. The original meaning of the name "Israel," as a symbol of acceptance with God by His forgiving grace (Genesis 32:28), forever remains the sacred root to which the prophets call the natural tribes of Israel to return (Hosea 12:6; Jeremiah 31:31-34; Ezekiel 36:26-28).

Whenever the Old Testament prophets portray the eschatological remnant of Israel, it is always characterized as a faithful, religious community which worships God with a new heart on the basis of the "new covenant" (Joel 2:32; Zephaniah 3:12, 13; Jeremiah 31:31-34; Ezekiel 11:16-21). This faithful remnant of the end-time will become God's witness among all the nations and includes also non-Israelites, regardless of their ethnic origin (Zechariah 9:7; 14:16; Isaiah 66:19; Daniel 7:27; 12:1-3).

The total picture of the Old Testament eschatological remnant reveals that Israel's covenant blessings as a whole will be fulfilled, *not* in unbelieving national Israel, but only in that Israel which is faithful to Yahweh and trusts in His Messiah. This remnant of Israel will incorporate the faithful remnants of all the gentile nations and thus fulfill the divine purpose of Israel's election.

### The Universal Purpose
### of Israel's Election

Moses had stressed the fact that God has chosen and redeemed Israel, not because of any moral virtue in the Israelites themselves, but exclusively because of God's faithfulness to His gracious promises made to the patriarchs Abraham, Isaac, and Jacob (Deuteronomy 7:7-9; Exodus 2:24-25). He who had brought Abraham out of Ur of the Chaldeans (Genesis 15:7), had brought the tribes of Israel out of Egypt (Exodus 20:2) in order to fulfill the Abrahamic covenant:

> I will make you into a great nation and I will bless you. I will make your name great, and you will be a blessing. I will bless those who bless you, and whoever curses you I will curse; and all peoples on earth will be blessed through you (Genesis 12:2-3; cf. 22:17-18; 26:4).[17]

We need to keep in view the organic unity of this multiple promise and its universal purpose: to bless all the peoples of the earth through Abraham and his offspring. This universal blessing undoubtedly serves to counteract the universal curse which had fallen upon the whole human race because of its rebellion against God (Genesis 3:17; 4:11-12). While "curse" stands for the destructive powers which ultimately lead to death, "blessing" represents the restoring, prospering, and prevailing powers which ultimately lead to life eternal (cf. Genesis 22:17; Numbers 23:7-10, 20-24; 2 Samuel 7:29). In this light it becomes clear that the divine election of Abram, and of Israel as a people, served the universal purpose of salvation. Israel's particular ethnic and geographic promises are subordinated to the purpose of saving mankind and not to a different and independent goal. The prophet Isaiah states:

> It is too small a thing for you to be my servant to restore the tribes of Jacob and bring back those of Israel I have kept. I will also make you a light for the Gentiles, that you may bring my salvation to the ends of the earth (Isaiah 49:6).

Jesus confirms: "Salvation is *from* the Jews" (John 4:22). Israel's particular election is therefore organically one with God's universal plan of salvation. As G. Vos summarizes, "The election of Abraham, and in the further development of things of Israel, was meant as a particularistic means toward a univeralistic end."[18]

From the very outset Israel was called to be a priestly light among the nations, "a kingdom of priests and a holy nation" (Exodus 19:6). All the other nations were called by God to share in the blessing given to Israel "if they acknowledged Israel or its king as bearer of the blessing."[19] God's plan of universal blessing and peace by means of Israel's election (Psalm 72:17; Jeremiah 4:2) becomes the subject of predictive prophecy in Isaiah:

> In the last days the mountain of the LORD's temple will be established as chief among the mountains; it will be raised above the hills, and all nations will stream to it. Many peoples will come and say, "Come, let us go up to the mountain of the LORD, to the house of the God of Jacob. He will teach us his ways, so that we may walk in his paths." The law will go out from Zion, the word of the LORD from Jerusalem. He will judge between the nations and will settle disputes for many peoples. They will beat their swords into plowshares and their spears into pruning hooks. Nation will not take up sword against nation, nor will they train for war anymore. Come, O house of Jacob, let us walk in the light of the LORD (Isaiah 2:2-5).

This prediction does not in the least eliminate or diminish the moral condition of loving obedience to the revealed Torah on the part of Israel or the Davidic king. In the name of God, Jeremiah confronted a backsliding Israel in Jerusalem with the original condition: "Obey me, and I will be your God and you will be my people" (Jeremiah 7:23).

Israel's election did not imply the rejection of the other peoples, but rather their inclusion. Israel was chosen, not just for its own salvation, but to lead the whole world to share in her saving knowledge and blessing. In short, Israel was chosen to represent the attractive character and saving will of Yahweh to the Gentiles. Commenting on Jeremiah 7:23, H. H. Rowley wrote these thought-provoking words:

> The purpose of the election is service, and when the service is withheld the election loses its meaning, and therefore fails. . . .

If she [Israel] ceased to acknowledge Yahweh to be her God, then she declared that she no longer wished to be His people. This is well brought out in Jeremiah's parable of the potter (Jer 18:1f.). The vessel that fails to realize the intention of the potter is refashioned into another vessel. . . . Her high calling to be the Chosen People was not the mark of the Divine indulgence or favouritism, but a summons to a task exacting and unceasing, and election and task were so closely bound together that she could not have the one without the other.[20]

If Israel would finally determine to be unfaithful to Yahweh, she would lose her privileges to receive God's blessings and be placed under the covenant curse, as stated so forthrightly in Leviticus 26 and Deuteronomy 28. The history of Israel, as recorded by Moses and the prophets, has been called "a history of failure" (R. Bultmann). Nevertheless, God's purpose for the world cannot be thwarted (Job 42:2). It is written, "I say: My purpose will stand, and I will do all that I please" (Isaiah 46:11). When Israel failed as a nation, the Lord Himself provided a perfect Israelite as the blessing and the light for both Israel and the world. The promised Messiah will not fail, because "the will of the LORD will prosper in his hand" (Isaiah 53:10).

The fundamental purpose of Israel's mission reaches its greatest clarity in Isaiah's four prophetic "Songs concerning the Servant of Yahweh" (Isaiah 42:1-4; 49:1-6; 50:4-9; 52:13–53:12). We take the position that the Servant stands for *both* the collective Israel and the representative Israelite in whom the people of Israel were embodied. Israel as a whole was called to be a missionary community, but ultimately only One would prove to fulfill Israel's mission, as Isaiah had outlined. The chosen Servant would serve the Lord, not only in spreading the knowledge of the true God to the ends of the earth (Isaiah 42:1-4), but also serve God in gathering Israel back to God (Isaiah 49:5-6). The Servant is called Israel (Isaiah 49:3) and also thought of as having a mission to Israel (Isaiah 49:5-6). To modern thought, this tension between identification and differentiation posits an antithesis but, as is being widely acknowledged today, "The Hebrew concept of corporate personality can reconcile both, and pass without explanation or explicit indication from one to the other in a fluidity of transition."[21] This means that in ancient Israel a representative individual could express the higher purpose of a group or nation. For instance, the *king* in Israel is called the "son" of God (2 Samuel 7:14; Psalm 2:7); while Hosea also calls the *nation* of Israel "son" of God (Hosea 11:1). This Hebrew concept of representation or "corporate personality" is the very foundation of the Christian doctrine of salvation by faith in Christ, as proclaimed by the apostle Paul: "For as in Adam all die, so in Christ all will be made alive" (1 Corinthians 15:22).

The prophet Isaiah distinguishes between an actual Israel, which is a "blind" and "deaf" servant of Yahweh (Isaiah 42:19-20), and the suffering servant of Yahweh as the faithful Israel (Isaiah 42:1-4; 49:1-6; 50:4-9; 52:13–53:12). As one scholar observes:

> But while the Servant is in some sense the representative or embodiment of Israel, he is distinguished from the nation as a whole, to which indeed his mission is first directed, as well as (thereafter) to the Gentile world.[22]

The individual Servant is strengthened by God for his mission and is vindicated against false charges from either Jewish or gentile opposition (Isaiah 50:4-9). The fourth Song of Yahweh's Servant, Isaiah 52:13–53:12, has been called "the culminating glory of Old Testament religion" (H. W. Robinson). The Servant would accept not only suffering and contempt, but also — unlike any other prophet — even death as the crowning act of his obedience, as "the very means by which he fulfills the purpose of God . . . and in consequence brings blessing and liberation to multitudes."[23]

> For he was cut off from the land of the living; for the transgression of my people he was stricken. . . . Yet it was the LORD's will to crush him and cause him to suffer, and though the LORD makes his life a guilt offering, he will see his offering and prolong his days, and the will of the LORD will prosper in his hand (Isaiah 53:8b, 10).

In this dramatic prophecy the new idea is presented of a suffering which is redemptive. As H. H. Rowley explains:

> It redeems not only the sufferer, but those who inflict it on him; and it redeems not only by its own virtue, merely because it is suffering, but because of the spirit in which it is endured. The Servant fulfills his mission to the world by suffering at the world's hands, and by yielding his life without struggle or complaint to be a sacrifice for those who slay him.[24]

Ultimately, the suffering of the chosen Servant is vicarious before God because "the LORD has laid on him the iniquity of us all" (Isaiah 53:6). This surprising message of triumph for Israel and the human race would only be understood and recognized by the Gentiles *after* the historical fulfillment of the death and resurrection of the Servant of Yahweh (Isaiah 52: 13-15).

The Servant of Isaiah 42–53 possesses the vital characteristics of the promised Davidic Messiah of Isaiah 11:1-10: "On the Davidic Messiah and the Servant alike the Spirit of Yahweh rests; both administer justice equitably, among the nations as well as in Israel."[25] This identification of the suffering Servant with the promised messianic King was never conceived as a possibility in Judaism. How can the glorious Messiah at one and the same time be one who judges the earth, slays the wicked with the breath of his lips, and also be one who passively suffers death by his enemies?

Here we come face to face with the revolutionary new understanding of Jesus of Nazareth concerning the mission of the promised Messiah. He united the three different concepts of Israel's prophecy—the coming Davidic King; the Son of Man (in Daniel 7); the suffering Servant of God—all in one Person: Himself.[26]

Jesus saw a definite order in the tasks of the Messiah: first an appearance in lowliness to fulfill the mission of the suffering Servant, and after this His appearance as King-Judge in divine glory. He even reproved His disciples of being slow of heart in believing this messianic program:

> Did not the Christ [or Messiah] have to suffer these things and then enter his glory? And beginning with Moses and all the Prophets, he explained to them what was said in all the Scriptures concerning himself (Luke 24:26-27).

God's purpose in His election of Abraham and Israel to redeem the world and reestablish it under the kingship of God was, in principle, fulfilled in the life, death, and resurrection of Messiah Jesus. Christ was the only perfectly obedient seed of Abraham, the only sinless Israelite who indeed deserved the endless blessings of God's covenant with Israel. Christ now offers the blessing of God's redemptive reign to all men, to Jews and Gentiles alike, without distinction (John 12:32; Galatians

3:14). God's plan with Israel on behalf of the Gentiles was therefore not thwarted or postponed, but rather prospered in the Messiah (Isaiah 53:10). God's plan progressed without delay, when the fullness of time had come (Galatians 4:4, 5) and Christ was exalted as the messianic Ruler at the right hand of God (Acts 2:36; 5:31; 1 Corinthians 15:25). In Christ all God's promises are "yes" (2 Corinthians 1:20). Christ has established His own messianic Israel, His *ekklesia* or Church, His spiritual kingdom or rulership in the present world (Matthew 16:18; 13:41).

### Notes on Chapter 6

[1]A. R. Hulst, *Wat betekent de naam "Israel" in het Oude Testament?*, Miniaturen No. 1, Bijlage Maandblad Kerk en Israel, Jrg. 16, No. 10 (Den Haag: Boekencentrum, 1962). See also his "Der Name 'Israel' im Deuteronomium," *OTS* 9 (1951):65-106.

[2]F. B. Meyer, *Israel: A Prince with God* (Ft. Washington, Penn.: Christian Literature Crusade, 1972), pp. 78-81.

[3]Ellen G. White, *Patriarchs and Prophets* (Mountain View, Calif.: Pacific Press Pub. Assn., 1917, 1943), p. 198.

[4]See G. F. Hasel, *The Remnant: The History and Theology of the Remnant Idea from Genesis to Isaiah*, Andrews University Monographs, Studies in Religion, Vol. 5, 3d ed. (Berrien Springs, Mich.: Andrews University Press, 1980).

[5]Ladd, *A Theology of the New Testament*, p. 108.

[6]Hulst, "Der Name 'Israel' im Deuteronomium," pp. 73, 103-104 (my translation).

[7]H.-J. Kraus, *The People of God in the Old Testament*, World Christian Books No. 22 (London: Lutterworth Press, 1963), p. 21.

[8]See Danell, *Studies in the Name 'Israel' in the Old Testament*, chapter 4.

[9]Hasel, *The Remnant*, p. 393.

[10]Ibid., p. 243.

[11]Ibid., p. 247.

[12]Ibid., p. 401.

[13]C. Westermann, *Isaiah 40–66: A Commentary* (Philadelphia: Westminster Press, 1977), pp. 314, 315. Cf. E. Jacob, *Theology of the Old Testament* (New York: Harper & Row, 1958), p. 324.

[14]O. Eisfeldt, *Geschichtliches und Ubergeschichtliches im Alten*

*Testament*, ThStKr Bd 109/2 (Berlin: Ev. Verlagsanstalt, 1947), pp. 14-15.

[15]Hulst, *Wat betekent de naam "Israel" in het Oude Testament?*, p. 20.

[16]See H. Eichrodt, *Ezekiel: A Commentary* (Philadelphia: Westminster Press, 1970), p. 280.

[17]See Kaiser, *Toward an Old Testament Theology*, pp. 13, 30f., for strong arguments for preferring the passive rendering "will be blessed" in Genesis 12:3 above the reflective rendering "will bless themselves."

[18]G. Vos, *Biblical Theology* (Grand Rapids, Mich.: Wm. B. Eerdmans Pub. Co., 1963, reprint), p. 90.

[19]J. Scharbert, in *TDOT*, vol. 3, p. 307.

[20]H. H. Rowley, *The Biblical Doctrine of Election* (London: Lutterworth Press, 1964), pp. 52, 51, 59.

[21]Robinson, *Corporate Personality in Ancient Israel*, p. 15.

[22]Bruce, *New Testament Development of Old Testament Themes*, p. 86.

[23]Ibid.

[24]H. H. Rowley, *The Missionary Message of the Old Testament* (London: Cary Kingsgate Press, 1955), pp. 61-62.

[25]Bruce, *New Testament Development of Old Testament Themes*, p. 90.

[26]See Rowley, *The Missionary Message of the Old Testament*, p. 54; Ladd, *The Last Things*, chapter 1.

# 7

## The Ecclesiological Interpretation
## of Israel's Remnant

Ecclesiology, or the doctrine of the Church, is claimed to be the "touchstone" or decisive test of dispensationalism.[1] C. C. Ryrie argues that the Church is distinct and separate from Israel in two respects: (1) in the Church the Gentiles are placed on equal footing with the Jews; (2) Christ dwells within the Church, His spiritual body.

The Church must have been unknown in Old Testament times, he infers, because it is called a "mystery" by the apostle Paul (Ephesians 3:4-6; Colossians 1:25-27). Furthermore, Paul calls the Church of Christ explicitly a "new man" (Ephesians 2:15), a creation which was the result of the death of Christ. The Church is built upon Christ's resurrection and ascension (Ephesians 1:20-23; 4:7-13) and became operative only on the day of Pentecost (Acts 2). The Church, he asserts, is *not* a subject of Old Testament prophecy, and therefore "the Church is not fulfilling Israel's promises"; consequently "Israel herself must fulfill them and that in the future."[2] The Church will be "raptured" away from the world before God again deals with Israel. Ryrie concludes, "The essence of dispensationalism, then, is the distinction between Israel and the Church."[3] He appeals to 1 Corinthians 10:32 to confirm his thesis that "natural Israel and the Church are also contrasted in the New Testament."[4]

However, the question is not, Does the New Testament contrast the Church with "natural Israel"? but rather, Is the Church called "the Israel of God" in the New Testament and is it presented there as the new Israel, the only heir of all God's promised covenant blessings for the present and the future? Further questions that should be examined are, *When* exactly did the Church begin, according to Christ? and, How do Christ and the New Testament writers apply God's ancient covenants with Abraham, with Israel, and with David?

### Christ's Gathering of Israel's Remnant
### The Beginning of the Church

The Christian Church was not created by Paul's preaching among the Gentiles, but by Christ personally within Palestinian Judaism. At His baptism in the Jordan River, Christ was "revealed to Israel" as the Messiah of prophecy (of Isaiah 42-53). God anointed Him with the Holy Spirit (Acts 10:38) and testified from heaven that Jesus was the Son of God, the chosen Servant of Yahweh. He would fulfill the prophetic messianic role of bearing the sins of the world as the Lamb of God (John 1:29-34, 41; Matthew 3:16, 17).

His coming to Israel was the highest test for the Jewish nation of its relation to the covenant of God. As the Messiah, He was to be the "stumbling stone," the "rock that makes them [Israel] fall" (Romans 9:32, 33; 1 Peter 2:8). Simeon had predicted:

> This child is destined to cause the falling and rising of many in Israel, and to be a sign that will be spoken against, so that the thoughts of many hearts will be revealed (Luke 2:34, 35).

Israel's relation to Yahweh was to be decisively determined before God by Israel's relation to the *first* advent of Christ and His atoning sacrifice. He came as God's unique Representative to speak and act on God's behalf to Israel and the world (John 12:48-50). Everyone's eternal destiny, life or death, is bound up with the individual's reaction to the claims of Jesus Christ:

> The Father loves the Son and has placed everything in his hands. *Whoever believes in the Son* has eternal life, but *whoever rejects the Son* will not see life, for God's wrath remains on him (John 3:35, 36; emphasis added).

> *Whoever believes in him is not condemned, but whoever does not believe stands condemned already because he has not believed in the name of God's one and only Son* (John 3:18; cf. 5:24, 25; emphasis added).

What counts before God for the individual Jew, counts for the Jewish nation collectively. Jesus told those Jews who claimed to be children of God and Abraham, yet planned to kill Him because He had proclaimed that Israel must be set free from sin by Him as the Son of God, "You belong to your father, the devil, and you want to carry out your father's desire" (John 8:44). For Jesus the true descendants of Abraham were ultimately defined, not by the blood of Abraham, but by the faith of Abraham. Sonship and fatherhood are primarily determined, not by physical, but by spiritual relationship (cf. Matthew 12:47, 50). The test for Israel had come in its reaction to Jesus as Messiah. Christ claimed that all Israel should come to *Him* to receive the rest of God or they would stand judged:

> Come to me, all you who are weary and burdened, and I will give you rest (Matthew 11:28; cf. Isaiah 45:22).

> He who is not with me is against me, and he who does not gather with me scatters (Matthew 12:30; cf. 18:20; 23:37).

Christ was sent first of all to gather "the lost sheep of the house of Israel" to Himself as the Messiah, just as the prophets had predicted that (the coming) David would gather Israel for Yahweh (Matthew 15:24; 10:5, 6; cf. Ezekiel 34:15, 16, 23, 24; Jeremiah 23:3-5). Christ was convinced that He was sent also to redeem the world (John 3:16) and that the Gentiles needed to rally to Him (cf. Isaiah 11:10; Matthew 11:28).

Christ proclaimed that His mission — to suffer death under God's judgment — was intended to benefit all peoples: "But I, when I am lifted up from the earth, will draw all men to myself" (John 12:32). The evangelist John explains that Jesus died "not only for that nation but also for the scattered children of God, to bring them together and make them one" (John 11:52). Referring to Isaiah's prophecy of a future gathering of Gentiles to the temple, Christ announced:

> I have other sheep that are not of this sheep pen. I must bring them also. They too will listen to my voice and there shall be one flock and one shepherd (John 10:16; cf. Isaiah 56:8).

As the messianic Shepherd, Christ declares here that He was sent to fulfill Israel's covenant promises of the gathering of Israel. As the Messiah He came to gather Israel to Himself (see Matthew 12:30), but more than that, to gather the Gentiles to Himself (see John 12:32). This called for a decision of faith in Him as the Messiah of Israel. For this universal mission He called from Israel His twelve apostles, who in their chosen number clearly represent the twelve tribes of Israel. By officially ordaining twelve disciples as his apostles (see Mark 3:14, 15), Christ constituted a new Israel, the messianic remnant of Israel, and called it His church (see Matthew 16:18). In the ordination of the twelve, Christ founded His church as a new organism, with its own structure and authority, endowing her with "the keys of the kingdom of heaven" (verse 19; cf. 18:17).

Christ's final decision regarding the Jewish nation came at the end of His ministry, when the Jewish leaders had determined to reject His claim of being Israel's Messiah. Christ's words in Matthew 23 reveal that Israel's guilt before God had reached its completion (Matthew 23:32). His verdict was therefore: "I tell you that *the kingdom of God will be taken away from you and given to a people who will produce its fruit*" (Matthew 21:43; emphasis added). This solemn decision implies that Israel would no longer be the people of God and would be *replaced* by a people that would accept the Messiah and His message of the kingdom of God. Which new "people" did Christ have in mind? On one earlier occasion Christ noticed, to His amazement, that a Roman centurion showed more faith in Him than anyone in Israel had ever done. Then He had said:

> I say to you that *many will come from the east and west, and will take their places* at the feast with Abraham, Isaac, and Jacob in the kingdom of heaven [kingdom of God, Luke 13:28]. But the subjects of the kingdom will be thrown outside, into the darkness, where there will be weeping and gnashing of teeth (Matthew 8:11, 12; emphasis added).

In this light it becomes evident that Christ did not promise the kingdom of God — the theocracy — to another "generation" of Jews in the far future, as dispensational writers favor,[5] but rather to Christ-believing people from all races and nations, "from the east and the west." In short, His Church ("My Church," Matthew 16:18) would replace the Christ-rejecting nation. It has been pointed out that Matthew is interested in showing the continuity of God's rule of salvation:

> The *basilei tou Theou* [kingdom of God] is a reality which overarches both the Old and New Testaments. God has conferred it on Israel and again taken it away after she became guilty. It is conferred anew on a people. As the old bearer was a

"people," so also the new one. Thus the continuity of the Kingdom entails the continuity of a people of God.[6]

The kingdom of God was manifested as a present reality in Christ's life and mission. The messianic hope of the Old Testament was actually fulfilled in Christ's victorious ministry over sin, Satan, and death, so that Christ publicly announced, "If I drive out demons by the Spirit of God, *then the kingdom of God has come upon you*" (Matthew 12:28; emphasis added). This is the kingdom of God that the Jews rejected. G. E. Ladd states, "When the nation as a whole rejected the offer, those who accepted it were constituted the new people of God, the sons of the Kingdom, the true Israel, the incipient church."[7] Jesus Himself identified the "people" whom God had chosen. To His disciples He said, "Do not be afraid, little flock, for your Father has been pleased to give *you* the kingdom" (Luke 12:32, emphasis added; cf. 22:29). Here Christ unmistakably identifies His disciples as the true Israel, because the Israel of God was called the flock or sheep of God by Israel's prophets (Isaiah 40:11; Jeremiah 31:10; Ezekiel 34:12-14). The true Israel finds her identity in accepting the yoke of Messiah Jesus (Matthew 11:29). Those who follow Christ are the true sons of the kingdom (Matthew 13:37, 38; cf. 8:12). F. F. Bruce confirms: "Jesus' calling of disciples around Himself to form the 'little flock' who were to receive the kingdom (Luke 12:32; cf. Daniel 7:22, 27) marks Him out as the founder of the New Israel."[8]

Jesus' preaching of faith and repentance as the condition for entering the kingdom (Mark 1:15) leads to the conclusion that "It can hardly be conceived of anything but the beginning of the gathering of a remnant of faith along the lines of the remnant hopes of the OT prophecies."[9] Christ created His Church, not *beside* Israel, but *as* the faithful remnant of Israel that inherits the covenant promises and responsibilities. Christ's Church is not separated from the Israel of God, only from the Christ-rejecting Jewish nation. Christ assumed the place of God when He promised:

> For where two or three are gathered together in my name, there am I in the midst of them (Matthew 18:20, RSV).

Here Jesus obviously discriminates the Christ-believing Israel — which is gathered to Him — from the Christ-rejecting

Israel that gathers only around Moses. Christ's statement is brought into sharper relief if it is contrasted with the familiar rabbinic saying: "When two sit together and concern themselves with words of the Torah, then the Shekina is among them" (Aboth 3, 2; in the Mishna).

The immediate consequence of Christ's taking the theocracy away from the nation of Israel was the bestowal of the covenant curse, as specified by Moses in Leviticus 26 and Deuteronomy 28, and by Daniel in chapter 9:26, 27 of his book. Weeping intensely over the city's horrible future under God's curse, Christ lamented:

> If you, even you, had only known on this day what would bring you peace—but now it is hidden from your eyes. The days will come upon you when your enemies will build an embankment against you and will dash you to the ground, you and the children within your walls. *They will not leave one stone on another, because you did not recognize the time of God's coming to you* (Luke 19:42-44; emphasis added).

> O Jerusalem, Jerusalem, you who kill the prophets and stone those sent unto you, *how often I have longed to gather your children together*, as a hen gathers her chicks under her wings, *but you were not willing. Look, your house is left to you desolate* (Matthew 23:37, 38; emphasis added).

Christ's coming to Jerusalem had been "the time of God's coming" to Israel. The consequences of the Messiah's withdrawal were immense for the Jewish nation. The loss of God's protective theocracy will reach till the very end of time (Daniel 9:26, 27; Luke 21:24; 1 Thessalonians 2:16). Christ emphatically urged His little flock, the faithful remnant of Israel, to flee out of the doomed city when the abominable desolator would approach the city (Mark 13:14; Matthew 24:15-20; Luke 21:20-24).

Only in Christ could Israel as a nation have remained the true covenant people of God. In rejecting Jesus as God's messianic King, the Jewish nation failed the decisive test of fulfilling God's purpose for the Gentiles. Christ, however, renewed God's covenant with His twelve apostles. He bestowed the divine calling of ancient Israel on His messianic flock, to be the light of the world (Matthew 5:14) and to "make disciples of all nations, baptizing them in the name of the Father and of the

Son and of the Holy Spirit" (Matthew 28:19). God was not dependent on the Jewish nation for the fulfillment of His divine purpose for all men. His plan could not be thwarted or delayed by Israel's rejection of the Messiah. The day of Pentecost proved that God was "on schedule." Precisely when the annual festival of Pentecost had arrived (Acts 2:1; literally: "was completed"), new, dramatic events took place in fulfillment of prophecy. From heaven Christ poured out the promised Spirit on the faithful remnant of Israel.

### The Church as the Remnant
### in Israel's Prophecies

The apostles did not regard the Church as a temporary interruption of God's plan, outside the scope of Israel's prophecy. Instead of any suggestion of a postponement of God's kingdom or a change of God's plan, the apostles stressed that every occurrence in Christ's life, death, resurrection, ascension, His outpouring of the Spirit of God, and His enthronement at the right hand of God, were all the unfolding and explicit fulfillments of Israel's prophecies. Christ's betrayal and death are explained by Peter on the day of Pentecost as the fulfillment of "God's set purpose and foreknowledge" (Acts 2:23). Even the persecution of Christ's Church in Jerusalem is viewed as what God's "power and will had decided beforehand should happen" (Acts 4:28; with an appeal to Psalm 2:1, 2).

With regard to Christ's ascension to heaven and His enthronement as the Davidic Ruler of both Israel and the nations, Peter appeals to David's prophetic Psalm 110, saying:

> For David did not ascend to heaven, and yet he said, The Lord said to my Lord: Sit at my right hand until I make your enemies a footstool for your feet. Therefore let all Israel be assured of this: God has made this Jesus, whom you crucified, both Lord and Christ (Acts 2:34-36).

Peter's application of Psalm 110 to Christ's present kingship has been called "an amazing bit of reinterpretation of Old Testament prophecy," because the promise of Psalm 110 refers to the king's throne in Jerusalem (see Psalm 110:2). Ladd explains:

> Peter, under inspiration, transfers the throne of David from its earthly site in Jerusalem to heaven itself. . . . Now he is

enthroned at God's right hand. Now that his messianic sufferings are past, he has entered in upon his messianic reign, and he will continue that reign until all his enemies have been subdued (1 Corinthians 15:25).[10]

Peter's interpretation is not a literal exegesis of Psalm 110, but the authorized christological application of David's prophecy. The Christian method of interpreting the Old Testament is to understand Israel's prophecy in the light of Christ and the New Testament. Then there is no postponement of Christ's kingdom at all, but only new progress and dramatic fulfillment (some three thousand Jews accepted Peter's interpretation and were baptized into Christ and His Church, Acts 2:41). Peter's interpretation of the outpouring of the Spirit as the direct fulfillment of Joel's prophecy for the last days (Acts 2:16-21) confirms the concept that the Church was *not* an unforeseen, unpredicted entity in the Old Testament. Rather it was the surprising fulfillment of Joel's remnant prophecy. Thus the Church is not an afterthought or interruption of God's plan with Israel for the world, but the divine progress and realization of the eschatological remnant of Israel. Shortly after the outpouring of God's Spirit on the Church, Peter stated categorically, "Indeed, all the prophets from Samuel on, as many as have spoken, have foretold these days" (Acts 3:24). In other words, since Pentecost all the Old Testament prophecies concerning the remnant of Israel have received their actual fulfillment in the formation of the apostolic Church. The Church is plainly prophesied in the remnant promises of the Old Testament.

Peter addressed the Christian churches of his time, scattered throughout the Middle East (1 Peter 1:1), with the honorable titles of Israel:

> You are a chosen people, a royal priesthood, a holy nation, a people belonging to God, that you may declare the praises of him who called you out of darkness into his wonderful light (1 Peter 2:9; cf. Exodus 19:5, 6).

Although the apostle does not use the name "Israel," everything Israel stood for, as the covenant people of God, he now applies to the Church. This is Peter's ecclesiological interpretation of God's covenant with Israel (Exodus 19:5, 6). This application is the outgrowth of the christological interpretation of the messianic prophecies. The ecclesiological application is only the organic extension of the christological fulfillment. As the body is organically connected to the head, so is the Church to the Messiah. The ecclesiological interpretation completely removes the ethnic and national restrictions of Israel's old covenant. The new-covenant people is no longer characterized by the bonds of race or country but exclusively by faith in Christ. This can be called Peter's spiritualization of Israel as a "holy nation." He thinks along the lines of a Passover typology when he stresses that Christians, as "God's elect," were "redeemed" by "the precious blood of Christ, a lamb without blemish or defect" (1 Peter 1:1, 18, 19). This Passover typology (see Exodus 12:5) is also used by the apostle Paul in 1 Corinthians 5:7. Furthermore, Peter's description of the Church as being "called out of darkness into his wonderful light" (1 Peter 2:9) strongly suggests an analogy with Israel's exodus from Egypt, the house of bondage (Exodus 4:23; 19:4; Isaiah 43:21). As ancient Israel experienced its exodus salvation in order to praise Yahweh's faithfulness and saving virtues, so the Church experiences her present salvation from the dominion of darkness in order to "declare the praises of him who called you to his wonderful light" (cf. also Colossians 1:13). This amounts to saying that the Christian community is the true Israel.[11]

When Peter continues to cite a specific prophecy made to Israel, he consistently follows the ecclesiological application:

Once you were not a people, but now you are the people of God; once you had not received mercy, but now you have received mercy (1 Peter 2:10; cf. Hosea 1:10; 2:23).

The prophet Hosea addressed these words as a promise to the ten apostate tribes of Israel before the Assyrian exile in 721 B.C. These tribes had come to live like the heathen nations and had therefore called upon themselves the covenant curse. Peter declares that Hosea's prophecy of God's future restoration of Israel has *now* been fulfilled in Christ's universal Church (1 Peter 2:9, 10)!

Paul also assures the Jews and the Gentiles in Asia Minor of "the good news":

What God promised our fathers he has fulfilled for us, their children, by raising up Jesus. As it is written in the second Psalm: 'You are my Son; today I have become your Father' (Acts 13:32-33).

Paul's foundation for the good news that Jesus has been coronated as King of all nations of the world, is his christological-eschatological interpretation of Psalm 2. Based on this christological application of the messianic prophecies, Paul and Barnabas declared that their gospel message — justification before God through faith in Christ — was commissioned to them by the God of Israel:

> For this is what the Lord has commanded *us*: I have made *you* a light for the Gentiles, that *you* may bring salvation to the ends of the earth (Acts 13:47, quoting Isaiah 49:6; emphasis added).

In Isaiah's original context, the predicted "light" of salvation for the Gentiles is a prediction of the coming Messiah who is described as an individual distinct from the nation of Israel. As the "Servant" of Yahweh, His first mission would be to "bring Jacob back to Him [Yahweh] and gather Israel to Himself" (Isaiah 49:5). In addition, the Servant was called to become a missionary to the Gentiles: "I will make *you* [the Servant] a light for the Gentiles, that you may bring my salvation to the ends of the earth" (Isaiah 49:6).

This messianic prophecy received its first christological application by Simeon when he took the child Jesus in his arms (see Luke 2:28-32). Paul and Barnabas, however, go a step further. They declare that they, as apostles of Christ, are now fulfilling this messianic commission. Standing before King Agrippa to defend his mission, Paul declares:

> I am saying nothing beyond what the prophets and Moses said would happen — that the Christ would suffer and, as the first to rise from the dead, would proclaim light to his own people and to the Gentiles (Acts 26:22, 23).

Paul sees himself so intimately one with Christ — even incorporated in Him (Romans 6:3, 5, 11) — that his christological application of Isaiah's messianic prophecies results in an apostolic application of the Messiah's mission. Israel's calling by Yahweh is therefore, for Paul, fulfilled in the apostolic Church. He joins Peter in citing Hosea's prophecy of Israel's restoration, in order to affirm its fulfillment in the universal Church of Christ (see Romans 9:24-26). Thus Peter and Paul stand together in declaring that Israel's remnant prophecies have found an ecclesiological fulfillment. This universal application to the Church community is not an abstract spiritualization, but denotes the true *literal* fulfillment. The reality of this fulfillment of God's original purpose with Israel is illustrated by Paul's assurance that unbelievers who visit a local church will be deeply impressed by God's presence and confess, "God is really among you!" (1 Corinthians 14:24, 25). This was God's plan for Israel's influence among the Gentiles (see Isaiah 45:14; Zechariah 8:23). It is presently fulfilled wherever two or more gather to worship God in the name of Christ (Matthew 18:20).

### *"The Israel of God"*
### *in the Context of Galatians*

Paul closes his epistle to the churches in Galatia with the benediction, "Peace and mercy to all who follow this rule, *even to the Israel of God*" (Galatians 6:16; emphasis added). What is meant by the phrase, "even *[kai]* to the Israel of God"? Grammatically speaking, *"kai"* can be translated by "even" or by "and." C. C. Ryrie states: "Actually an absolute decision cannot be made from the verse itself, but general usage would favor the recognition of two classes in this verse."[12] With this last statement, however, he ignores a basic principle of literal exegesis. Whenever the grammatical syntax is inconclusive, the historical context may illuminate the particular meaning of a term. The historical background of this epistle indicates that Paul is vehemently rejecting any different status or claim of the Jewish Christians beside or above that of gentile Christians before God. Baptized Jews and Gentiles are all one in Christ, are "all sons of God through faith in Christ Jesus." Consequently, "there is neither Jew nor Greek" in Christ (Galatians 3:26-28). "If you belong to Christ, then you are Abraham's seed, and heirs according to the promise" (Galatians 3:29). How could language state it any more conclusively and unambiguously? Yet, Paul does not want to be misunderstood and therefore has more to say to those who still claim special promises for ethnic Israel. In Galatians 4:21-31 the apostle radically denies any claim of ethnic Israel to any covenant promise. This passage has rightly been called "the sharpest polemic against Jerusalem and Judaism in the New Testament."[13] Paul goes so far as to equate "the present Jerusalem," the nation of Israel, with the status before God of Ishmael, who was *totally disinherited* because he persecuted Isaac:

> It is the same now. But what does the Scripture say? "Get rid of the slave woman and her son, for the slave woman's son will never share in the inheritance with the free woman's son." Therefore, brothers, we are not children of the slave woman, but of the free woman (Galatians 4:29-31).

In this context Paul applies Isaiah's prophecy of Israel's return from exile (Isaiah 54:1) to the creation of the Church (see Galatians 4:27). In its original setting, Isaiah assured Israel in captivity that the Lord, as Israel's "Husband" (Isaiah 54:5), would soon bring the "barren woman" (Israel) back from her "widowhood," with deep compassion (verse 7). As a result, Israel would multiply again and prosper as never before (verses 2-3). With apostolic authority, Paul declares that Isaiah's restoration promise has found its concrete fulfillment in the Church. His application is: *"Now you, brothers, like Isaac, are children of promise"* (Galatians 4:28; emphasis added). This fulfillment of Israel's restoration promise has been achieved by Christ — who is now in "the Jerusalem above" (verse 26) — in Christians who are born again by His Spirit (verse 29).

H. Ridderbos affirms:

> Paul sees the fulfillment of this promise [of Isaiah 54:1] in the gathering of the believers in Christ. It is a gathering made not from among the Jews only, but from among the Gentiles also.[14]

The key to the understanding of Paul's principle of prophetic interpretation is found exclusively in Jerusalem's persistent rejection of Christ as its Messiah. As in the judgment of Jesus Jerusalem was "filling up" the measure of Israel's sin (Matthew 23:37), so Paul judges that the deliberate opposition of the Jewish leaders to his proclamation of Christ to the Gentiles for their salvation continues "to fill up the measure of their sins" (1 Thessalonians 2:16). And he adds, "God's wrath has come upon them at last" [or: *completely;* or: *forever*] (1 Thessalonians 2:16, RSV).

Paul's use of the term "the Israel of God" in Galatians 6:16 must receive its specific meaning in harmony with the whole tenor of Paul's epistle to the Galatians, which he summed up in the words:

> Neither circumcision [being a Jew] nor uncircumcision [being a Gentile] means anything; what counts is a new creation. Peace

and mercy to *all* who follow this rule, even to the Israel of God (Galatians 6:15, 16; emphasis added).

Paul pronounces God's blessing of peace and mercy upon *all* who follow the rule, or principle, of being a new creation by faith in Christ. He clearly makes an all-inclusive statement for Christians (verse 15). Is it conceivable that he suddenly would distinguish within the Church between a Jewish class and a gentile class of Christians? J. Barton Payne must admit that the dispensational exegesis of "even the Israel of God" (Galatians 6:16) as referring to a special class of people within the Church, is inadmissible.

> To render it *and* [Galatians 6:16], as if a distinct group of Hebrew-Christians were contemplated, would oppose the thrust of the epistle as a whole. That distinction has now come to an end within God's people.[15]

Paul's expression "the Israel of God" is a profoundly religious qualification and is clearly synonymous with his earlier expression for *all* Christians, "You are Abraham's seed and heirs according to the promise" (Galatians 3:29). Dispensational theologians grant that Paul, by the term "the Israel of God", meant believers in the Lord Jesus Christ.[16] Because of their dispensational concern to keep Israel and the Church separate, however, they insist that Paul *must* have had Jewish Christians in mind as a distinct class within the Church. But to single out Jewish believers within the Church as "*the* Israel of God" is a concept that is in basic conflict with Paul's message to the Galatians. He declares categorically that "there is neither Jew nor Greek" within the Church, and that the Church as a whole — all who belong to Christ — is *the* seed of Abraham, *the* heir of Israel's covenant promise (3:26-29).

Because of this historical-theological context, the New International Version and similar translations of the Bible (as the Revised Standard Version; the Amplified New Testament; the New Testament by J. B. Phillips, etc.) are justified to translate the *"kai"* in Galatians 6:16 as an explanatory "and," by "even." Understood this way, the Church and "the Israel of God" are completely identified.[17] Paul's benediction in Galatians 6:16 becomes, then, the chief witness in the New Testament in declaring that the universal Church of Christ is *the* Israel of God, *the* seed of Abraham, *the* heir to Israel's covenant promise (cf. Galatians 3:29; 6:16). Ryrie's assertion, "Only when a believer belongs to the race Israel can he in any sense be called a spiritual Israelite,"[18] is an idea not derived from Paul's Epistle to the Galatians and counteracts its clear message.

P. Richardson has suggested that Paul's phrase "the Israel of God" (Galatians 6:16) refers to "all those Israelites who are going to come to their senses and receive the good news of Christ. . . . There is an Israel (of God) within (all) Israel." He paraphrases Galatians 6:16, "Pray God give peace to all who will walk according to this criterion, and mercy also to his faithful people Israel."[19] This interpretation assumes that Paul accepts two kinds of faithful Israel: an Israel that has accepted Christ—and thereby became "a new creation" (Galatians 6:15)—and an Israel of God that has not yet accepted Christ but is nevertheless God's "faithful people Israel."

Richardson appeals to the structural similarity of Galatians 6:16 and the Jewish Benediction in the *Shemoneh Esreh* ("mercy upon us and upon all Israel thy people"). He suggests that Paul might unconsciously allude to this Jewish benediction, but admits that both are not exactly identical. He therefore concludes: "The Galatians sentence conveys the impression of being an interpreted reflection of the benediction."[20] The basic deficiency of this approach is that it does not seek its hermeneutical key in the message of Galatians itself but in an external similarity with a non-biblical source. Neglecting the theological thrust of Paul's Epistle to the Galatian churches, Richardson introduces two kinds of faithful Israel into Galatians 6:16: one that has already accepted Christ and one that has not yet accepted Christ. Such a projection of two kinds of faithful Israel beside the unfaithful Israel fails to appreciate the importance of Christ as the sole norm for determining *"the"* faithful Israel of God since the cross of Christ.

Paul's christology and ecclesiology compel him to define all Christ-believers as the "new creation" of God, the "one new man" in Christ (Ephesians 2:15). Reborn Christ-believers—from both Israel and the Gentiles—are therefore, in Paul's theology, the only *faithful* Israel of God.

### Gentile Christians Are Fellow Citizens in Israel

Paul's Epistle "to the saints in Ephesus" enlightens our understanding of the relationship of Israel and the Church.

Written explicitly for gentile Christians (Ephesians 2:11, 17; 4:17), the apostle informs them that the integration of Gentiles into Israel as sons or heirs of God was not a matter of divine afterthought. Rather it was God's plan or predestination (Ephesians 1:5, 11) from "before the creation of the world" (Ephesians 1:4). Both Jewish and gentile children of God will be united forever "under one head, even Christ" (Ephesians 1:10). To be a Christian is to live from the knowledge that one partakes of Israel's covenant blessings. Through the gospel, Christians have received "citizenship in Israel" and rejoice in the same hope as Israel (Ephesians 2:12; 4:4).

> Consequently, you are no longer foreigners and aliens, but fellow citizens with God's people and members of God's household, built on the foundation of the apostles and prophets, with Christ Jesus himself as the chief cornerstone (Ephesians 2:19, 20).

Through the cross, Christ has reconciled both Jews and Gentiles "to God" (Ephesians 2:16). He thereby destroyed also "the barrier, the dividing wall of hostility" between Jews and Gentiles themselves, "by abolishing in his flesh the law with its commandments and regulations" (Ephesians 2:14, 15). This is an undeniable reference to Christ's abrogation of the Mosaic law with its earthly temple ritual. The formation of a messianic Israel, made up from all believers in Christ among men, was Christ's mission. "*His purpose was to create in himself one new man out of two* [Jews and Gentiles], thus making peace" (Ephesians 2:15; emphasis added). This purpose was realized through the cross of Christ (2:16) and commissioned to be proclaimed by "God's holy apostles and prophets."

> This mystery is that through the gospel the Gentiles are heirs *together* with Israel, members *together* of one body, and sharers *together* in the promise in Christ Jesus (Ephesians 3:6; emphasis added).

Paul stresses here three times—with the word "together"—that Jewish Christians and gentile Christians are totally equal within Israel and the covenant promise. (In the original it is even more conspicuous: *synkleronoma, syssoma, symmetocha*). No theological system is justified, therefore, in rebuilding the dividing wall between Israel and the Church. The reception of Gentiles into Israel's household has been compared with the reception of the prodigal son into his father's house, in Jesus' parable (Luke 15:11-32).[21] The father embraced the lost son when he returned in shame, while the elder son begrudged the father's generosity. So must the largely gentile Church in Paul's time realize that Gentiles have entered into the house of Israel as their Father's house and are entitled to partake fully of Israel's covenants as fellow citizens and co-heirs (cf. Romans 8:17). The sonship of Gentiles is an adoption into an already existing household.

Paul differentiates between "we, who were the first to hope in Christ" (Ephesians 1:12)—or Israel—and the Gentiles, who were aliens, "without hope and without God in the world" (Ephesians 2:12). Of Jews he says, *"we"* were predestined in Christ *"for the praise of his glory"* (Ephesians 1:12). Of Gentiles he says, "And *you also* were included in Christ . . . *to the praise of his glory"* (Ephesians 1:13, 14). Both Jews and Gentiles are thus called to the same destiny: to praise God's glory. Paul stresses in Ephesians 1 the assuring concept that Christ only carried out, and the Spirit only revealed, what God had chosen and determined in eternity.[22] The cross was the appointed means to fulfill God's preconceived plan. The Church, as the united worship of God by Jews and Gentiles in one body, is not a temporary solution for an emergency situation caused by the rejection of Christ by the nation of Israel. The *uniting* of two previously separated branches of the human race in Christ is *the* mystery, the substance and essence of God's eternal plan. This was revealed in principle—although not on such a scale and in such clarity—in the prophetic writings of Israel (Ephesians 3:5; Romans 1:2; 16:25, 26). The gospel of Christ was not wholly undisclosed in Israel's prophetic writings. It was only dimly understood before Christ's time (see 1 Peter 1:10-12; Luke 24:15-17, 44). In the light of God's new revelation in Christ, the apostles were able to understand God's eternal plan of salvation in its universal scope and to grasp its christocentric structure (Ephesians 1:9, 10; cf. 2 Corinthians 3:13-18).

As all things were created and are sustained by Christ, so all things in the universe will finally be reunited and again fully integrated into one organic whole by Him, on the basis of His reconciling blood shed at the cross (Colossians 1:20). This cosmic unity of heaven and earth has *now* been achieved in Christ (Ephesians 1:22) and therefore signifies also the decisive end of racial barriers, of every dichotomy in Abraham's true seed and Israel's spiritual household before God (Ephesians 2:16-22). All eyes are not on Israel as a nation but on Christ and His messianic Israel, which has welcomed gentile Christians into Israel as fully equal fellow citizens.

### The Ecclesiological Application
### of Israel's Covenant

The burden of the inspired author of the Letter to the Hebrews is to especially exhort Jewish Christians with the assurance that Christ, through His self-sacrifice and present priesthood, is the realization of God's covenant with Israel.

> But the ministry Jesus has received is as superior to theirs [of the Levitical priests] as the covenant of which he is mediator is superior to the old one, and it is founded on better promises (Hebrews 8:6).

Hebrews assumes an intimate connection between *priesthood* and *covenant*. The old covenant had "an earthly sanctuary" with its own priesthood (Hebrews 9:1). Christ "was designated by God to be high priest in the order of Melchizedek" (Hebrews 5:10), after His resurrection, in the heavenly sanctuary (Hebrews 8:1, 2). This change of priesthood—from the Levitical to that of Melchizedek—entailed a necessary change of sanctuary and its ceremonial law (Hebrews 7:12). While the old covenant by itself could not cleanse the heart from defilement, "Jesus has become the guarantee of a better covenant" (Hebrews 7:22). Not only does He possess "a permanent priesthood" (7:24, 25); His covenant is also based on better, more effective promises of God. The new covenant functions better than the old covenant for God's people. Christ appears "for us in God's presence" (9:24) on the basis of the merits of His atoning self-sacrifice, offered once for all (Hebrews 7:27). Jesus is able to bestow on all who approach His throne the blessings promised by God to Israel of old: deliverance from an evil conscience, and personal assurance of salvation (Hebrews 9:14; 10:22).

In contrast with Israel's old covenant, which failed, the new covenant, promised through Jeremiah (31:31-34), will not fail because Christ is the surety or guarantee of it (Hebrews 7:22). Christ effects three basic promises of God: (1) *He internalizes*

God's moral law in the hearts of His people, which is better than laying the law as an external yoke upon Israel (Hebrews 8:10); this implies the regeneration of the heart so that it becomes inclined to obey God through the power of the indwelling Spirit, as the parallel promise in Ezekiel makes clear (Ezekiel 36:26, 27); (2) *He individualizes* the saving knowledge of God, so that each Israelite, without exception, has a personal, immediate relation with God (Hebrews 8:11); and (3) *He forgives* the sins of God's people and "will remember their sins no more" (Hebrews 8:12). These are the "better promises" of Jeremiah's prophecy, which Christ came to fulfill (Hebrews 8:6). By His inauguration of this new covenant, "He has made the first one obsolete; and what is obsolete and aging will soon disappear" (Hebrews 8:13). We are reminded that "the author's comment was written from the prophet's (Jeremiah's) perspective, not from his own; he knew that the old covenant had already disappeared as a valid expression of the relationship between God and his people (7:12)."[23] In other words, Jeremiah already announced the termination of the old covenant as soon as God introduced the concept of a new covenant. The question arises, To what people does Hebrews apply Jeremiah's new-covenant promise: to the Jewish people as a nation in the future, or to individual Jews and Gentiles in the Church at the present time?

Dispensational authors are not in every respect united in their interpretations. J. F. Walvoord reports[24] that J. N. Darby held that the new covenant belonged to the Israelites only, but that L. S. Chafer conceived of two different new covenants: a new covenant (Jeremiah 31) for national Israel, to be fulfilled only in the future millennium, and a new covenant (Hebrews 8), which refers to the Church in the present age. The *Scofield Reference Bible* (first edition, 1917), however, states that the new covenant has a twofold application: first to Israel, to be fulfilled in the millennium, and secondly, to the Church presently. The *New Scofield Reference Bible* has changed its former view and now declares that the new covenant will only be ratified in a future, repentant Israel (p. 1317). Walvoord also insists that the new covenant is with Israel and that its fulfillment will only be realized "in the millennial kingdom after the second coming of Christ."[25]

It is quite obvious that dispensationalism finds it difficult to do justice to the immediate context of Hebrews 8 because here Jeremiah's new covenant is applied undeniably to all Christians. Walvoord claims, "It is, in fact, the only passage which provides any difficulty to the premillennial [more accurately: dispensational] view, and this difficulty vanishes if the passage is carefully studied."[26] His so-called "careful" study in his book *The Millennial Kingdom* (chapter 18, "The New Covenant with Israel") is greatly disappointing, however, because no consideration whatsoever is given to the sacred duty of exegesis and no effort made to relate the passage of Hebrews 8:8-13 to the vital context and message of the Letter itself! Hardly touching the opinions of others, he merely defends his dispensational view and concludes: "The concept of *two new covenants* is a better analysis of the problem and more consistent with premillennialism as a whole."[27] This curious projection of "two new covenants" is more the defense of a problematic dogma than the result of careful exegesis of Holy Scripture. Walvoord's effort to deny that the "better covenant" of Hebrews 8 is Israel's predicted "new covenant" amounts to a clear denial of the biblical message:

> The only argument is that which was always true—the prediction of a new covenant automatically declares the Mosaic covenant as a temporary, not an everlasting covenant. . . . It declares a "better covenant" than the Mosaic covenant has been made possible (Heb 8:6), but it does not state . . . that this better covenant is "the new covenant with the house of Israel", or that Israel's new covenant has been introduced.[28]

This incredible dissection of the sacred text completely aborts the vital assurance which Hebrews 8 wants to bring to the Jewish Christians, namely, that God's new covenant with Israel *has found* its true fulfillment in Christ's enthronement at the right hand of God as the better High Priest for Israel. Hebrews 8 is neither reiterating "that which was always true," nor promising some future fulfillment of Jeremiah's new covenant. It rather proclaims the gospel message that the promised "new covenant" has been ratified by the atoning sacrifice of Christ and is now powerfully effective in the risen Christ (see Hebrews 4:14-16; 5:5, 6, 10; 6:19, 20; 7:11-27; 8:1, 2; 9:14, 24; 12:24; 13:20). Three key passages in particular seem to refute Walvoord's conclusion that Israel's new covenant has not yet been introduced by Christ.

Jesus has become the guarantee of a better covenant (Hebrews 7:22).

For this reason Christ is the mediator of a new covenant, that those who are called may receive the promised eternal inheritance (Hebrews 9:15).

But you have come to Mount Zion, to the heavenly Jerusalem, the city of the living God . . . to the church of the firstborn, whose names are written in heaven . . . to Jesus the mediator of a new covenant (Hebrews 12:22, 23, 24).

These inspired messages do not receive due consideration in Walvoord's argumentation. Hebrews 7:22 is systematically omitted in his discussion of texts on the new covenant, so that the vital message that Christ "has become the guarantee of a better covenant" is not even mentioned.[29] Concerning Hebrews 9:15, he remarks: "Christ is the Mediator 'of a new covenant', which is true, of course, both for a covenant with the church or a covenant with Israel."[30] Avoiding an explanation of Hebrews 9:15 by its context, Walvoord forces a basically different concept on this text: that Christ will become the Mediator "of a new covenant" for the Jewish nation at the second advent. He simply concludes that most dispensationalists agree that "a new covenant has been provided for the church, but not *the* new covenant for Israel."[31] C. C. Ryrie goes so far as to acknowledge that the new covenant which Jesus instituted for the Church at the Lord's Supper (Matthew 26:28; Mark 14:24) bestows *all the important blessings promised to Israel* in Jeremiah 31:31-34 on "those who believe on Christ in this age." But then he starts to backtrack:

One cannot deny that the Church receives similar blessings to those of the new covenant with Israel, but *similarity is not fulfillment.* . . . Could it not be that there is a new covenant for the Church as well as a new covenant for Israel? . . . The new covenant of Hebrews 8:7-13 belongs to the Jewish people and not to the church.[32]

Dispensationalism is forced to project two different new covenants into one and the same prophecy of Scripture! Is this still the claimed "normal and literal sense," "the ordinary literal sense"?[33] If the Church's "new" covenant is *not* the new covenant promised to Israel, then where is the Church's first covenant in Scripture (cf. Hebrews 8:13)?

No wonder that J. B. Payne finds the dispensational claim for Hebrews 8-10—the denial of the efficacy of Jeremiah's new covenant in the Church—"difficult to support." It suffers "from the inherent unlikelihood of such unelaborated subtlety of thought," namely, that Jeremiah's words apply to the Church only by analogy, but not in reality. Such reasoning definitely undermines the argument of Hebrews:

> Its readers were being confronted with the temptation of laps-
> ing back into Mosaic ceremonialism; and to explain that Jere-
> miah had predicted that in the millennium ceremonialism
> would be replaced by a more spiritual form of worship would
> hardly be as convincing as to quote the prophet to prove its
> replacement at the time then present.[34]

Payne shows that Hebrews 8:13; 9:14; and 10:16-17 require that the new covenant of Jeremiah 31 "is one, and . . . belongs to the church." The forgiveness of sins which Jeremiah prom-ises in the new covenant is now mediated by Christ to all who "have confidence to enter the sanctuary by the blood of Jesus" (Hebrews 10:19).

Regarding Hebrews 12:24, Walvoord's only comment is: "Reference is apparently to the covenant with the Church and not to Israel's new covenant."[35] One may ask, however, If the Church is separated from Israel's covenant, why, then, has the Church come "to Mount Zion, to the heavenly Jerusalem," in coming to Jesus as mediator of a new covenant (Hebrews 12: 22-24)? How can one deny here the notion of an essential ful-fillment? The whole Letter of Hebrews is carried, not by the idea of analogy, but by the notion of the eschatological fulfill-ment of Israel's covenant and typological sanctuary mediation (Hebrews 1:1-3, 13). In Jesus' life and ministry has finally ar-rived what all Israel's symbols and types foreshadowed. The author of Hebrews therefore dwells, not on some imagined analogy between two new covenants, but on the salvation-historical contrast of Christ's new covenant with Israel—the twelve apostles were all Israelites—and the Mosaic old cove-nant. Daniel P. Fuller is therefore clearly in harmony with the basic structure of the Hebrews Letter when he concludes:

> He clearly contrasts this "new Covenant" with the old Mosaic
> Covenant in Hebrews 7:22-23; 9:15; 12:18-24, and cites Jere-
> miah 31:31-34 in support of this contrast in Hebrews 8:8-13

and 10:16-17. Such passages offer considerable evidence for concluding that this inspired writer regarded Jesus' work as a fulfillment of the new covenant promised in Jeremiah 31:31-34. But then a promise for Israel would find some fulfillment in the Church, and this would refute dispensationalism's basic premise that God's dealings with Israel remain separate from his dealings with the church.[36]

It is true that Christ's reign over the Church, which is effective in inclining the hearts and lives of individual believers (Jews and Gentiles) to the obedience of faith, is not yet the glory of the future messianic kingdom. The second coming brings its own, more glorious consummation of the new covenant in the kingdom of glory. But this greater glory should never lead us to deny the truth and reality of the spiritual fulfillment of Christ's present kingdom (see Romans 14:17; 1 Corinthians 4:20; Colossians 1:13). Walvoord attempts to support his futuristic application of Jeremiah's "new covenant" promise for the Jewish nation, in the millennium, by an astounding disregard for the grammatical-historical principle of exegesis in dealing with God's promise of a new covenant in Jeremiah 31. He states:

> The covenant promised fulfillment after the days of Israel's trouble [Jeremiah 30:7] or the great tribulation which Christ predicted (Matt 24:21). It is further synchronized with the time of Israel's regathering which is regarded as a preparation for fulfillment of the covenant (cf. Jer 31:1-20) and constitutes the immediate context of the revelation of the new covenant.[37]

The historical setting in which Jeremiah predicted Israel's salvation from "a time of trouble" (Jeremiah 30:7) is clearly stated as the promised deliverance from the Babylonian captivity (Jeremiah 30:3; 29:10). Chapters 30 and 31 of Jeremiah contain an anthology of God's restoration promises, written shortly after Nebuchadnezzar had deported the king of Judah, along with ten thousand Jews, to exile in 597 B.C. (Jeremiah 29). These restoration promises inspired the exiled Jews with new hope for the end of the predicted seventy years of captivity (Jeremiah 25:11; 29:10). Through Jeremiah the Lord promised a new exodus from Babylon for a repentant, godly Israel.

> This is what the LORD says: "When seventy years are completed for Babylon, I will come to you and fulfill my gracious promise

to bring you back to this place. . . . You will seek me and find me when you seek me with all your heart. "I will be found by you," declares the LORD, "and will bring you back from captivity. I will gather you from all the nations and places where I have banished you," declares the LORD, "and will bring you back to the place from which I carried you into exile" (Jeremiah 29:10, 13-14).

This is the historical setting to which the new-covenant promise of Jeremiah 31:31-34 must be related in its historical exegesis, but which is neglected in Walvoord's interpretation.

This new-covenant promise of Jeremiah already began to have an initial fulfillment in Israel's return to the promised land under Prince Zerubbabel (Ezra 1:1-5; Haggai 2:20-23). But this immediate historical fulfillment did not exhaust the meaning of Jeremiah's promise. Only when Christ regathered the faithful Israelites to Himself, did Jeremiah's new covenant receive its spiritual but essential fulfillment in the messianic Israel, the Church (Matthew 12:30; John 12:32; Hebrews 8: 1-2; 10:15-22).

C. C. Ryrie, however, considers the ecclesiological application of Israel's new covenant to be no fulfillment at all. He argues, "If the Church is not a subject of Old Testament prophecy, then the Church is not fulfilling Israel's promises, but instead Israel herself must fulfill them and that in the future."[38] He even states, "The Church is not fulfilling in any sense the promises to Israel."[39] This is a rather curious assertion if compared with his admission in the same book that "the four important blessings promised to Israel in Jeremiah 31:31-34, are all promised to those who believe on Christ in this age" (regeneration, indwelling of the Holy Spirit, teaching of the Holy Spirit, and forgiveness of sins).[40] "Some of the blessings of the new covenant with Israel are blessings which we enjoy now as members of the body of Christ."[41]

But in its ethnic, Jewish aspect, Ryrie asserts, the claimed ecclesiological fulfillment does "alter" or "change" the literal fulfillment.[42] He even calls the ecclesiological application an *abrogation* of Israel's new covenant.[43] He wonders, "Does the New Testament change all this? If it does, premillennialism [read: dispensationalism] is weakened."[44] He admits that the dispensational construction of two new covenants is ultimately nothing more than an inference needed to support its doctrine of ethnic literalism in prophecy. "The induction that there are two new covenants strengthens the premillennial position."[45] Ryrie's premise that the ecclesiological fulfillment implies the abrogation of Israel's new covenant is a *non sequitur*, an unwarranted jump to a conclusion which has no foundation or justification in the New Testament.

The ecclesiological interpretation cannot be regarded as the abrogation of Israel's new covenant, because Christ Himself instituted the sacrament of the Last Supper as the fulfillment of Jeremiah's predicted covenant, in His words, "This cup is the new covenant in my blood which is poured out for you . . . for the forgiveness of sins" (Luke 22:20; Matthew 26:28; cf. Jeremiah 31:34).

With regard to insisting on ethnic literalism in prophetic fulfillment, the apostle Paul emphatically corrects such a self-imposed necessity by pointing to the familiar remnant theology of the prophets themselves. Believing Gentiles are included in the eschatological remnant of Israel.

> It is not as though God's word had failed. For not all who are descended from Israel are Israel. Nor because they are his descendants are they all Abraham's children. On the contrary, "It is through Isaac that your offspring will be reckoned." In other words, it is not the natural children who are God's children, but it is the children of the promise who are regarded as Abraham's offspring (Romans 9:6-8).

> Now you, brothers, like Isaac, are children of promise (Galatians 4:28).

> So too, at the present time there is a remnant chosen by grace (Romans 11:5).

According to Hebrews 8-12, the Church of Jesus represents the true fulfillment of Jeremiah's predicted new covenant. Far from being an abrogation of Israel's new covenant, it is rather a type and guarantee of the final consummation of the new covenant, when true Israelites of all ages will join in the wedding supper of the Lamb in the New Jerusalem (Matthew 8:11, 12; 25:34; Revelation 19:9; 21:1-5). We conclude, therefore, with J. Barton Payne: "The church represents the culmination of Hebrew history; it constitutes the fulfillment of the predicted new testament to be made 'with the house of Israel and with the house of Judah' (Jer 31:31, Heb 8:8, 10:17-19)."[46]

### Notes on Chapter 7

[1]Ryrie, *Dispensationalism Today*, pp. 132, 133.

[2]Ryrie, *The Basis of the Premillennial Faith*, p. 126.

[3]Ryrie, *Dispensationalism Today*, pp. 46-47.

[4]Ibid., p. 138.

[5]See Pentecost, *Things to Come*, pp. 91, 465. Ladd, *A Theology of the New Testament*, p. 200 note, comments, "This, however, is a forced interpretation."

[6]W. Trilling, *Das Wahre Israel. Studien zur Theologie des Matthaus-Evangeliums*, Stud. A. und N.T., Bd X (München: Kösel Verlag, 1964), p. 65 (my translation).

[7]Ladd, *A Theology of the New Testament*, p. 113. In chapter 8, "The Kingdom and the Church," Ladd presents a splendid study on the difference and the interrelationship of the Kingdom of God and the Church.

[8]F. F. Bruce, in *The New Bible Dictionary*, ed. J. D. Douglas (Grand Rapids, Mich.: Wm. B. Eerdmans Pub. Co., 1979; reprint ed.), p. 558.

[9]G. F. Hasel, "Remnant," in *ISBE*, new ed., section III C2.

[10]Ladd, *The Last Things*, pp. 17, 18. Cf. also Bruce, *New Testament Development of Old Testament Themes*, p. 79.

[11]B. Reicke, *The Epistles of James, Peter, and Jude*, The Anchor Bible, vol. 37 (Garden City, N.Y.: Doubleday, 1964), p. 93.

[12]Ryrie, *The Basis of the Premillennial Faith*, p. 69.

[13]J. C. DeYoung, *Jerusalem in the New Testament* (Kampen: Kok, 1960), p. 106.

[14]H. Ridderbos, *The Epistle of Paul to the Churches of Galatia*, NICNT (Grand Rapids, Mich.: Wm. B. Eerdmans Pub. Co., 1957), p. 179.

[15]Payne, *Encyclopedia of Biblical Prophecy*, p. 100, n. 183.

[16]J. F. Walvoord, *Israel in Prophecy* (Grand Rapids, Mich.: Zondervan, 1962), p. 59. Ryrie, *The Basis of the Premillennial Faith*, p. 69.

[17]So also U. Luz, *Das Geschichtsverständnis bei Paulus* (München: C. Kaiser, 1968), p. 269; Ridderbos, *The Epistle of Paul to the Churches of Galatia*, p. 227; Ladd, *A Theology of the New Testament*, p. 539, who refers to other NT scholars. However, not all agree (on Galatians 6:16). See W. Hendriksen, *Israel in Prophecy* (Grand Rapids, Mich.: Baker Book House, 1974), pp. 33-34.

[18]Ryrie, *Dispensationalism Today*, p. 149.

[19]P. Richardson, *Israel in the Apostolic Church* (Cambridge:

Cambridge University Press, 1969), pp. 82, 83, 89.

[20]Ibid., p. 80.

[21]M. Barth, *Israel und die Kirche im Brief des Paulus an die Epheser*, Theol. Existenz Heute, NF NR 75 (München: Kaiser Verlag, 1959), p. 8.

[22]See ibid., p. 14.

[23]M. M. Bourke, in *The Jerome Biblical Commentary*, ed. R. E. Brown, J. A. Fitzmyer, and R. E. Murphy (Englewood Cliffs, N.J.: Prentice-Hall, 1968), p. 396 (no. 47).

[24]J. F. Walvoord, *The Millennial Kingdom* (Grand Rapids, Mich.: Zondervan, 1974), pp. 109, 110.

[25]Ibid., p. 209.

[26]Ibid., p. 215; cf. also his admission: "There are problems that remain in the premillennial [read: dispensational] understanding of this passage [Hebrews 8]," *Israel in Prophecy*, p. 54.

[27]Walvoord, *The Millennial Kingdom*, p. 219 (emphasis added). So also Ryrie, *The Basis of the Premillennial Faith*, p. 118.

[28]Walvoord, *The Millennial Kingdom*, pp. 216, 217.

[29]Both his *The Millennial Kingdom* and his *Israel in Prophecy* ignore the existence of Hebrews 7:22.

[30]Walvoord, *The Millennial Kingdom*, p. 218.

[31]Ibid., p. 214.

[32]Ryrie, *The Basis of the Premillennial Faith*, p. 117, 118, 122.

[33]See Walvoord's claims in *Israel in Prophecy*, pp. 44, 48, 93, 121.

[34]Payne, *Encyclopedia of Biblical Prophecy*, p. 328, n. 24.

[35]Walvoord, *The Millennial Kingdom*, p. 218.

[36]Daniel P. Fuller, *Gospel and Law: Contrast or Continuum? The Hermeneutics of Dispensationalism and Covenant Theology* (Grand Rapids, Mich.: Wm. B. Eerdmans Pub. Co., 1980), p. 165.

[37]Walvoord, *The Millennial Kingdom*, p. 211.

[38]Ryrie, *The Basis of the Premillennial Faith*, p. 126.

[39]Ibid., p. 136.

[40]Ibid., p. 118.

[41]Ibid., p. 124.

[42]Ibid., p. 105.

[43]Ibid., p. 125.

[44]Ibid., p. 115.

[45]Ibid., p. 125.

[46]Payne, *Encyclopedia of Biblical Prophecy*, p. 100.

# 8

## The Church and Israel
## in Romans 9–11

The doctrine of the Church is of decisive importance in dispensationalism. The Church is considered to be distinct from Israel and not a new spiritual Israel.[1] God has different purposes and programs for Israel and the Church "within His overall plan." C. C. Ryrie states unambiguously: "The Church is not fulfilling in any sense the promises to Israel. . . . The Church age is not seen in God's program for Israel. It is an intercalation."[2] The New Testament does not "enmesh them [God's promises to Israel] into the Church."[3] "And all this," he claims, "is built on an inductive study of the use of two words ["Israel" and "Church"], not a scheme superimposed on the Bible."[4] He concludes:

> Use of the words *Israel* and *Church* shows clearly that in the New Testament national Israel continues with her own promises and the Church is never equated with a so-called "new Israel" but is carefully and continually distinguished as a separate work of God in this age.[5]

Can these assertions be substantiated from the New Testament, using the grammatical-historical method of exegesis, as dispensationalism claims? What are the rules of such exegesis?

### The Role of the Context
### in Biblical Distinctions

A basic principle of exegesis that is sometimes ignored in doctrinal constructions is the determining role of the context — allowing each text or term to receive its literal meaning from its own immediate context. The danger is always present that the interpreter will superimpose the meaning of a term in one historical context upon the same term in a different historical context of Scripture. It is plain that when two texts seemingly contradict each other at face value, each needs to be understood from its own historical and literary context (for example, see Romans 3:28 and James 2:24).

Thus, the term "Israel" as used in Paul's letter to the Romans must be determined by the context of Romans, and his use of the same term in his letter to the Galatians must be understood by the context in Galatians. These historical contexts differ considerably and may not be ignored or denied for the sake of constructing doctrinal uniformity. That would be a forced, dogmatic exegesis, which is no longer open to the nuances of the biblical contexts.

### "Israel" in the Context of Romans

It seems clear that in Romans 9-11 Paul is especially concerned with his kinsmen, "the people of Israel" (9:3, 4). Besides referring frequently to ethnic Israel outside the Church, he distinguishes also between Christ-believing Jews and Christ-believing Gentiles within the Church (Romans 11: 5, 13). Why this distinction within the church at Rome? Did he distinguish between Israel and the Gentiles on the principle that God has two kinds of people, each with a different eschatological promise and destiny? The internal evidence points to the contrary. For example, Paul warns the two factions within the church at Rome, Jews and Gentiles, not to boast to each other about some alleged superiority or prerogative (see Romans 11:18, 25; 12:3).[6] Paul's differentiation of ethnic origins within the Christian community did not lead him to distinguish between different covenant promises for Israel and the Gentiles. The very opposite is the case. The thrust of Paul's epistle is to remind the church of the original purpose of Israel's election: to be a blessing to all the Gentiles of the world by sharing with them the saving light of Israel's God and Messiah (Isaiah 42:1-10; 49:6).

Against the background of this plan of God, Paul reports the surprising fact that "Gentiles who did not pursue righteousness have obtained it, a righteousness that is by faith [in Jesus as Messiah], but Israel, who pursued a law of righteousness, has not attained it" (Romans 9:30, 31). The decisive test for standing in the proper covenant relation with God is therefore now to exercise faith in Christ as the Messiah of Israel (Romans 9:33). Such faith alone assures the covenant blessings. The Church has access to God through no other covenant than the new covenant promised to Israel's faithful remnant (Romans 9:24-29).

Ellen G. White recognizes this fundamental openness of God's covenant with Israel to the Gentiles:

> The blessings thus assured to Israel are, on the same conditions and in the same degree, assured to every nation and to every individual under the broad heavens.[7]

In Romans 9-11 Paul reaches the climax of his epistle[8] in his exposition of how believing Gentiles relate to the Israel of God. He portrays the conversion of Gentiles to Christ as the ingrafting of wild olive branches (Gentiles) into the one olive tree of the Israel of God (Romans 11:17-24). In this way Paul visualizes the spiritual unity and continuity of God's covenant with Israel and His new covenant with the Church of Christ. Through faith in Christ, Gentiles are legally incorporated in the olive tree, the covenant people of God, and share in the root of Abraham (verse 18). The lesson of the parable of the cultivated olive tree in Romans 11 is that the Church lives from the root and trunk of the Old Testament Israel (Romans 11:17-18).

Paul's specific burden in Romans 11 is, however, the revelation of a divine "mystery" concerning ethnic Israel:

> Israel has experienced a hardening in part until the full number [the *pleroma*] of the Gentiles has come in. And so [*houtos*, in this way] all Israel will be saved, as it is written: . . . (Romans 11:25, 26).

Most commentators agree that Paul places here the salvation of ethnic Israel in a dynamic interrelation [*houtos*] with the salvation of the Gentiles. He anticipates an interaction between the salvation of "all Israel," or their "fullness" (Romans 11:26, 12), and the ingathering of the fullness of the Gentiles to Christ (Romans 11:25). Paul does not suggest an order of successive dispensations. He sees *many* Jews respond favorably to the salvation of *many* Gentiles who rejoice in God's mercy through Christ. He describes this mysterious relationship with a definite apocalyptic perspective, although he recognizes also the need for a present fulfillment (three times: "now"):

> Just as you [gentile Christians] who were at one time disobedient to God have *now* received mercy as a result of their disobedience [Jewish rejection of Christ], so they too have *now* become disobedient in order that they too may *now* receive mercy as a result of God's mercy to you. For God has bound all men over to disobedience so that he may have mercy on them all (Romans 11:31, 32; emphasis added).

One can observe in this amazing climax a striking interdependence of the salvation of the Jews and that of the Gentiles. As one scholar aptly states: "God grants no mercy to Israel without the Gentiles, but neither does he do so to the Gentiles without Israel."[9]

Enraptured by this amazing vision of God's faithfulness to His covenant promise to Israel, in spite of Israel's faithlessness — God's call to Israel is "irrevocable" (11:29) — Paul opens up a surprising perspective of God's saving purpose for the human race as a whole. Divine mercy flowed from Israel to the Gentiles in order that "all Israel" would be aroused to long also for the same mercy in which the Gentiles rejoice. In Paul's view, Israel has not fallen beyond recovery. "Not at all! Rather, because of their transgression, *salvation has come to the Gentiles to make Israel envious*" (Romans 11:11; emphasis added)! It is God's intention to bring natural Israel back to Himself *by means of* the Church of Christ. This way of saving many Jews from ethnic Israel for Christ is part of the marvellous "mystery" of God.

Only in this interdependence of Israel and the Church can the same gospel of salvation for all men — justification by grace through faith in Christ — be maintained. It needs to be stressed:

> There is no question of another conversion than that which results from the preaching of the gospel in history (cf. chs. 10:14ff.; 11:11, 14, 22) and from the activity presently coming to them from the believing gentile world (ch. 11:31).[10]

For this reason the Church is called to be actively involved in Jewish evangelism. E. G. White encourages Christians to witness to the Jewish people and to expect God's blessing.

> The time has come when the Jews are to be given light. The Lord wants us to encourage and sustain men who shall labor in

right lines for this people; for there are to be a multitude convinced of the truth, who will take their position for God. The
time is coming when there will be as many converted in a day as
there were on the day of Pentecost, after the disciples had
received the Holy Spirit.[11]

How does dispensationalism connect the Pauline hope for
ethnic Israel with the gospel preaching of the cross of Christ,
when its axiom states that "the glory of God is to be realized not
only in salvation but also in the Jewish people"?[12] How will
Israel be saved, according to dispensational eschatology? This
question is pressed by Bruce Corley:

> Are we to wait for an apocalyptic miracle to happen seven years
> after the "fulness of the Gentiles" has been raptured out of the
> world? Will the Jews come by preferential treatment or through
> justification by faith? The former opinion cuts the heart out of
> the Pauline gospel.[13]

Paul allows no other way for "all Israel" to be saved than
the way all the Gentiles are saved: by faith in Christ, by the
confession from the heart that Jesus is the risen Lord of Israel
(10:9, 10). He explicitly states God's condition for Israel's
salvation: "*If they do not persist in unbelief,* they will be
grafted in, for God is able to graft them in again" (11:23; emphasis added). Ethnic Israel had largely come to claim God's
covenant promises by trusting in its blood relation to father
Abraham and thus to expect God's eschatological blessings as
an *unconditional* guarantee (see Matthew 3:7-9; John 8:33-34).

Against this attitude of boasting in Israel's ethnic advan-
tage (see Romans 2:25-29), the apostle urgently proclaims:

> For there is no difference between Jew and Gentile — the same
> Lord is Lord of all and richly blesses all who call on him, for,
> "Everyone who calls on the name of the Lord will be saved"
> (Romans 10:12, 13; cf. 3:22-24).

The apostle removes every theological distinction between Jew
and Gentile before God, because "Christ is all, and is in all" (Colossians 3:11; cf. Galatians 3:26-29). Paul's cutting edge against
natural Israel is the point that Israel's religious self-righteousness,
of making claims before God while rejecting Christ and His gospel
of the kingdom (Romans 9:31-10:4), was the very cause of her fall
and rejection (Romans 11:11, 15). But this does not mean that
God has rejected *His* people Israel (Romans 11:11)!

### Paul's Application of Israel's
### Remnant Theology

The apostle appeals to the well-known "remnant" promises of Israel's prophets, to maintain his thesis that God's covenant promises have *not* failed, although Israel as a nation did fail to accept the kingship of Jesus Christ. "It is not as though God's word had failed. For not all who are descended from Israel are Israel" (Romans 9:6). Thus, Paul continues the Old Testament distinction of a spiritual Israel within the nation Israel. The prophets called this spiritual Israel "the remnant," and it was to be the bearer of God's covenant promises. In the faithful remnant, Israel continued always as the people of God in salvation history. God provided a faithful remnant by His sovereign grace and thus showed that in every judgment on Israel He did not reject those of His people that trusted and obeyed Him. God's covenant promises can never be used as claims on God outside a living faith-obedience relation to the Lord. God's promise and Israel's faith belong inseparably together, as Paul states, "The promise comes by faith, so that it may be by grace" (Romans 4:16).

Dispensationalism accepts the conditional nature of God's promise for the individual Israelite, but insists on *unconditional* promises for national Israel. Ryrie comments on Paul's distinction of spiritual and natural Israel in Romans 9:6:

> In the Romans passage Paul is reminding his readers that being an Israelite by natural birth does not assure one of the life and favor promised the believing Israelite who approached God by faith.[14]

He affirms that in Paul's view, a natural Israelite has no right to claim God's covenant promises of "life and favor" that God has assured in both the Abrahamic and Mosaic covenants. Why not? Because faith in the Lord and His Messiah is the required condition for receiving His blessings (see Romans 11:23). It must be acknowledged, however, that this condition of faith is also realized and maintained in Israel's remnant, chosen by God's sovereign will. One commentator on Romans explains:

> A "remnant" is not just a group of separate individuals taken out of a people doomed to overthrow; it is itself the chosen

people, it is Israel *in nuce.* . . . In the "remnant" Israel lives on as the people of God. . . . God's free and sovereign grace decides who shall belong to the "remnant". . . . But according to God's election, the "remnant" had been brought to faith in Christ. It comes before God with no claims; it knows it is wholly dependent on God's grace. Therefore, as the spiritual Israel, it now receives the fulfillment of the promise.[15]

Paul does not operate with the dispensational contrast of individual Israelites versus national Israel, in which the individual has only conditional promises and the nation has only unconditional promises within the same covenant. Paul continues the Hebrew theology that "only the remnant will be saved" (Romans 9:27; citing Isaiah 10:22-23 where Israel's remnant returns "to the mighty God," verse 21). Paul's message is that God is faithful to His word because He has again graciously provided a believing remnant of Israel, the apostolic church, through the creative power of His promise. "So, too, at the present time there is a remnant chosen by grace" (Romans 11:5). The legitimate heirs of the Mosaic and Abrahamic covenants are not the unbelieving natural descendants of Abraham ("Israel after the flesh," 1 Corinthians 10:18, KJV), but exclusively the spiritual children of Abraham, those who belong to Christ.

In other words, it is not the natural children who are God's children, but it is the children of the promise who are regarded as Abraham's offspring (Romans 9:8).

If you belong to Christ, then you are Abraham's seed and heirs according to the promise (Galatians 3:29).

The believing remnant of Israel in Paul's time was created by faith in the proclamation that Jesus of Nazareth was the Christ of prophecy. As Paul writes, "Faith comes from hearing the message, and the message is heard through the word of Christ" (Romans 10:17). There is no ethnic superiority or preference for membership in the remnant of Israel, as Paul understood it.[16] The name "Christians" (Acts 11:26) simply means "the messianic people," all those from Israel and the Gentiles who are baptized into Christ (Galatians 3:26-29).

Paul therefore applies Hosea's promises of Israel's restoration to the formation of the Church of Christ as a whole, for their eschatological fulfillment (Romans 9:25, 26; cf.

Hosea 2:23; 1:10). The Church now occupies the place of Christ-rejecting ethnic Israel—the lopped-off branches in Romans 11:17—and is therefore endowed with Israel's covenant, the blessings and responsibilities, as well as the curses if apostasy will occur. The spiritual blessing of God's presence among His people is intended to arouse the jealousy of natural Israel, because God's redemptive calling of Israel is irrevocable (Romans 11:29).

### Does Paul Look for Israel's Restored Theocracy in Palestine?

Can the words of Paul, "And so all Israel shall be saved" (Romans 11:26) be construed to teach the restoration of Israel's theocracy in Palestine? The *New Scofield Reference Bible* seems to say this in its comments on Romans 11:26, "According to the prophets Israel, regathered from all nations, restored to her own land and converted, is yet to have her greatest earthly exaltation and glory" (p. 1226).

Paul appeals to the Old Testament in order to substantiate his challenging statement:

> As it is written: "The deliverer will come from Zion; he will turn godlessness away from Jacob. And this is my covenant with them when I take away their sins" (Romans 11:26, 27).

Through the living witness of gentile Christians, many Jews will come to faith in Christ and thus be regrafted into the true Israel of God (Romans 11:23). Israel is thus saved in the same way as the Gentiles are saved ("so," Romans 11:26).

Such a conversion of Jews is in agreement with other Old Testament promises. Paul therefore appeals to a combination of passages of Isaiah 59:20, 21; 27:9, and of Jeremiah 31:34, which predict a spiritual renewal of Israel through God's forgiveness of their sins. These passages also express the *condition* of repentance and obedience for Israel's restoration as theocracy. God's promise of redemption in Isaiah reads in full:

> "*The Redeemer will come to Zion, to those in Jacob who repent of their sins*," declares the LORD (Isaiah 59:20; emphasis added).

God promised that He would come as Redeemer to "Zion" for "those who repent of their sins." Repentance was required of Zion or Israel because of its systematic social injustices (Isaiah

59:2-8) which caused Israel's exile among the nations. Repentance was already stated by Moses as the condition for any return of Israel as theocracy to the promised land (see Deuteronomy 30:1-10). Accordingly, Paul stresses the spiritual nature of Israel's redemption by calling it a redemption from "godlessness" and of God's taking away "their sins" (Romans 11:26, 27).

Jeremiah had promised Israel a "new covenant" in which each Israelite would know the Lord personally in the forgiveness of sins (Jeremiah 31:31-34). But again the condition is stated undeniably: "I will put my law in their minds and write it on their hearts" (verse 33). These are the very gospel blessings that Christ offers to both Jew and Gentile through His death, resurrection, and exaltation as the King of Israel (Acts 5:31). Christ is the divine Redeemer who finally has come to Zion. The text of Isaiah 59:20 states literally that the Redeemer will come "to Zion"; the Greek Septuagint reads "for the sake of Zion." Paul modifies this phrase of Isaiah by stating that the Deliverer will come "from Zion" (Romans 11:26), because Christ had now come from Israel. "'Out of Zion' refers to Christ's first advent," comments Lenski.[17] Salvation is from a Jewish Messiah (John 4:22). Christ still comes to Israel through the gospel preaching, in order to redeem them from their sins of unbelief and hardening of heart (see Matthew 11:28). In this way all believing Israelites will be saved (Romans 11:26).

Paul's perspective on natural Israel in Romans 11 is one of hope and assurance that still many—"the fullness" of— Israelites will return to their covenant God through faith in Christ. He says nothing, however, about Israel's physical return to the land of Palestine. F. F. Bruce observes that Paul is saying "nothing about the restoration of an earthly Davidic kingdom, nothing about national reinstatement in the land of Israel. What he envisaged for his people was something infinitely better."[18] The better promise is, of course, salvation from sin and the assurance of acceptance with God. The testimony of the New Testament scholar Herman Ridderbos, during the 1971 "Jerusalem Conference on Biblical Prophecy," is significant in this respect:

> I cannot find any scriptural guarantee for the national restoration and glory of Israel as the people of God. . . . Romans 11:26 proclaims that all Israel will be saved; I understand this to mean that pleroma [fullness] of believers in Israel; by God's

grace all those who believe will be gathered into His kingdom, together with the pleroma from all other nations.[19]

## Notes on Chapter 8

[1]Ryrie, *Dispensationalism Today*, p. 154.

[2]Ryrie, *The Basis of the Premillennial Faith*, p. 136.

[3]Ryrie, *Dispensationalism Today*, p. 96.

[4]Ibid.

[5]Ibid., p. 140.

[6]W. D. Davies, "Paul and the People of Israel," *NTS* 24 (1978): 4-39, states, "We have already suggested that in Romans ix-xi Paul faced an emerging hostile attitude among Gentile Christians toward Jewish Christians and Jews; that is, he faced anti-Judaism. This attitude he rejected" (p. 29).

[7]White, *Patriarchs and Prophets*, pp. 500, 501.

[8]See K. Stendahl, ed., *Paul Among Jews and Gentiles* (Philadelphia: Fortress Press, 1976), pp. 78-96.

[9]H. N. Ridderbos, *Paul: An Outline of His Theology* (Grand Rapids, Mich.: Wm. B. Eerdmans Pub. Co., 1975), p. 360.

[10]Ibid., p. 358.

[11]In *What Ellen G. White Says About Work for the Jewish People* (Washington, D.C.: North American Missions Committee, General Conference of Seventh-day Adventists, 1976). Quotation from *Review and Herald*, June 29, 1905, p. 8.

[12]Ryrie, *Dispensationalism Today*, p. 104; cf. p. 155.

[13]B. Corley, "The Jews, the Future, and God (Romans 9-11)," *Southwestern Journal of Theology* 19:1 (1976):42-56; quotation is from p. 51, note 44. See also Ladd, *A Theology of the New Testament*, p. 539; Ridderbos, *Paul: An Outline of His Theology*, section 58.

[14]Ryrie, *Dispensationalism Today*, p. 138.

[15]A. Nygren, *Commentary on Romans* (Philadelphia: Fortress Press, 1978), pp. 393, 394.

[16]M. Bourke, *A Study of the Metaphor of the Olive Tree in Romans XI* (Washington, D.C.: Catholic University of America Press, 1947), pp. 80-111.

[17]R. C. H. Lenski, *The Interpretation of St. Paul's Epistle to the Romans* (Columbus, Ohio: Wartburg Press, 1945), p. 729.

[18]F. F. Bruce, *The Epistle of Paul to the Romans*, Tyndale New Testament Commentary (Grand Rapids, Mich.: Wm. B. Eerdmans Pub. Co., 1971), p. 221. So also, J. Murray, *The Epistle to the Romans*, NICNT, Vol. 2 (Grand Rapids, Mich.: Wm. B. Eerdmans Pub. Co., 1977), p. 99; C. E. B. Cranfield, *The Epistle to the Romans*, The International Critical Commentary, Vol. 2 (Edinburgh: Clarke, 1979), p. 579.

[19]In *Prophecy in the Making*, ed. C. F. H. Henry (Carol Stream, Ill.: Creation House, 1971), p. 320.

# 9

## Israel's Territorial Promise
## in New Testament Perspective

The dispensational insistence on a dichotomy[1] of Israel and the Church manifests itself most conspicuously in the projection of separate hopes and compartmentalized eschatological programs for each. In this view, the Church can only hope for *heaven* and Israel only for *Palestine* as their respective eternal inheritances.

Dispensationalism calls God's covenant promise to Israel in Deuteronomy 30:1-10, "the Palestinian covenant,"[2] because God had clearly laid down the boundaries of the promised land in His covenant with Abraham: "To your descendants I give this land, from the river of Egypt to the great river, the Euphrates" (Genesis 15:18; cf. Deuteronomy 11:24). The destiny for natural Israel in this Middle East land is seen as being unfolded further in Isaiah 32, "See, a king will reign in righteousness and rulers will rule with justice. . . . My people will live in peaceful dwelling places, in secure homes, in undisturbed places of rest" (Isaiah 32:1, 18).

In sharp contrast with Israel's "Palestinian" covenant, the Church can claim only heaven as her destiny and hope. God "has blessed us in the heavenly realms with every spiritual blessing in Christ" (Ephesians 1:3). "God raised us up with Christ and seated us with him in the heavenly realms in Christ Jesus" (Ephesians 2:6).

The marked contrast between Isaiah 32 and Ephesians 2 brought John N. Darby, in 1868, to deduce "an obvious change of dispensation,"[3] on the basis of literal interpretation. It led him to the conclusion that the royal reign of righteousness and peace on earth was God's plan for the Jewish nation only.

### The Land Promised to the
### Israel of God Only

The Old Testament describes the land promised to the patriarchs and Israel consistently in theological terms: as God's gracious gift or blessing to His covenant people (Genesis 12:1, 7; 13:14-17; 15:18-21; Deuteronomy 1:5-8; Psalm 44:1-3). The land *itself* is called, as it were, to observe a sabbath to the Lord (Leviticus 25:2), "to symbolize Yahweh's creation and ownership of the land."[4] It remained "*His* holy land" (Psalm 78:54) as long as God dwelt in the midst of Israel (Numbers 35:34). The holiness of Israel's land is entirely derivative. The destiny of land, city, and temple depends, therefore, on Israel's religious relation to the Lord (see Leviticus 26). God's judgment on Israel entails His judgment on Israel's land, because it is His land or inheritance. "The land must not be sold permanently, because the land is mine and you are but aliens and my tenants" (Leviticus 25:23). Both the covenant people and its land ultimately depend on Yahweh. Consequently, "Israel cannot claim an immediate relation to its land, cannot have it at its disposal in an autonomous way, cannot idolize the land into an absolute possession."[5] Israel does not own the land. Hosea therefore announces this judgment of God on the Ten Tribes, "They shall not remain in the land of the LORD" (Hosea 9:3). Jeremiah explains:

> I brought you into a fertile land
> to eat its fruit and rich produce.
> But you came and defiled my land
> and made my inheritance detestable.
> —Jeremiah 2:7

Israel's obligation to Yahweh was basically, "I thought you would call me 'Father' and not turn away from following me" (Jeremiah 3:19; cf. 2:8; Psalm 105:43-45). Although the land was the gift of grace to Israel, the covenant people could only abide or stay within the land of God if they would obey the Lord (see Deuteronomy 4:40; Isaiah 1:19). The gift cannot be received without its Giver. Without this theological dimension or condition, Israel's political existence could not be the Israel of God, the theocracy. When Israel became persistently unfaithful to its covenant God, the Lord therefore took His inheritance back from Israel (Jeremiah 17:1-4; 15:13-14). That means, in the Old Testament, Israel's dispersion among the Gentiles and the destruction of the land (Isaiah 1:5-9; Jeremiah 4:23-26). With the rejection of Israel, as the faithless nation, God thus also rejected its land as no longer under His blessing.

Israel's existence as the theocracy is inseparably tied to its dwelling in the land of Palestine. Exile of Israel was caused by God's withdrawal of His covenant blessing. This truth is confirmed by God's gracious promise of a "new covenant" with all the Twelve Tribes,[6] in conjunction with the promise of a new exodus from the lands of the Assyrian and Babylonian captivity, a new settling in the land of the forefathers (Jeremiah 30-32), and the coming of the Messiah, the greater David (Jeremiah 23:5, 6). These astounding promises of Jeremiah reveal that God's faithfulness to His covenant with Israel continued within and through His judgment of the disobedient tribes.

Nevertheless, Israel's return from exile was still conditioned by its return to Yahweh. "A remnant will return, a remnant of Jacob will return to the mighty God" (Isaiah 10:21; see also Isaiah 4:2-6; Jeremiah 3:12-13; 31:21-22). These prophetic judgment oracles point up the fact that Israel as covenant people cannot possess Palestine without Yahweh. As Peter Diepold observes regarding the Old Testament, "Although the land is a gift of the grace of Yahweh, it still counts that Yahweh's donation can only be realized in obedience to the revelation of His will."[7]

The newness of Jeremiah's new-covenant promise is the marvellous assurance that God, by His sovereign grace, will provide such a new Israel in which the spiritual requirements of loving obedience and experiential knowledge of God are fulfilled. Such a promise is nothing less than an eschatological promise, because it denotes a radically new beginning of God's history with Israel. Yet, even in Jeremiah's promises of chapters 30-32, the restoration of Israel in the promised land cannot be realized without a new covenant relationship with God. A secular, political reconstitution of Israel as a nation is nowhere envisioned in Old Testament prophecy. Only when Yahweh is acknowledged in His Messiah, the new David, as the sole Lord and Ruler, will Israel dwell in Palestine as the faithful remnant, as the Israel of God (Isaiah 9:7; 11:10-12; Ezekiel 37:21-27; Jeremiah 23:5-8). Then the land will be restored in justice and peace, not in its old, sinful form, because God's Shekinah glory will be manifested among His people (Ezekiel 37:27-28).

### The Unity of Biblical Eschatology

Instead of seeking our own independent solution to the different aspects of biblical eschatology, we are duty-bound to ask how Christ, the true Interpreter, and the New Testament writers understood the Old Testament hope for peace and righteousness. In His Sermon on the Mount, Christ promised the kingdom of heaven to "the poor in spirit" (Matthew 5:3; called the kingdom of God, in Luke 6:20); and to "the meek," or "the humble," He promised the earth (Matthew 5:5). Two conclusions must be drawn: (1) To His spiritual followers Jesus assigns the whole *earth* together with the kingdom of *heaven* (or of God)[8] as their inheritance; (2) He applies Israel's territorial inheritance to the Church by enlarging the original promise of Palestine to include the earth made new. In ancient Israel, David assured the Israelites who endured suppression by evil men, that God would vindicate their trust in Him:

> But the meek will inherit the land and enjoy great peace . . .
> The righteous will inherit the land and dwell in it forever.
> —Psalm 37:11, 29

Clearly, Christ applies Psalm 37 in a new, surprising way: (1) This "land" will be larger than David thought; the fulfillment will include the entire earth in its recreated beauty (see Isaiah 11:6-9; Revelation 21-22); (2) The renewed earth will be the inheritance of all the meek from all nations who accept Christ as their Lord and Savior. Christ is definitely not spiritualizing away Israel's territorial promise when He includes His universal Church. On the contrary, He widened the scope of the territory until it extended to the whole world.

The apostle Paul understood the territorial covenant promise just as Jesus did, as being universal from the outset and as a gift of grace. He writes:

> It was not through law that Abraham and his offspring received the promise that he would be *heir of the world*, but *through the righteousness that comes by faith* (Romans 4:13; emphasis added).

Paul declares that this world-wide territorial promise was the essence of the Abrahamic covenant and would be granted by means of righteousness by faith. God's invitation to Abraham to look "north and south, east and west" in the land of Canaan sets no limits.

"All the land that you see I will give to you and your offspring forever. I will make your offspring like the dust of the earth, so that if anyone could count the dust, then your offspring could be counted" (Genesis 13:14, 15-16).

In order to understand Paul, one must view the land of Palestine as a down payment, or pledge, assuring Israel as a nation the larger territory necessary to accommodate the countless multitudes of Abraham's offspring. The Abrahamic covenant contained the promise of an offspring and of a land for that offspring. These promises have found a gradually increasing fulfillment since Israel's settlement in the land of Canaan under Joshua (Joshua 21:45). W. C. Kaiser, Jr., interprets Israel's conquest of Canaan as follows:

This, in turn, became a token or pledge of the complete land grant yet to come in the future even as the earlier occupations were simultaneously recognized as "expositions, confirmations, and expansions of the promise."[9]

Paul reckons Abraham to be the father of all believers who are justified by faith in Christ among all the nations of the world (see Romans 4:13, 16-24). Abraham "is the father of us all" (both believing Jews and believing Gentiles). "As it is written: 'I have made you a father of many nations.' He is our father in the sight of God" (Romans 4:16, 17). Paul interprets God's promises to Abraham concerning land and offspring "in the sight of God" as being fulfilled through Christ. That is not according to the hermeneutic of literalism, but Paul's theological exegesis. The land becomes the world; the nations become the believers who trust in God and who are justified by faith, as was Abraham. The conclusion of D. P. Fuller regarding Romans 4 is therefore exact: "Paul understood that Abraham would father a multitude of nations through Christ."[10] This is in agreement with Paul's statement that the land or world that is promised "comes by faith, so that it may be by grace and may be guaranteed to all Abraham's offspring" (Romans 4:16). Israel's territorial promises are made sure in Christ and guaranteed through Him to all believers, whether Jew or Gentile. Consequently, Israel's covenant is conditional with respect to those who qualify as recipients. The condition is: faith in Jesus as the Messiah of Israel.

This conclusion militates against the assertion of the dispensationalist J. Dwight Pentecost: "This covenant made by God with Israel in regard to their relation to the land must be seen to be an unconditional covenant."[11] On the other hand, the *New Scofield Reference Bible* (p. 251) acknowledges the explicit conditional nature of Deuteronomy 30:1-10, stating, "The Palestinian Covenant gives the conditions under which Israel entered the land of promise."

W. C. Kaiser explains this tension in perhaps the best words: "The conditionality was not attached to the promise but only to the participants who would benefit from these abiding promises. . . . The promise remained permanent, but the participation in the blessings depended on the individual's spiritual condition."[12] This conditional aspect on the part of the recipients does not infringe in the least upon the unconditional foundation of God's promise regarding the kingdom of God, in terms of a redeemed earth (Isaiah 11:6-9; Amos 9:13-15). Isaiah describes this in cosmic terms: "Behold, I will create new heavens and a new earth . . . for I will create Jerusalem to be a delight and its people a joy" (Isaiah 65:17; cf. 66:22). Here the prophet unites heaven and earth together as one glorious inheritance for eschatological Israel. The New Testament declares emphatically that Abraham and his believing descendants looked forward by faith to something far more permanent and glorious than the conquest of Palestine or a rebuilt Jerusalem:

> By faith he [Abraham] made his home in the promised land like a stranger in a foreign country. . . . For he was looking forward to the city with foundations, whose architect and builder is God. . . . All these people [spiritual Israel] were still living by faith when they died. They did not receive the things promised. . . . If they had been thinking of the country they had left, they would have had opportunity to return. *Instead, they were longing for a better country—a heavenly one.* Therefore God is not ashamed to be called their God, for *he has prepared a city for them* (Hebrews 11:9, 10, 13, 15, 16; emphasis added).

Thus basically one eschatology binds Israel and the Church together.

### The Inadequacy of the Hermeneutic
### of Literalism

The hermeneutic of ethnic and geographic literalism in prophecy is based on the assumption that prophecy is nothing but history ahead of time. Consequently, it ascribes to the prophetic portrayals the exactness of a photographic picture in advance. This assumption allows no room for greater and better things to come, things that "no mind has conceived" but God alone (1 Corinthians 2:9; Isaiah 64:4). Literalism denies the inherent biblical structure of an escalating typology. Christ came in humbleness, yet He was greater than Jonah, greater than Solomon, greater than the temple (Matthew 12:40, 42, 6). He raised the Jewish hope far above expecting a Messiah who was literally identical with a king, prophet, or priest in Israel. As the divine Messiah, He stood infinitely above those ancient prototypes, already in His humble incarnation but especially in His coming glorification. An exact reproduction of Israel's theocratic kings should not be expected. If understood as types of greater and better things to come, "the representation *must* have been, to a large extent, figurative and symbolical."[13] One may therefore also view the promised land — Palestine — as "a miniature world in which God illustrated His kingdom and His way of dealing with sin. The land which God promised to Abraham and his seed . . . was a type of the world (Romans 4:13)."[14] The full scope of Israel's prophets was not nationalistic, but universal, with an increasing cosmic dimension which took in heaven and earth (Isaiah 65:17; 24:21-23).

The decisive principle for the eschatological application of Israel's territorial promise is, however, the way Christ and the New Testament as a whole apply this covenant promise. The classical passage that teaches the universal enlargement of Israel's restricted holy territory is found in Jesus' revelation to the Samaritan woman. Recognizing that Jesus was a prophet, the woman asked Him which mountain was holy in God's sight, the mountain of Samaria (Mount Gerizim) or Mount Zion in Jerusalem? Christ replied, "Believe me, woman, a time is coming when you will worship the Father neither on this mountain nor in Jerusalem" (John 4:21). Since the coming of the Messiah, *He* is now the holy Place, to which all Israel and the Gentiles must gather (Matthew 11:28; 23:37). "For where two or three are gathered in my name, there am I in the midst of them," Christ declared (Matthew 18:20, RSV). Looking into the future ages, He added later, "But I, when I am lifted up from the earth, will draw all men to myself" (John 12:32). Christ does not differentiate between a Jewish-Christian and a gentile-Christian hope in eschatology. The spiritual descendants of Abraham from all the nations will be brought together into "one flock" under "one Shepherd" (John 10:16).

An underlying principle seems to govern Christ's applications of Israel's promises: the removal of the old *ethnic* restriction among the new-covenant people entails the removal of the old *geographic* Middle East center for Christ's Church. Wherever Christ is, there is the holy space. This is the essence of the New Testament application of Israel's holy territory. For the holiness of old Jerusalem, the New Testament substitutes the holiness of Jesus Christ. It "Christifies" the old territorial holiness and thus transcends its limitations. This should not be regarded as the New Testament rejection of Israel's territorial promise, but rather as its fulfillment and confirmation in Christ.

The basic continuity of the Old and New Testament eschatology is visualized dramatically in the Epistle to the Hebrews. This apostolic writer assures the new-covenant Israel that in coming to Jesus Christ, "You have come to Mount Zion, to the heavenly Jerusalem, the city of the living God. You have come . . . to the church [*ekklesia*] of the firstborn, whose names are written in heaven. You have come to God . . . , to Jesus the mediator of a new covenant . . ." (Hebrews 12:22-24). Through the atoning blood of Christ's death, the Church is now constantly by faith entering the heavenly sanctuary and drawing near to the very throne of grace to receive help (Hebrews 4:16; 10:19-22).

This imagery of Christian worship is not presented as an analogy or a parallel worship beside Israel but as the proclamation of an essential fulfillment of Israel's ancient types and shadows. The retaining of the Hebrew imagery and terminology serves the purpose of stressing the basic unity and continuity of divine worship in its progressive revelation and historical realization in Christ (Hebrews 1:1-3). The present spiritual fulfillment does not annul or cancel the future apocalyptic consummation of Israel's promises. The cross of Christ nevertheless has transformed them all, once and forever, by the Christocentrism of the gospel hermeneutic. The continuity of the Old Testament terms and Middle East images in Hebrews assures the Church of Christ that God's promise has neither failed nor been postponed but is experienced now in Christ (Hebrews 6:5) and will be fulfilled in an even more glorious way in its apocalyptic consummation (Hebrews 13:14).

### One Hope for Abraham, Israel, and the Church

Abraham and his believing offspring were promised, not just Palestine, in the present sinful condition, but "a better country" with a heavenly city (Hebrews 11:10, 16). In short, they looked beyond Palestine to a *new* heaven and earth, and to a *new* Jerusalem. Furthermore, this eternal inheritance is not restricted to the Israel of God from the houses of Judah and Israel. Hebrews teaches explicitly that Israel and the Church will be united in one inheritance: "God had planned something better for us [the Church] so that only together with us would they [Israel] be made perfect" (Hebrews 11:40; cf. 13:14).

This apostolic Letter applies the new covenant, which God had promised to the twelve tribes of Israel (Jeremiah 31:31-34), to the universal Church of Christ (Hebrews 8:1-13). The author even declares that the Mosaic covenant is now antiquated, the Levitical law abrogated, and that the earthly temple, with its ritual of sacrifices, is "set aside" as "obsolete" by Christ (Hebrews 8:13; 10:9). All believers must turn their eyes to Jesus as the King-Priest on the throne of grace, because the Holy Spirit has now disclosed that the true mediation is transferred from the earthly to the heavenly sanctuary (Hebrews 9:8; 10:19-22). Through Christ we all may now enter into the vivifying rest of God, assured of the hope of a place of rest for eternity (Hebrews 4:3, 9).

In Christ "we are receiving a kingdom that cannot be shaken" (Hebrews 12:28) and are "looking for the city that is to come" (Hebrews 13:14). But the unassailable certainty of the coming of the New Jerusalem and the unshakable kingdom of God does not antiquate the spiritual condition of accepting Jesus as Lord and Christ. Jesus stressed the conditional nature of participating in the coming messianic banquet in unambiguous terms:

> I say to you that many will come from the east and the west,
> and will take their places at the feast with Abraham, Isaac, and
> Jacob in the kingdom of heaven [of God, in Luke 13:28]. But
> the subjects of the kingdom will be thrown outside, into
> darkness, where there will be weeping and gnashing of teeth
> (Matthew 8:11, 12; cf. Luke 13:28, 29).

In other words, according to Christ, natural (unbelieving)
Israel has no part whatsoever in the kingdom promise. Believing Gentiles will take their empty seats at the eschatological
festival of Abraham's offspring.

The Church of Christ has no other hope, no other destiny,
no other inheritance than the one that God gave to Abraham
and Israel—a redeemed heaven and earth (Isaiah 65:17). This
could not be confirmed more conclusively than by the words of
the apostle Peter:

> That day will bring about the destruction of the heavens by
> fire, and the elements will melt in the heat. But *in keeping with
> his promise* we are looking forward to a new heaven and a new
> earth, the home of righteousness (2 Peter 3:12, 13; emphasis
> added).

With apostolic authority Peter transfers the hope of Israel to
the Church. The new heaven and new earth—promised to Israel in Isaiah 65:17—has now become the promised inheritance of the Church.

The question arises, How can the Church triumphant,
glorified and taken to paradise with God at the second advent
of Christ (see 1 Thessalonians 4:16, 17; John 14:1-3), receive
the earth as her eternal home? The answer is found in Revelation 21-22, where divine inspiration reveals that the New Jerusalem, by God's power, will descend from heaven to the earth:

> Then I saw a new heaven and a new earth, for the first heaven
> and the first earth had passed away, and there was no longer
> any sea. I saw the Holy City, the new Jerusalem, coming down
> out of heaven from God, prepared as a bride beautifully
> dressed for her husband. And I heard a loud voice from the
> throne saying, "Now the dwelling of God is with men, and he
> will live with them. They will be his people, and God himself
> will be with them and be their God." He who was seated on the
> throne said, "I am making everything new!" Then he said,
> "Write this down, for these words are trustworthy and true"
> (Revelation 21:1-5).

A new earth is the final goal of all redemptive history. Man's ultimate destiny centers in a regenerated earth (Matthew 5:5; 19:28). According to Paul, "The creation itself will be liberated from its bondage to decay and brought into the glorious freedom of the children of God" (Romans 8:21). Only then will Abraham's hope be fulfilled and all his children, in Israel and the Church, live together throughout eternity as one family in one city. The apocalyptic realization of God's inheritance and His glorious dwelling among His people (Revelation 21:3) will be the eternal consummation of His covenants with Abraham (Genesis 17:7), with Moses (Exodus 6:7; Deuteronomy 29:13), with David (2 Samuel 7:24), and of His new covenant with Israel (Jeremiah 31:1, 31; Ezekiel 36:28; 37:23).

In Revelation 21-22, God's continuing covenant promises find at last their perfect fulfillment in the new earth of the age to come.[15] Through Christ both Israel and the Church are one and meet together in one new city, the New Jerusalem, which has gates named after the twelve tribes of Israel and foundations bearing the names of the twelve apostles of Christ's Church (see Revelation 21:12-14). The lesson for Christians is profound, as John Bright concludes:

> So, like Israel of old, we have ever to live in tension. It is the tension between grace and obligation: the unconditional grace of Christ which is proffered to us, his unconditional promises in which we are invited to trust, and the obligation to obey him as the church's sovereign Lord.[16]

### Notes on Chapter 9

[1]Ryrie, *Dispensationalism Today*, pp. 154, 155.

[2]*NSRB*, p. 251 (on Deuteronomy 30).

[3]Documentation in Fuller, *Gospel and Law: Contrast or Continuum?*, pp. 15, 16.

[4]W. D. Davies, *The Gospel and the Land: Early Christianity and Jewish Territorial Doctrine* (Berkeley, Calif: University of California Press, 1974), p. 29.

[5]P. Diepold, *Israels Land*, BWANT NR 15 (Stuttgart: W. Kohlhammer, 1972), p. 109 (my translation).

[6]Davies, *The Gospel and the Land*, p. 43, remarks that Jeremiah's heart's desire was "that the northern Israel as well as

Judah should ultimately return from exile (Jeremiah 3:12f.; 31:4-5; 31:9, 15-20)."

[7]Diepold, *Israels Land*, p. 183 (my translation).

[8]The *New Scofield Reference Bible* views the terms (a) "kingdom of heaven" and (b) "kingdom of God" as largely overlapping in meaning, but nevertheless as distinct: (a) stands for God's rulership from heaven over earthly people alone, however in the sphere of an external profession of God by people; (b) stands for the cosmic, universal kingdom of God (pp. 994, 1002). Ryrie soft-pedals this strange literalism by saying, "This distinction is not the issue at all. The issue is whether or not the Church is the kingdom . . ." (*Dispensationalism Today*, p. 173). The real issue, however, is whether Christ's present reign on the throne of God is the present fulfillment of the Davidic covenant.

[9]Kaiser, *Toward an Old Testament Theology*, pp. 90, 91.

[10]Fuller, *Gospel and Law: Contrast or Continuum?*, p. 133.

[11]Pentecost, *Things to Come*, p. 98.

[12]Kaiser, *Toward an Old Testament Theology*, pp. 94, 110.

[13]P. Fairbairn, *Prophecy and Proper Interpretation* (Grand Rapids, Mich.: Guardian Press, 1976; reprint of 1865), p. 229.

[14]L. F. Were, *The Certainty of the Third Angel's Message* (Berrien Springs, Mich.: First Impressions, 1979), p. 86.

[15]See Ladd, *A Theology of the New Testament*, p. 632.

[16]J. Bright, *Covenant and Promise: The Prophetic Understanding of the Future in Pre-Exilic Israel* (Philadelphia: Westminster Press, 1976), p. 198.

# 10

## Problematic Texts

---

*Amos 9:11-12 As Applied in Acts 15:16-18*

During the first apostolic council in Jerusalem the question was discussed whether Christ-believing Gentiles should be circumcised and required to obey the law of Moses in order to be saved (see Acts 15:1, 5, 6). Peter then testified that God had shown him, in the conversion of Cornelius and his household (see Acts 10), that God "made no distinction between us and them, for he purified their hearts by faith" (Acts 15:9). He concluded, "We believe it is through the grace of our Lord Jesus that we are saved, just as they are" (verse 11).

After Barnabas and Paul had confirmed this conclusion by recounting their own experiences, James, the brother of Jesus, agreed that God apparently had taken "from the Gentiles a people for himself" (verse 14). James used a phrase that was reserved for Israel as the covenant people of Yahweh (Deuteronomy 7:6; 14:2; 28:9, 10; Isaiah 43:7). Christ-believing Gentiles are thus included in God's covenant people. James did not think that he had detected a new arrangement of salvation for Gentiles. His response is rather: "The words of the prophets [plural] are in agreement with this, as it is written" [quoted Amos 9:11, 12, in the Septuagint version] (Acts 15:15). This interpretation of Amos by James confirms Peter's application of Joel 2:28-32 to the Church (in Acts 2:16-21). The gentile mission of the apostolic Church forms an essential part of God's predicted purpose. Amos' prophecy of the restoration of Israel is given an ecclesiological application. Gentiles

must, therefore, be fully accepted into Israel's messianic remnant (Romans 11:5), the Church, by faith alone. God bestowed His Holy Spirit on Gentiles in Caesarea even before they
were baptized (Acts 10:44-47)! Amos predicted explicitly that
faithful remnants of Edom and other nations shall be blessed
together with the restored Israel:

> In that day I will restore David's fallen tent. I will repair its
> broken places, restore its ruins, and build it as it used to be, so
> that they may possess the remnant of Edom and all the nations
> that bear my name, declares the LORD, who will do these things
> (Amos 9:11-12).

James' point in citing this passage at the conclusion of the
apostolic council is that Amos' prediction had come true since
Pentecost through the inflow of gentile believers into the
Church. The fact that James alters the Hebrew text in quoting
Amos' prophecy has given an opportunity to the *Scofield Reference Bible* to impose its dispensational program of events on
the introductory words of Amos as cited by James: "After this I
will return and rebuild David's fallen tent" (Acts 15:16). The
words "after this I will return" are interpreted as meaning

> . . . the time after the present world-wide witness (Acts 1:8),
> when Christ will return. James showed that there will be Gen-
> tile believers at that time as well as Jewish believers; hence he
> concluded that Gentiles are not required to become Jewish
> proselytes by circumcision.[1]

This view envisions three successive dispensations in the
text of Amos 9:11: (1) the calling out of a people from among
the Gentiles during the present Church Age; (2) "After this,"
meaning after this Church Age, the regathering of national
Israel and the restoration of the Davidic throne on earth during the millennium; and (3) after this the salvation of the remnant of Israel and that of all the Gentiles.[2]

This dogmatic construction has received no support from
biblical exegetes at large. The reason is that responsible exegesis of Scripture does not allow the dispensational interpretation when the passage is connected with the original context in
the book of Amos and with the immediate context of Acts 15:
13-15.

In the setting of the book of Amos, the phrase, "After this
I will return and rebuild David's fallen tent," refers clearly to

the time of Israel's restoration after the Babylonian captivity. J. F. Walvoord declares, however, that the words in the Amos quotation, "After these things I will return" (Acts 15:16), mean to say that after God's judgment on Israel—their scattering and discipline—Christ will return.[3] This conclusion violates the literal, historical exegesis of Amos 9, which requires the application of God's judgment to Israel's exile to Assyria and Babylon (see Amos 5:27). This judgment began in the days of Amos himself, in 722 B.C. After the Babylonian exile the Lord returned in favor to Jerusalem and restored His theocracy to the faithful remnant of Israel (see Zechariah 8). Zechariah added the promise that the Messiah would come to rule Israel and the world in universal peace (Zechariah 9:9, 10). God's final judgment on Israel would depend on Israel's response to the atoning sacrifice of the Messiah (Daniel 9:26, 27; see chapter 11, below). It is James' contention in Acts 15 that Amos' prophecy has found its ongoing fulfillment since the first coming of the Messiah, in the mission of the apostolic Church.

In the appearance of Christ, God did return to Israel. J. Barton Payne explains:

> The reference [the rebuilding of David's fallen tent] must be to His first coming; for Acts 15:16 emphasizes that it is this event which enables the Gentiles, from the apostolic period onward, to seek God. . . . [Then] came the engrafting of the uncircumcised Gentiles into the church, to which Acts 15 applies the OT passage, so it cannot refer to times yet future.[4]

God restored the throne of David in the resurrection, ascension, and inauguration of Christ Jesus as Lord and Redeemer of Israel (Acts 2:36; 5:31). Christ is already the Priest-King at the right hand of God (Acts 2:33-36; Hebrews 1:3, 13), to whom is given all authority in heaven and on earth (Matthew 28:18). As the Davidic kings were sitting "on the throne of the LORD" (1 Chronicles 28:5; 29:23), so Christ is now seated with His Father on His throne (Revelation 3:21). The Davidic throne is no longer unoccupied or ineffective, but is transferred from Jerusalem to the throne room in heaven, where Christ is presently the Davidic King (Acts 2:34-36; 1 Corinthians 15:25; Ephesians 1:20-22). The throne of David and the throne of the Lord cannot be separated, as dispensationalism presumes. Amos' prediction of the restoration of the throne of David was fulfilled in Christ's enthronement in heaven. This is the apostolic message.

G. E. Ladd confirms this conclusion:

> James cites the prophecy of Amos 9:11-12 to prove that Peter's experience with Cornelius was a fulfillment of God's purpose to visit the Gentiles and take out of them a people for his name. It therefore follows that the "rebuilding of the dwelling of David" which had resulted in the Gentile mission, must refer to the exaltation and enthronement of Christ upon the (heavenly) throne of David and the establishment of the church as the true people of God, the new Israel. Since God had brought Gentiles to faith without the Law, there was no need to insist that the Gentiles become Jews to be saved.[5]

The New Testament application of Amos 9:11-12 is called the christological-ecclesiological interpretation of Israel's restoration promise. A closer look reveals another interesting feature. While Amos prophesied the physical conquest of the Davidic rulership over the remnant of Edom, James translates this political-military kingship into Christ's higher, spiritual conquest and reign over the hearts of gentile believers. Amos' phrase "so that they may possess the remnant of Edom" becomes in Acts 15:17, "that the remnant of men may seek the Lord." Martin J. Wyngaarden analyzes Acts 15:16-18 as follows:

> Here Christ's exalted reign from heaven represents the glorious restoration of the dynasty, the remnant of Edom becomes the residue of men, the military possession of Edom makes room for the voluntary seeking of the Gentiles after the Lord, with the absence of the physical warfare suggested by the imagery of Amos.[6]

He characterizes this transformation as the New Testament spiritualization, authorized by the Holy Spirit. The universal apostolic church is *the* restoration of Israel.

### Isaiah 11:10-12: What is the Fulfillment of Israel's "Second" Gathering?

> In that day the Root of Jesse will stand as a banner for the peoples; the nations will rally to him, and his place of rest will be glorious. In that day the LORD will reach out his hand a second time to reclaim the remnant that is left of his people from Assyria, from Lower Egypt, from Upper Egypt, from Cush, from Elam, from Babylonia, from Hamath, and from the

islands of the sea. He will raise a banner for the nations and gather the exiles of Israel; He will assemble the scattered people of Judah from the four quarters of the earth (Isaiah 11:10-12).

The *New Scofield Reference Bible* considers this passage a proof text for its expected future reconstitution of Israel as a national theocracy in Palestine at the second coming of Christ (*NSRB* 723). J. F. Walvoord supports this futurism with an appeal to Isaiah's sequence of describing first the messianic kingdom (verses 6-9) and then the gathering of Israel (verses 10-15).[7] On the basis of this literary sequence, Walvoord argues, the messianic gathering of Israel will take place only when the Messiah appears in glory, at the beginning of the millennium. This futuristic interpretation fails to do justice, however, both to the grammatical-historical exegesis of Isaiah 11 and to the New Testament theological interpretation. For an orderly discussion of this messianic prophecy we must relate Isaiah 11 (1) to the time of its own dispensation; (2) to the first coming of Christ; and (3) to the second coming of Christ.

*1. The Initial Fulfillment of Isaiah 11.*

Isaiah made his prophecy about a "second" gathering of the Israel of God around 701 B.C., when Assyria had already deported many tribes of Israel beyond the Euphrates River (721 B.C.). Isaiah sees Israel largely in exile in Assyria and Babylon (at that time a province of Assyria). He predicts the good news that the God of Israel will regather "the remnant that is left of His people" among the Middle East nations. Isaiah relates this future gathering explicitly to Israel's former gathering, when Moses miraculously dried up the Red Sea so that Israel had a free pathway out of Egyptian bondage.

> There will be a highway for the remnant of his people that is left from Assyria, *as there was for Israel when they came up from Egypt* (Isaiah 11:16; emphasis added).

The prophet Isaiah stands between Israel's past exodus from Egypt under Moses and its future exodus from Babylon (see diagram, following page).

When the Davidic prince Zerubbabel gathered the faithful remnant of Israel from Babylon (Ezra 1:5) and returned to Jerusalem in 536 B.C., God actually began to fulfill Isaiah's promise to reclaim God's faithful remnant a "second" time

| PAST | PRESENT | FUTURE |
|---|---|---|
| *First Exodus of Israel:* From Egypt | Isaiah predicts ⟶ | *Second Exodus of Israel:* From Babylon |
| *Time:* Under Moses | *Time:* Around 700 B.C. | *Time:* Fulfilled in Israel's Return to Palestine under Zerubbabel in 536 B.C. |

from their scattering among the gentile nations (see Ezra 1-2). It is certainly correct to conclude that this gathering of Israel under Zerubbabel in 536 B.C., and later in 457 B.C. under Ezra, was not the complete fulfillment of Isaiah 11:11-15, because the Messiah had not yet appeared. Nevertheless, Zerubbabel was a prince from the house of David and therefore a type of the Messiah. This makes the exodus of Israel under Zerubbabel basically an *initial fulfillment* of the messianic gathering prophecy. It only reinforced Isaiah's promise of the *eschatological* gathering of all Messiah-believing people from Israel and all the nations by the coming of Christ Himself.

Isaiah's prediction that "the LORD will dry up . . . the Euphrates River" (11:15) in order to deliver Israel has also found a striking historical fulfillment. The Persian general Cyrus diverted the waters of the Euphrates north of the city of Babylon in order to bring about its sudden fall in 539 B.C. The deeper meaning of Isaiah's prophecy of this drying up of the Euphrates' waters on behalf of Israel is brought to light in the New Testament Apocalypse (Revelation 16:12), in connection with the remnant church of the time of the end.[8]

## 2. The Christological-Ecclesiological Fulfillment of Isaiah 11

Isaiah opens with the prediction of the coming of the Messiah in a twofold manifestation. One appearance is likened to a little shoot from the stump of Jesse, strengthened by the anointing of the Spirit of the Lord (verses 1-3). The second appearance is His appearance as the glorious Judge who "will strike the earth with the rod of his mouth; with the breath of his lips he will slay the wicked" (verses 4-5). The New Testament reveals that these two appearances of the Messiah refer to two different historical advents of Christ to the world. Because it is the same Messiah, both advents basically share in the same Lordship or kingdom of Christ. The peace and righteousness of the messianic kingdom, as described in Isaiah 11:6-9, therefore find their fulfillments in keeping with the appearances of Christ. The first coming of Christ brings internal peace with God and with fellow men, through Christ's reconciling sacrifice and Spirit (see Colossians 1:19-20; Ephesians 2:14-18). The second coming will add external peace and universal righteousness through His Judgment of the world and His new creation (2 Thessalonians 1:5-10; 2 Thessalonians 2:8; Revelation 21:1-5).

Isaiah's forecast of the gathering of Israel is deeply God-centered and Messiah-centered. The gathering is primarily to the Messiah Himself, and only secondarily to the land of Israel. Furthermore, the gathering is not for Israel only but explicitly for all believing Gentiles (Isaiah 11:10). The historic fulfillment of this messianic gathering to God's "place of rest" began already with the first advent of Christ (see Matthew 12:30; John 12:32; Hebrews 4:14-16).

The apostle Paul cites the essence of Isaiah 11:1, 10, to assure the church in Rome that Isaiah's prediction of the messianic rest is now experienced through faith in Christ (Romans 15:8, 9, 12). Thus Paul gives Isaiah 11:10 an undeniably christological-ecclesiological application. Isaiah's prophetic remnant of Israel is a Christ-believing remnant, not a purely ethnic-political nation which rejects Jesus as the Messiah. Christ is the "Banner" to which the remnant will rally. Christians from ethnic Israel and the Gentiles are already now drinking "water from the wells of salvation" with messianic joy (Isaiah 12:3; John 7:38, 39; 15:11).

### 3. The Apocalyptic Consummation of Isaiah 11

The deepest intention of Isaiah's prophecies concerning Israel's gathering from the dispersion undoubtedly implies an apocalyptic perspective. Only when the faithful remnant will be restored in Paradise (Isaiah 11:1-9) will the gathering of all Israel be completed. Only when all the wicked are judged by the Messiah's righteousness (Isaiah 11:4) will Isaiah's promise be completely realized: "They will neither harm nor destroy on all my holy mountain, for the earth will be full of the knowledge of the LORD as the waters cover the sea" (Isaiah 11:9). This universal perspective is expanded in Isaiah 24-27, the so-called Isaiah-Apocalypse, which has been called "one of the most beautiful and magnificent parts of the OT" (E. Sellin). This apocalyptic unit culminates in God's trumpet call to gather Israel into His everlasting kingdom.

> In that day the LORD will thresh from the flowing Euphrates to the Wadi of Egypt, and *you, O Israelites, will be gathered up one by one.* And in that day a great trumpet will sound. Those who were perishing in Assyria and those who were exiled in Egypt *will come and worship the LORD on the holy mountain in Jerusalem* (Isaiah 27:12-13; emphasis added).

This final remnant of Israel is not pictured as an ethnic group or political entity, but as a religious remnant. The purpose of God's last trumpet is to gather each Israelite so that all Israel may "worship Yahweh" in His holy temple in truth and Spirit, in everlasting freedom from all oppression.

Do Christ and the New Testament writers envision such an apocalyptic gathering of the Israel of God at the glorious second advent of Christ? Christ saw His second coming as the final harvest of His mission to draw all men to Himself through His cross (John 12:24, 32; 14:1-3). He announced that He would return in power and great glory to judge Israel and the nations of the earth in regard to their faith in or rejection of His messianic mission to die for their sins (John 5:22-24). He would judge them all by their relation to His own people (Matthew 25:31-46). When He returns, "He will send his angels with a loud trumpet call, and they will gather his elect from the four winds, from one end of the heavens to the other (Matthew 24:31).

Christ refers here, not to an ethnic Israel, but to "His elect." This messianic Israel will be gathered, not to the Middle East, but "from the four winds, from one end of the heavens to the other," to Himself (cf. John 14:2, 3; 1 Thessalonians 4:16, 17). This is Christ's final application of Isaiah's gathering promises (cf. Matthew 8:11, 12).

### 4. Dispensational Interpretations of Isaiah 11:11-15

The Hebrew Christian Arthur W. Kac defends the thesis that the formation of the modern State of Israel in A.D. 1948 was the initial or "preparatory" fulfillment of Isaiah's prophecy. God has now gathered Israel a "second time" from the nations to their homeland (Isaiah 11:11) in order to reconstitute Israel as "a fully independent sovereign State."[9] What, then, does Kac see as the first gathering of Israel? He rejects Israel's deliverance from Egypt as God's first gathering of His people, because Israel's stay in Egypt was "voluntarily for some four hundred years" (see, however, Genesis 15:13-16!). Kac asserts: "The first dispersion of the Jewish people was accomplished by Babylon and the first Return had taken place at the end of the Babylonian exile. The passage cited above [Isaiah 11:11] speaks of a second ingathering and it implied a second dispersion."[10] He even states that the restoration "promises . . . never found fulfillment after the conclusion of the Babylonian exile."[11] Consequently Kac draws up the following order of events in Isaiah 11:11 (see diagram):

| Isaiah Predicts Two Future Gatherings | First, a Gathering of Israel from Babylon | A Second Gathering of Israel from all Nations |
|---|---|---|
| Time: 700 B.C. | Fulfilled after 537 B.C. | Fulfilled since A.D. 1948 |

Kac seems not to accept any fulfillment of Isaiah's promise for the period after the Babylonian exile. He states categorically that God's gathering promises "never found fulfillment after the conclusion of the Babylonian exile," yet he admits that "the first return had taken place at the end of the Babylonian exile." It is generally acknowledged that Israel's return from Babylon was a true, although partial, fulfillment of Isaiah's gathering prophecy. According to the literal exegesis, Isaiah did not predict that God would gather Israel "two times" but "a second time". The implication is, of course, that the first gathering had taken place in Isaiah's past (see Isaiah 11:16). Another indication of a basic lack of historical exegesis on Kac's part is found in the remark that the prophecy of Zechariah, chapter 8, was made "after the ingathering of the Babylonian Exile had already taken place," and consequently "implies another Restoration."[12] Kac simply overlooks the fact that Zechariah's prophecy was made in 518 B.C. (Zechariah 7:1) and was later fulfilled in Israel's further gathering from

Babylon under Ezra in 457 B.C. (Ezra 7). This was, in fact, the restoration which Zechariah promised.

More serious, however, is the fact that Kac violates the fundamental New Testament principle of interpreting Old Testament prophecies that pass from the old into the new dispensation. The cross and the resurrection of Christ irrevocably transform the nature of Israel and all its eschatological fulfillments (see chapter 7 above).

Kac's ethnic, political application of the eschatological Israel has robbed the "remnant" of its profound religious-theological essentials and left only a restored secular nation, the modern State of Israel. How this present State of Israel "is preparatory to Israel's final and complete redemption," and how this "will issue forth in the transformation of the kingdom of this earth into the Kingdom of God,"[13] he leaves an open question. He "associates" the present State of Israel with the return of the Lord Jesus Christ, in an unexplained and mysterious way.

The official dispensational position on Isaiah 11 is presented in the *New Scofield Reference Bible*: "This chapter is a prophetic picture of the glory of the future kingdom, which will be set up when David's Son returns in glory (Luke 1:31-32; Acts 15:15-16)" (p. 723). J. F. Walvoord also declared that Israel's gathering will only take place at the second coming of Christ, based on Isaiah's order of description.[14] Later he stated:

> The final regathering of Israel, of which the present occupa-
> tion of a portion of the Holy Land is the first stage, will have its
> culmination when Israel's Messiah returns to the earth in power
> and glory to reign.[15]

Like Kac, Walvoord now applies Isaiah's "second" gathering to the secular State of Israel, since A.D. 1948. Isaiah's order of description apparently is no longer pressed literally (Messiah's kingdom of justice first, then Israel's gathering). The restored Israel is thus basically robbed of its theological essence.

The late Old Testament scholar J. Barton Payne presents an interpretation of Isaiah's gathering prophecies that basically belongs to the hermeneutic of dispensationalism. In his *Encyclopedia of Biblical Prophecy* (Harper, 1973), Payne briefly acknowledges that the promised gathering of Israel in

Isaiah 11:11 presupposes "the first time having been at their exodus from Egypt" (p. 299). His concern is with the time of the fulfillment of the predicted "second" gathering of ethnic Israel. To him this will be "the regathering of converted Jews, after Christ has set up His future kingdom." He calls it "God's millennial regathering of Israel" (p. 300), "the millennial return of Israel to Palestine" (p. 398; on Hosea 1:11; 2:23). Payne completely overlooks the historical fulfillment of Isaiah 11 in Israel's return from Babylon. He points exclusively to a future apocalyptic fulfillment for ethnic Israel in the Middle East at the second advent of Christ. His outline of Isaiah 11:11 is (see diagram):

| The First Gathering Israel from Egypt | Isaiah Predicts ⟶ | "Second" or Millennial Gathering of Converted National Israel to Palestine |
|---|---|---|
| Under Moses | Time: 700 B.C. | Millennium |

The confusion of dispensational literalsm becomes more evident when one notices that Kac's exegesis of Isaiah 11 concludes that the first gathering of Israel was not from Egypt but from Babylon. The second gathering, then, began in A.D. 1948. Payne, however, declares that the first gathering was from Egypt and that the second will start at the second coming of Christ. There exists, furthermore, confusion about the nature of the remnant of Israel. Kac operates with a secular, natural Israel only, while Payne speaks of "converted Jews," who will be converted "by Christ's appearance in the clouds" above the city of Jerusalem (p. 140). All dispensationalists agree, however, that eschatological Israel must be Jewish people who will return to Palestine so that Christ can reestablish the Davidic kingdom for them in old Jerusalem.

We need to inquire now on what basis Payne retains the ethnic and geographic restrictions in his eschatological fulfillment. Payne's basic argument is that the Church will be raptured from earth to heaven so that the Messiah will reign on earth over Israel only. Payne's presupposition is that Israel and the Church must be separated forever, in spite of Christ's teaching and the New Testament revelation. He asserts more in particular:

> A basis for distinguishing between those to whom He comes, whether to the church, in its rapture, or to the Jews, in their regathering, is to be found in the Scripture's teaching that the latter are to be brought back by other people (Isa 14:2, 49:22) and by the use of standard means, e.g., a highway, 11:16, 35:8. The church, in contrast, experiences its rapture by the direct act of God. It may be identified by such supernatural elements as the sounding of His great trumpet (Isa 27:12-13; Matt 24:31; 1 Thess 4:16; "the last trumpet," 1 Cor 15:52).
>
> *Geographical allusions*, indicating the localized presence of Jesus Christ, *form a basic key to the identification of Millennial prophecies*.[16]

Our fundamental critique of Payne's prophetic interpretation is that he operates with a preconceived hermeneutic of literalism. He *subordinates Christ and the New Testament eschatology to the ethnic and geographic aspects of the old covenant*, instead of making Christ the superior norm by which all ethnic and geographic allusions are transformed and transcended (see chapters 7 and 9, above). We illustrate this with an example of Payne's statements:

> When Zechariah 8:22, for instance, speaks of many nations seeking the Lord, one might think of them in the church age, as in Zechariah 2:11; but the nations in chapter 8 "come to seek Yahweh in Jerusalem."[17]

A close look at Zechariah 2 reveals, however, that Zechariah 2:11 is in no respect different from Zechariah 8:22, contrary to Payne. Just as in Zechariah 8, Zechariah 2 addresses the "daughter of Zion" (2:10) and refers to "Judah as his [Yahweh's] portion in the holy land, and [He] will again choose Jerusalem" (2:12).

Furthermore, the geographic designations of "Jerusalem," "Mount Zion," etc., always signify the religious reality of Yahweh's presence within the Old Testament prophecies, hence the theological qualification "holy" hill, "holy" city, "holy" land. The presence of the Shekinah glory of Yahweh determines whether Jerusalem, or any place, is under the covenant blessing. In Psalm 46 Israel sang about Jerusalem: "God is within her, she will not fall; . . . The LORD Almighty is with us; the God of Jacob is our fortress" (Psalm 46:5, 7). If the glory of Yahweh would ever depart from the temple because of Israel's abominations, then the curse of God would replace the blessed protection; the "unholy" place would be destroyed (see Leviticus 26:31-33; Ezekiel 8-9). This happened with Jerusalem in Ezekiel's time. After God's presence had left Jerusalem's temple through the East Gate (Ezekiel 11:22, 23), Nebuchadnezzar destroyed Jerusalem and the temple in 586 B.C. This happened again when Jerusalem refused to be gathered to the Messiah Himself (Matthew 23:37). Christ then announced, "Look, *your house is left to you desolate*" (Matthew 23:38). This punitive curse—caused by the withdrawal of the Messiah from Jerusalem—fell on the doomed city in A.D. 70, by means of the Roman general Titus. Thus the prophecy of Daniel 9:26, 27, which predicted Jerusalem's destruction because of the rejection of the Messiah, was dramatically fulfilled.

The New Testament does not predict another restoration of Yahweh's glory in old Jerusalem, which to this day rejects Christ's substitutionary atonement at the cross. It proclaims, however, the good news to Israel and the Gentiles that all who accept the crucified, risen, and exalted Christ as their Lord and Savior have thereby come to "the true tabernacle" (Hebrews 8:1, 2), and

> to *Mount Zion, to the heavenly Jerusalem,* the city of the living God . . . *to the church* of the firstborn, whose names are written in heaven . . . to Jesus the mediator of a new covenant (Hebrews 12:22, 23, 24; emphasis added).

Paul concludes that the present city of Jerusalem is "in slavery with her children," theologically speaking. Our Jerusalem is "above" and is "our mother" (Galatians 4:25, 26).

If dispensationalism would take Christ as its guiding norm of prophetic interpretation instead of geographic literalism, it could no longer regard old Mount Zion as the holy center of prophecy. The glory of Christ far exceeds that of the old temple (Matthew 12:6; John 4:21). The progressive revelation of God's Shekinah in Christ is the decisive principle of Christian eschatology. The apostolic principle of the christological-ecclesiological interpretation can hardly be called an "indiscriminate spiritualization of all the terms and promises relating to the land."[18]

It is not legitimate to conclude that simply because the *geographic* promises to Israel were "stated and restated so many times," that this frequency by itself "makes it clear that God intended them to be taken at their face value."[19] Is *our* concept of "literalism" the divine norm for the understanding of the fulfillment of Israel's eschatological prophecies? Or should Christ be our norm for the true understanding of the Old Testament, under the guidance of the Holy Spirit in the New Testament?

### Matthew 23:39: Will the Jews be Saved When They See the Messiah in His Glory?

O Jerusalem, Jerusalem, you who kill the prophets and stone those sent to you, how often I have longed to gather your children together, as a hen gathers her chicks under her wings, but you were not willing. Look, your house is left to you desolate. For I tell you, *you will not see me again until you say, "Blessed is he who comes in the name of the Lord"* (Matthew 23:37-39, emphasis added; cf. Luke 13:35).

Dispensational writers use the final statement of Jesus' anti-Pharisaic discourse (Matthew 23:39) as an eschatological promise for the restoration of a Jewish theocracy. In their view, Christ merely postponed the fulfillment of the Davidic kingdom for national Israel because His contemporary generation rejected Him as the Messiah.[20] Walvoord regards Matthew 23:39 as Christ's promise of an apocalyptic regathering of a godly remnant of Israel at His second coming:

In pronouncing judgment upon His generation, Christ was in effect predicting the final dispersion and their ultimate regathering when the godly remnant of Israel in repentance would say: "Blessed is he that cometh in the name of the Lord."[21]

In other words, Christ's judgment on Israel was only a temporary punishment, not His final judgment.

Dispensationalism appeals to the conversion of Paul near Damascus (Acts 9:3-6) as an illustration for the future national conversion of Israel.[22] J. D. Pentecost sees Matthew 23:39 also as a parallel with Paul's statement in Romans 11:26, "And so all Israel will be saved, as it is written: 'The deliverer will come from Zion.'" He assumes hereby, "It is to be noted that the remnant of Romans 11:26 is not converted until the second advent of Christ."[23]

Texts receive their specific meaning from their contexts. A closer look at the context of Matthew 23:39 leads us to the conclusion that Jesus' seven woes in Matthew 23 contain an inescapable note of finality; it is the final reckoning of theocratic Israel:

> *Fill up, then, the measure of the sin of your forefathers!* . . . And so upon you will come all the righteous blood that has been shed on earth, from the blood of righteous Abel to the blood of Zechariah son of Berakiah, whom you murdered between the temple and the altar. I tell you the truth, all this will come upon this generation (Matthew 23:32, 35, 36; emphasis added).

This character of final judgment becomes explicit also in Christ's parable of the Tenants of the Vineyard (Matthew 21:33-42), which summarizes Israel's history of rebellion against God until it reaches its climax in the violent rejection of the Son of the landowner, the messianic fulfillment of the stone rejected by the builders in Psalm 118:22, 23. Matthew does not separate the Jewish leaders from the Jewish nation, as if God's punishment is final for the leaders but only temporary for the Jewish nation.

Matthew adds the unambiguous interpretation:

> Therefore I tell you, the kingdom of God will be taken away from you and given to a *nation* [*ethnos*] producing the fruits of it (Matthew 21:43, RSV).

This inspired interpretation of Jesus' parable of the unfaithful tenants clearly implies the rejection of Israel as a national theocracy. The loss of this privileged status as the exclusive people of God is also stated explicitly in Jesus' eschatological saying of Matthew 8:11, 12. The real punishment of the guilty nation was not the destruction of temple and city or the dispersion of the Jewish people among the nations. It was the *withdrawal* of the Messiah's presence, God's taking away His kingdom or covenant blessing from the nation. For a chosen people, no neutral position is ever possible. The Jewish nation could be only for Him or against Him (Matthew 12:30). In Christ, Jerusalem was faced with either her Savior or her Judge.

> He who falls on this stone will be broken to pieces, but he on whom it falls will be crushed (Matthew 21:44).

> Look, your house is left to you desolate. For I tell you, you will not see me again until you say, 'Blessed is he who comes in the name of the Lord' (Matthew 23:38, 39).

"Your house" seems to refer directly to the temple, of which Jesus had said a short while earlier, "It is written, 'My house will be called a house of prayer, but you are making it a den of robbers'" (Matthew 21:13). In its broader sense, the whole city and nation were inextricably bound up with the temple. The whole nation would be left "desolate" because Christ would leave that generation and give it up to judgment (cf. Jeremiah 7:14, 15). This causal relation of Jerusalem's rejection of Christ and her destruction seems to be implied in Jesus' words: "For I tell you, you will not see me again . . ." One scholar interprets these words to mean: "Your house will be abandoned because the Messiah withdraws Himself."[24]

But dispensationalism insists on interpreting Jesus' following words, "Until you say, 'Blessed is he who comes in the name of the Lord'," as a promise that an eschatological remnant of Israel will acknowledge Christ when He returns in glory. They will be saved because they confess, "Blessed is he who comes in the name of the Lord." Must we then assume that Christ predicts a forced acceptance of Himself by Jews at His glorious second advent? Such a new way of salvation — "by sight" instead of "by faith" — goes against the very grain of the eternal gospel of God (see Romans 10:17). Christ never coerces the human will or heart to accept Him; He could have achieved that already at His first advent. The projection of such a forced control over Jewish hearts at the second advent is an unwarranted speculation. The implication would be a stain on God's character:

> God does not force the will of His creatures. He cannot accept an homage that is not willingly and intelligently given. A mere forced submission would prevent all real development of mind or character; it would make man a mere automaton.[25]

The Jews are saved in no other way than by believing the gospel message of the crucified and risen Savior (see chapter 8).

The question arises, Was not Saul of Tarsus converted by a glorious vision of Christ on the Damascus road? Paul's Damascus experience was Christ's calling of Saul to become His "chosen instrument." He was to give witness of the risen Christ to all peoples with the same apostolic authority as the other apostles to whom the risen Savior had appeared (Galatians 1:12, 15, 16). Christ commissioned Saul:

> I am sending you to open their eyes and turn them from darkness to light, and from the power of Satan to God, so that they may receive forgiveness of sins and a place among those who are sanctified by faith in me (Acts 26:17, 18).

Paul fulfilled this high calling by "proving from the Scriptures that Jesus was the Christ" (Acts 9:22; 17:3; 18:5, 28). Christ's self-revelation to Saul near Damascus was not of the same type as that which will take place at His glorious second advent. First of all, Saul alone saw "a light from heaven" flash around him and he alone heard a distinct voice speak to him, while "the men travelling with Saul stood there speechless; they heard the sound but did not see anyone" (Acts 9:7; cf. 22:9). Furthermore, even Saul did not know whom he was facing, and therefore asked, "Who are you, Lord?" (Acts 9:5; 22:8; 26:15). By contrast, when Christ returns to the earth in His divine glory, "every eye will see him, even those who pierced him; and all the peoples of the earth will mourn because of him" (Revelation 1:7; cf. Matthew 24:30). Instead of another opportunity for salvation for those who have rejected Him as the Lamb of God, we hear them all cry out, "Hide us from the face of him who sits on the throne and from the wrath of the Lamb! For the great day of their wrath has come, and who can stand?" (Revelation 6:16, 17; cf. Hebrews 10:29-31).

The second advent will be too late for true repentance. Paul urges, therefore: "I tell you, now is the time of God's favor, now is the day of salvation" (2 Corinthians 6:2). Christ's words to the leaders of Israel's Sanhedrin are similar to those in Matthew 23:39:

> But I say to all of you: In the future you will see the Son of Man sitting at the right hand of the Mighty One and coming on the clouds of heaven (Matthew 26:64).

These are not words that promise another chance to repent and to be saved at the second coming of Christ. They rather suggest that the Jews who have rejected Him will have to acknowledge at His glorious appearing as Messiah-Judge that this Jesus, whom they now despise, is the true messianic King of

Israel. Only then will they see Him again, the Blessed One "who comes in the name of the Lord." Then they will meet Him as their Judge (see also Matthew 7:21-23). Such a climax exactly fits the series of "woes" in Matthew 23. No perspective on a sudden conversion can be projected onto Christ's solemn forecast in Matthew 23:39 from the immediate or wider contexts in the Gospels.

In addition, the text gives no hint of a political future for Israel.[26] Jesus' words are spoken in the context of divine judgment on the nation. They seem to suggest the irrevocable condition for the peace of Israel: Christ must be accepted first as the suffering Servant-Messiah, as the rejected stone of Psalm 118:22, before He can be greeted with joy as, "Blessed is he who comes in the name of the LORD" (Psalm 118:26; cf. Luke 19:41-44). He cannot be accepted merely as the gloriously appearing Messiah. Christ is not interested in being accepted on the basis of His divine miracles. When the Jews "intended to come and make him king by force" (John 6:15) because He was the wondrous messianic Prophet of Deuteronomy 18:15 (John 6:14), Christ did *not* accept such a coronation. Christ draws all men to salvation only through His cross:

> But I, when I am lifted up from the earth, will draw all men to myself. He said this to show the kind of death he was going to die (John 12:32, 33).

If Jews persist in their unbelief and rejection of Christ as the suffering and risen Messiah, they will irrevocably meet Him as their Judge (Matthew 8:11-12). Only those Jews who have come to faith in Christ through the proclamation of the apostolic gospel will ultimately rejoice when they will see Christ in His glorious second advent. This is further developed by Paul in Romans 11:25-27 (see chapter 8).

### Luke 21:24: Is Jerusalem No Longer Trampled On by the Gentiles since A.D. 1967?

> They will fall by the sword and will be taken as prisoners to all the nations. Jerusalem will be trampled on by the Gentiles until [achri] the times of the Gentiles are fulfilled (Luke 21:24).

The dispensational writer J. D. Pentecost offers this interesting exposition:

The "times of the Gentiles" has been defined by the Lord as that period of time in which Jerusalem was under the dominion of Gentile authority (Luke 21:24). This period began with the Babylonian captivity when Jerusalem fell into the hands of the Gentiles. It has continued unto the present time and will continue through the tribulation period, in which era the Gentile powers will be judged. *The dominion of the Gentiles ends at the second advent of Messiah to the earth.*[27]

The *New Scofield Reference Bible* likewise explains the end of the "times of the Gentiles" as being "the destruction of Gentile world power by a 'stone cut out without hands' (Dan 2:34-35, 44), i.e., the coming of the Lord in glory (Rev 19:11, 21)."[28] Others, however, apply the end of the "times of Gentiles" to the moment when the Jewish army recaptured the old city of Jerusalem from the Arabs in the six-days war of 1967. J. Ockenga even sees the June 6, 1967, date as "a remarkable manifestation of the fulfillment of God's Word" in Leviticus 26:18, 24, 28, where Moses announced that God would punish an apostate Israel for their sins "seven times over."[29] He converts the idiomatic expression "seven times" into seven symbolic years and then applies a day-for-a-year symbolism so that it becomes more than 2556 actual years. Starting with the siege of Jerusalem by Nebuchadnezzar on March 7, 588 B.C., the years end exactly on June 6, 1967. Remarkable indeed! He speculatively concludes:

> The termination of the times of the Gentiles is that period when the generation then living shall not pass away until all of the prophecies concerning the second coming of our Lord shall have been fulfilled (Luke 21:23).[30]

In other words, Ockenga predicts that the generation living in 1967 will not pass away before Christ returns in glory.

Other students of the prophetic Word apply Jesus' phrase "times of Gentiles" only to Jerusalem's destruction by the Roman army in A.D. 70,[31] or extend them until the second coming of Christ. J. B. Payne, for instance, concludes: "These 'times,' then, would still appear to be going on today because, even though the Israeli army captured the Old City of Jerusalem in 1967, the present policy is as little receptive of Christ and is as 'Gentile' in the NT sense (see Rom 2:28; Phil 3:2) as was the preceding Arab rule."[32]

On the other hand, some have interpreted these "times of Gentiles"—there are *no* definite articles in the Greek phrase—as a period of opportunity for Gentiles to enter the kingdom of God. They have further connected Jesus' phrase with Paul's words that the fullness of the Gentiles will come in "and so all Israel will be saved" (Romans 11:25, 26).[33] The conclusion has been drawn that when such "times of Gentiles" shall be completed, all ethnic Israel (Jerusalem) "will be saved." The expectation of such an interpretation of Luke 21:24—by means of Romans 11—is no longer a political resurgence of Israel, but only Israel's spiritual return to God through faith in the gospel. However, the context of Luke 21:20-24 is exclusively political, not spiritual. Moreover, Luke 21:24 is based on Daniel's predictions of the trampling underfoot of Israel's sanctuary (Daniel 8:13) and of the destruction of Jerusalem (Daniel 9:26, 27). The times of Gentiles are therefore characterized as times of persecution and unrest for ethnic Israel.

The question remains, What is the implication of the expression "until the times of the Gentiles are fulfilled" (Luke 21:24)? Does it indicate a future restoration of Jerusalem and the temple to the Jewish nation at the second advent of Christ, as it was before A.D. 70? C. F. Baker argues that "if this city is trodden down UNTIL a certain time, there must of necessity come a time following that when the city will not be trodden down. . . . If this Scripture teaches anything, it teaches that the earthly Jerusalem is to be restored."[34] Such a reasoning seems logical at first but is not necessarily scriptural because it does not relate Scripture to Scripture, as responsible exegesis requires. The conjunction "until" does not always imply a promise of restoration to a preceding situation. The precise meaning of "until" depends on the context in which it is used. The statement of W. Hendriksen is more biblically oriented:

> Here in Luke 21:24 the meaning is simply this, that for Jerusalem the condition of being trampled underfoot *will not cease* a hundred years or fifty years or even ten years before Christ's return, but will last on and on and on, *until* Christ's second coming. Somewhat similar is the meaning of this little word in Rom 11:25; 1 Cor 11:26; 15:25; and Rev 2:25.
>
> It is clear, therefore, that neither the word *until* nor anything else in this passage is or implies a prediction of

national restoration in store for the Jews either just before or in connection with Christ's return.[35]

It is definitely true that the conjunction "until" (*achri*) does not contain, in itself, the suggestion of a change to a previous situation. This can be shown from its use in other places of Scripture:[36]

Be faithful unto death, and I will give you the crown of life (Revelation 2:10, RSV).

Only hold fast what you have, until I come (Revelation 2:25, RSV).

He who conquers and who keeps my works until the end . . . (Revelation 2:26, RSV).

For He must reign until he has put all his enemies under his feet (1 Corinthians 15:25, RSV).

In all these passages "until" (*achri*) is not used to suggest a future change in the believer's attitude or in Christ's rulership. The message is clearly that after death or after the second advent, no change in the faithfulness of the believer must occur—that no reversal to a previous situation will take place. The context alone indicates whether the conjunction "until" intends to convey the idea of change. With regard to Luke 21:24, the apocalyptic discourse as a whole (Luke 21) nowhere suggests any restoration of old Jerusalem to a previous glory or theocracy. It is therefore "more likely that no sequel to the 'times of the Gentiles' is envisaged other than the ultimate consummation."[37]

The book of Daniel predicts that war and desolation— meaning the absence of the messianic glory—are decreed to continue for Jerusalem "until the end" (Daniel 9:26, 27). The only restoration of Jerusalem promised in the New Testament is the New Jerusalem built by God Himself as the metropolis for His faithful people on the new earth (Revelation 21-22; see chapter 9).

### Notes on Chapter 10

[1]*NSRB*, p. 1186 (on Acts 15:16). Scofield concludes that the Hebrew text in Amos 9:11 must be a corrupt text, of a later date than Acts 15 (p. 938, on Amos 9:12). The words "In that day" (Amos 9:11) of the Hebrew text obviously give no support to the dispensational exegesis (see Wyngaarden, in note 6).

[2]*NSRB*, p. 1186.

[3]Walvoord, *Israel in Prophecy*, p. 92. So also G. D. Young, in *Prophecy in the Making*, ed. C. F. Henry (Carol Stream, Ill.: Creation House, 1971), p. 166.

[4]Payne, *Encyclopedia of Biblical Prophecy*, p. 417 (nos. 23, 24).

[5]Ladd, *A Theology of the New Testament*, p. 355. See further the refutation of the dispensational exegesis of Acts 15:15-18 by A. C. Schultz in *The New Testament and Wycliffe Bible Commentary*, 4th ed. (New York: Yversen-Norman Assn., 1973), p. 483. Also by P. E. Hughes, *Interpreting Prophecy: An Essay in Biblical Perspectives* (Grand Rapids, Mich.: Wm. B. Eerdmans Pub. Co., 1976), p. 107; and M. J. Wyngaarden, *The Future of the Kingdom* (Grand Rapids, Mich.: Baker Book House, 1955), pp. 110-112, 168-169.

[6]Wyngaarden, *The Future of the Kingdom*, p. 168. He defends successfully the authenticity of the Hebrew text in Amos 9:12 on pp. 112-113, note.

[7]Walvoord, *Israel in Prophecy*, p. 66.

[8]See *SDABC*, vol. 7 (1957), p. 842-844. Extensively by Were, *The Certainty of the Third Angel's Message*, chapter 25.

[9]A. W. Kac, *The Rebirth of the State of Israel: Is It of God or of Men?*, ref. ed. (Grand Rapids, Mich.: Baker Book House, 1976), pp. 39, 372.

[10]Ibid., p. 38.

[11]Ibid., p. 39.

[12]Ibid., p. 41.

[13]Ibid., p. 372.

[14]Walvoord, *Israel in Prophecy*, pp. 66.

[15]Walvoord, *Prophecy in the Making*, p. 338.

[16]Payne, *Encyclopedia of Biblical Prophecy*, pp. 114, 115 (emphasis added).

[17]Ibid., p. 115.

[18]Walvoord, *Israel in Prophecy*, p. 72.

[19]Ibid.

[20]Pentecost, *Things to Come*, pp. 142, 248, 266 (quoting L. S. Chafer).

[21]Walvoord, *Israel in Prophecy*, p. 106; cf. his *The Millennial Kingdom*, p. 268.

[22]Pentecost, *Things to Come*, pp. 298, 299.

[23]Ibid., p. 298.

[24]Trilling, *Das Wahre Israel*, p. 86 (my translation). See also Luke 19:41-44.

[25]Ellen G. White, *Steps to Christ* (Mountain View, Calif.: Pacific Press Pub. Assn., 1908, 1921, 1956), p. 44.

[26]R. T. France, "OT Prophecy and the Future of Israel," *Tyndale Bulletin* 26 (1975):53-78. Quotation on p. 76, n. 41.

[27]Pentecost, *Things to Come*, p. 315 (emphasis added).

[28]*NSRB*, p. 1368 (on Revelation 16:19).

[29]J. Ockenga, "Fulfilled and Unfulfilled Prophecy," in *Prophecy in the Making* (Carol Stream, Ill.: Creation House, 1971), p. 309.

[30]Ibid., pp. 309, 310.

[31]L. A. DeCaro, *Israel Today: Fulfillment of Prophecy?* (Grand Rapids, Mich.: Baker Book House, 1974).

[32]Payne, *Encyclopedia of Biblical Prophecy*, p. 100. See also note 12, chapter 2.

[33]See I. H. Marshall, *Luke, Historian and Theologian* (Exeter, England: Paternoster Press, 1970), pp. 186-187.

[34]Baker, *A Dispensational Theology*, p. 606.

[35]Hendriksen, *Israel in Prophecy*, p. 28.

[36]See W. Bauer, *Greek-English Lexicon of the New Testament*, trans. and ed. W. F. Arndt and F. W. Gingrich (Chicago: University of Chicago Press, 1957).

[37]Cf. France, "OT Prophecy and the Future of Israel," p. 76.

# 11

## God's Ultimatum to Israel

## The Seventy Weeks of Daniel

The importance of the seventy-weeks prophecy of Daniel 9 is widely admitted. Says dispensationalist Alva J. McClain, "Probably no single prophetic utterance is more crucial in the fields of Biblical Interpretation, Apologetics, and Eschatology."[1] Yet, this most telling messianic prophecy in the whole Bible is also considered by some to be "one of the most difficult [to understand] in all the Old Testament."[2]

Nevertheless, the book of Daniel testifies to the divine inspiration of the Hebrew Bible and of predictive prophecy in particular. A reckoning of the seventy weeks of Daniel 9 as 490 years leads irrevocably to the conclusion that the promised Messiah of Israel already appeared *before* the destruction of Jerusalem in A.D. 70. It is understandable that the Talmud places a curse on those who attempt to compute the seventy weeks of Daniel.[3]

[24]"Seventy 'sevens' are decreed for your people and your holy city to finish transgression, to put an end to sin, to atone for wickedness, to bring in everlasting righteousness, to seal up vision and prophecy and to anoint the most holy.

[25]Know and understand this: From the issuing of the decree to restore and rebuild Jerusalem until the Anointed One, the ruler, comes, there will be seven 'sevens,' and sixty-two 'sevens.' It will be rebuilt with streets and a trench, but in times of trouble. [26]After the sixty-two 'sevens,' the Anointed One will be cut off and will have nothing. The people of the ruler who will come will destroy the city and the sanctuary. The end will come like a flood: War will continue until the end, and

desolations have been decreed. [27]He will confirm a covenant with many for one 'seven,' but in the middle of that 'seven' he will put an end to sacrifice and offering. And one who causes desolation will place abominations on a wing of the temple until the end that is decreed is poured out on him (Daniel 9:24-27, NIV).

Christ's admonition to His apostles to read and understand "the prophet Daniel" concerning the coming "abomination that causes desolation" in Jerusalem (Matthew 24:15) indicates that the prophecy of Daniel determined Christ's future outlook. There can be no doubt that Christ applied the desolating abomination of Daniel 9:27, not to the past outrages of Antiochus Epiphanes in 167-164 B.C. (as 1 Maccabees 1:54ff. does), but to His own immediate future, when the Roman army would destroy Jerusalem and the temple in His own generation (see Luke 21:20-24). Jesus' contemporary application of Daniel 9:26, 27 was confirmed in A.D. 70 when the Roman armies under General Titus placed their idolatrous ensigns as an "abomination" in Jerusalem and destroyed the temple.[4] The position of L. F. Hartman that "the quasi-prophecy of Daniel 9:26" refers exclusively "to the climax of Epiphanes' persecution of the Jews, when he abolished the legitimate sacrifices of Yahweh in the Temple of Jerusalem and set up on its altar the statue of Zeus Olympios,"[5] is answered by J. G. Baldwin: "Commentators who argue that Antiochus Epiphanes fulfilled this prophecy are at a loss to account for the fact that he destroyed neither the Temple nor the city of Jerusalem [as required by Daniel 9:26]."[6]

Thus Christ applied the seventy-weeks prophecy of the coming Messiah and the subsequent devastations of Messiah's enemy to His own time and not to either the past or the indefinite future. Christ related the fall of Jerusalem in A.D. 70 to Israel's final refusal to accept Him as her King and Savior (see Matthew 21:33-43; 23:37, 38; Luke 19:41-44). This correlation between the coming of the Messiah and the destruction of both city and sanctuary is the crucial message of Daniel 9:26, 27. The seventy-weeks prophecy is basically a messianic prophecy announcing the consequences of Jerusalem's rejection of her Messiah. It is God's ultimatum to national Israel.

### The Unbreakable Unity of the Seventy Weeks

"Seventy 'sevens'" were decreed, or determined, by God as a final probationary period for Jerusalem and the Jewish people after the seventy years of the Babylonian exile had terminated (see Daniel 9:24). There can be no doubt about the duration of this period: seventy times seven "years," or 490 years (see RSV). No day-for-a-year symbolism needs to be supposed here because Gabriel uses no symbols in his detailed chronological explanation. G. F. Hasel observes, "There is virtually unanimous agreement among interpreters of all schools of thought that the phrase 'seventy weeks' or literally 'sevens seventy' . . . means 490 years."[7]

Gabriel explained to Daniel that the history of Israel within this 490-year span would develop in three distinct phases: one of seven weeks, a second of sixty-two weeks, and a third of one week (see verses 25 and 27). However, nowhere does the angel imply a gap between any of these three phases. To suggest an indeterminate time interval between the seven and sixty-two weeks, or between the sixty-two and the one last week, is an unnatural assumption that militates against the expressed unit and goal of the seventy weeks (see verse 24).

The normal, natural, exegetical assumption is that the seventy consecutive weeks are an unbreakable unity. They are presented as a unit, just as are the seventy years of Babylonian exile in Daniel 9:2. E. J. Young concludes, "If there is no warrant for inserting a gap in Jeremiah's prophecy, what warrant is there for doing so in the prophecy of the seventy sevens? Had there been a gap in Jeremiah's prophecy (Jer 25:10) Daniel could never have understood the years of the captivity."[8] "Never," concludes Philip Mauro, "has a specific number of time-units, making up a described stretch of time, been taken to mean anything but continuous or consecutive time-units."[9] Because the other predicted time periods are consecutive, the natural expectation can only be that the seventy weeks of Daniel are also consecutive.

J. F. Walvoord, however, draws a parallel between the Old Testament messianic prophecies and the time prophecies in Daniel in order to support the idea of a gap between the sixty-ninth and seventieth week of Daniel 9. But the fact that the Old Testament prophets customarily fuse the first and second advents of Christ together in their messianic prophecies without considering the interval between the two (Isaiah 9:6; 61:1, 2; Zechariah 9:9, 10) gives us no rationale to create a gap between the specific *time* periods in Daniel 9. The chronological unit of the seventy weeks is not "parallel" to the non-chronological messianic promises, in spite of Walvoord's assertion.[10] The regular messianic promises do not always intend to present the proper historical order of the two advents of Christ and even sometimes *reverse* the order (see Genesis 3:15; Zechariah 9:9). Such examples can never serve as an argument to create a gap between Daniel's sixty-ninth and seventieth prophetic week. E. Hengstenberg represents the classical church interpretation: "The period of 70 hebdomads, or 490 years, is here predicted as one that will continue uninterruptedly from its commencement to its close. . . . What can be more evident than this? Exactly 70 weeks in all are to elapse; and how can anyone imagine that there is an interval between the 69 and the 1 week, when these together make up the 70?"[11] The dispensational break in the unit of the seventy weeks destroys the very point in specifying seventy consecutive weeks.

### Reasons for Dissecting the Weeks?

It is "of major importance" to dispensationalism, according to Walvoord,[12] to separate the last week from the total unit of seventy weeks and project it into the indefinite future. Acknowledging that this "startling" dissection needs some good reason, McClain asks, "How can such a method be justified?"[13] He offers five reasons.

First, Daniel's expression "After the sixty-two 'sevens,' the Anointed One will be cut off" (chap. 9:26) indicates that the death of the Messiah must take place *before* the seventieth week. It also occurs *after* the sixty-two weeks; consequently it must fall *between* the sixty-ninth and seventieth week! Only after the death of Christ and after the (next mentioned) destruction of Jerusalem (verse 26) do we come to the final week in verse 27. This literalistic reading of verses 26 and 27 is determined by the idea that Daniel necessarily presents a strictly chronological sequence in these two passages. Such an assumption is accepted as a self-evident axiom. J. F. Walvoord states: "The anointed one, or the Messiah, is cut off after the sixty-ninth week, but not in the seventieth."[14] However, this last phrase, "but not in the seventieth," appears nowhere in Daniel 9:26, 27; it is Walvoord's unwarranted assumption. This presupposition has been severely criticized both from the standpoint of literary analysis and of theological exegesis.[15]

When Daniel announced that seventy weeks are determined for national Israel and that the Messiah will be "cut off" after the first sixty-nine weeks, the natural presumption can only be that the death of the Messiah will take place sometime *during the last week*. J. Barton Payne concludes, "What could be more naturally assumed that that it [the cutting off of the Messiah] concerns the 70th week?"[16]

McClain's second argument is, "In the record of the prophecy, the destruction of the city [verse 26] is placed *before* the last week [verse 27]."[17] Therefore, the events of the seventieth week cannot occur prior to the destruction of Jerusalem. For this reason dispensationalism sees verse 27 as a prediction about another enemy of God, the end-time antichrist, who would suddenly rise more than nineteen centuries after the death of Christ and after the destruction of Jerusalem in A.D. 70. This argument is valid only on the assumption that verses 26 and 27 are phrased in a modern style of prose that describes events in strictly chronological order. But recent studies (see note 15) have made it clear that dispensationalism's literalistic reading fails to recognize the Hebrew poetic style of "repetition with elaboration" in Daniel 9:24-27, which J. B. Payne calls a "revelational pattern."[18] This stylistic pattern appears also in verses 24 and 25. Payne argues that "Daniel 9:25, 26 cannot be taken as subsequent to 9:24; instead verses 25, 26 pick up [repeat and elaborate] the summary of the entire seventy weeks given in verse 24." This seems quite obvious. The relation of verse 27 to verse 26 is also obvious. Payne remarks: "That verse 27 thus repeats verse 26 is recognized by interpreters of every stamp and is confirmed by the verbal correspondences that appear, particularly in the last parts of the respective verses."[19] With this recognition, we see the atoning death of Christ again mentioned in verse 27 and now more precisely located "in the middle" of the last prophetic week, not in an unmentioned gap. Verses 26 and 27 relate to each other according to the structure: Messiah versus Destroyer (verse 26), Messiah versus Desolator (verse 27). The simple poetic style of Hebrew parallelism in verses 26 and 27 (which is also the poetic arrangement in verse 25)[20] is the most thorough reply of grammatical exegesis to the imposition of a dissecting gap.

But the question remains, Did not the destruction of Jerusalem and the sanctuary (verse 26) occur in A.D. 70, almost forty years after the death of Christ and thus *outside* the seventy weeks of years? This objection would be valid if the destruction of Jerusalem and the sanctuary were mentioned in verse 24 as one of the six predicted goals of the seventy-weeks prophecy. This is not so. The time of the Messiah's anointing and of His atoning death are precisely predicted to occur within the 490 years, but the time of Jerusalem is not. This divine judgment was delayed until forty years after the cross of Christ, so that many thousands of Jews could hear the meaning of the cross of Christ and be saved through faith and repentance.

McClain's third reason for separating the seventieth week is, "The fulfillment of the tremendous events in verse 24 cannot be found anywhere in known history."[21] He means that no end of sinning and no beginning of everlasting righteousness can be noticed among the Jewish people. No atonement for wickedness, no sealing up of vision and prophecy, no anointing of a most holy thing are discernible. But such an observation is rejected by most conservative Bible interpreters as missing the mark. Verse 24 must be understood as being accomplished by the Anointed One Himself on behalf of Israel (verses 25-27). Christ's death and resurrection to a new priesthood accomplished a perfect atonement for Israel's sin and provided an everlasting righteousness for Israel. True Israelites did enter into the benefits of His sacrificial death and are therefore clothed with the white garments of His righteousness. Christ's baptism (His anointing by the Spirit) and death authenticated Daniel's prophetic vision. His ascension to heaven meant the consecration of a new high-priesthood[22] in the sanctuary of heaven, manifested on earth in the outpouring of the anointing Spirit of God on the day of Pentecost (see Acts 2:33; Hebrews 7:12, 22; 8:1, 2; 9:23, 24). Thus E. J. Young declares of Daniel 9:24, 27, "The passage is Messianic through and through."[23] And J. G. Baldwin concludes her exegesis in these words: "The first coming of Christ is the focal point of the forward look, though the second coming in judgment is also envisaged."[24] This view does justice to both aspects of the messianic prophecy of Daniel 9:24-27—the central focus on the Messiah's coming to fulfill the sixfold goal of verse 24, and the final judgment of God poured out on the desolator at "the end" (verse 27). Dispensationalism categorically denies that Christ's first advent (His baptism, His death and resurrection) fulfilled any of the six goals of this magnificent messianic prophecy.

McClain's fourth reason for a gap interpretation is the argument from analogy with the nonchronological messianic prophecies. This has already been discussed above.

His fifth argument: "The testimony of our Lord Himself shows that the Seventieth Week is still future."[25] McClain bases this statement on the assumption that the future desolator spoken of in the second part of verse 27 is the same power referred to earlier in the verse as putting an end to sacrifice and offering "in the middle" of the seventieth week. Thus he argues that while Daniel placed the "abomination of desolation" (KJV) exactly in the middle of the last week, in Matthew 24:15, 21, 29, 30 "our Lord placed it at 'the end,' just before His second coming in glory." He concludes: "Therefore, *the Seventieth Week must also come at the end of the present age just prior to Christ's coming in glory.* This is the interpretation of Christ Himself, and it should settle the matter."[26] McClain reaches this conclusion on the basis of several unwarranted presuppositions. The first is the failure to recognize the style of Hebrew parallelism in verses 26 and 27, whereby it becomes clear that verse 27 speaks more elaborately about the same two powers—the Messiah and His opponent—as does verse 26. Not the antichrist, but the Messiah Himself is predicted to end the sacrificial system in the middle of the seventieth week, exactly three and one-half years after His baptism as the Anointed One. The Gospel of John verifies the precise historical fulfillment of this prophecy in Christ's life; the time between His baptism and cross was exactly three and one-half years.[27]

### Did Christ Put an End to Israel's Sacrifices?

McClain insists that "the death of Christ did not cause the Jewish sacrifices to cease. They continued, in fact, until the destruction of Jerusalem nearly forty years later. . . . The sacrifices should have ceased immediately. But they did not."[28] This reasoning reckons only with a human point of view. From God's point of view, as recorded in the New Testament, Daniel's description discloses one of the most profound and decisive revelations of the Messiah's mission. It is the very goal of the seventy-weeks prophecy, God's method of fulfilling the six-fold goal of Daniel 9:24. The abolishing of the whole Levitical priesthood and sacrificial service was already announced in Psalm 110:1, 4, an earlier messianic prophecy. Here David had declared that the future messianic Ruler would also be "a priest forever, in the order of Melchizedek."

The New Testament presses the challenging question:

> If perfection could have been attained through the Levitical priesthood (for on the basis of it the law was given to the people), why was there still need for another priest to come—one in the order of Melchizedek, not in the order of Aaron? For when there is a change of the priesthood, there must also be a change of the law" (Hebrews 7:11, 12).

Only the Messiah Himself could legitimately abolish, once and forever, the system of symbols that pointed forward to the atoning self-sacrifice of the spotless Lamb of God. "He sacrificed for their sins once for all when he offered himself" (Hebrews 7:27). "But now he has appeared once for all at the end of the ages to do away with sin by the sacrifice of himself. . . . Christ was sacrificed once to take away the sins of many people" (Hebrews 9:26-28). "He sets aside the first [sacrifices and offerings] to establish the second [the will of God]" (Hebrews 10:9).

There can never be a valid return to the old covenant and its earthly temple worship. Christ has terminated the "shadow" and inaugurated a "better covenant" that offers His righteousness as the everlasting righteousness (see Hebrews 7:22; cf. 10:12; Romans 3:22, 25). "By calling this covenant 'new,' he has made the first one obsolete; and what is obsolete and aging will soon disappear" (Hebrews 8:13).

Christ confirmed God's covenant with Israel when He instituted the Lord's Supper the night before His death. Taking the cup, He declared: "'This is my blood of the covenant, which is poured out for many for the forgiveness of sins'" (Matthew 26:28). Thus Christ confirmed God's covenant with many in Israel for one week (seven years): three and one-half years before His death by His own ministry and three and one-half years by that of His apostles in Jerusalem.[29]

The fulfillment of Daniel's prediction that "in the middle of that 'seven' he [the Anointed One of Daniel 9:25, 26] will put an end to sacrifice and offering" (chap. 9:27), was strikingly confirmed by an act of God Himself. When Jesus died, "at that moment the curtain of the temple was torn in two from top to bottom" (Matthew 27:51; cf. Mark 15:38). The death of Christ signified the end of Israel's sacrificial temple ritual by an unmistakable act from heaven. The legitimacy of the temple sacrifices had come to an end.

The Jews as a whole did not accept this divine decision and immediately reinstituted their bloody sacrifices. But the Shekinah glory had now departed from their temple; it was therefore no longer the temple of God, and Jerusalem was no longer the holy city. Instead of God's blessing, His curse now rested on *their* house ("your house," Matthew 23:38; cf. 1 Thessalonians 2:16). Total destruction by the Roman armies would soon follow. "They will not leave one stone on another, because you did not recognize the time of God's coming to you (Luke 19:44; cf. 21:20-24). This fatal consequence of Israel's rejection of the Messiah—the destruction of Jerusalem in A.D. 70—was part and parcel of Daniel's prophecy. Christ explained: "For this is the time of punishment in fulfillment of all that has been written" (Luke 21:22). We agree, therefore, with the view of G. F. Hasel: "Although with the death of Jesus Christ the Jewish sacrifices did not cease, the sacrifices offered after His death could no longer be regarded as legitimate and valid in God's sight (Heb 7:11; 8:13; 9:25, 26; 10:8, 9)."[30]

### When Did Christ Become the Anointed One?

McClain further challenges the messianic interpretation of Daniel 9:26 by stating, "They cannot point to the place in history where it [the Messiah's covenant with Israel] began nor where it ended."[31] This leads us to consider the significance of Daniel's repeated title of "Anointed One" for Israel's Redeemer.

The first sixty-nine weeks of years were to reach "until the Anointed One, the ruler, comes" (Daniel 9:25). This is one of the most explicit messianic prophecies in the Hebrew Bible. The Messiah is designated by the double characteristic of *Anointed One* and *Ruler*, identifying Him as the royal Messiah or Priest-King (cf. Isaiah 61:1-3; Zechariah 6:13; Psalm 110: 4). Dispensationalists regularly neglect Daniel's emphasis on the coming Prince as the *Anointed One* (chap. 9:25, 26) and select the term "ruler" (verse 25) as the exclusive focus of this time prophecy. McClain pinpoints April 6, A.D. 32, as the time when Jesus "offered Himself as the Prince and King of Israel" at His triumphal entry into Jerusalem, just a few days before His crucifixion.[32] The fact is, however, that Jesus was not "anointed" at that time!

The real question is, When did Jesus offer Himself as the *Anointed One?* The New Testament replies with unmistakable clarity that "God anointed Jesus of Nazareth with the Holy Spirit and power" (Acts 10:38) and proclaimed this Anointed One to be His Son (see Mark 1:9-11; cf. Psalm 2:6, 7) on the day of Jesus' baptism by John the Baptist. Luke, the historian, dates Christ's baptism "in the fifteenth year of the reign of Tiberius Caesar" (chap. 3:1; see verses 2, 3, 21), apparently the only event in Christ's life that is historically dated in the New Testament. Jesus' own testimony in the synagogue at Nazareth, shortly after His baptism, confirms this conclusion. He read the prophecy of Isaiah 61:1, "The Spirit of the Lord is on me, because he has anointed me," and then commented, "Today this scripture is fulfilled in your hearing" (Luke 4:16, 21). Thus Christ offered Himself to Israel as the "Anointed One," the Messiah, immediately after His baptism three and one-half years before His crucifixion. In contrast, Jesus' triumphal entry into Jerusalem was clearly intended to draw the attention of Israel and the world to the redemptive significance of His impending crucifixion on behalf of all men.

Right after His baptism, however, Christ announced to Israel, "The time is fulfilled" (Mark 1:15, KJV). We agree, therefore, with J. B. Payne's conclusion: "Here [at Christ's baptism] arises a Messianic consummation that did find fulfillment in history and that does fit the chronology [of Daniel 9:25]."[33] It needs to be stressed that Jesus became the predicted Messiah at His baptism only in order to fulfill the sixfold divine mission described in Daniel 9:24. This goal was accomplished basically in His atoning death on the cross exactly three and one-half years later. This was, of course, "the middle" of the seventieth week of Daniel 9:27. On the cross, just before He died, Christ exclaimed in triumph to the Father, "'It is finished'" (John 19:30). His mission, as described in Daniel 9:24, was completed. Since the goal of the seventy-weeks prophecy is so intensely messianic, "the principal emphasis is not upon the beginning and ending of this remarkable period but upon the mighty events which were to transpire therein, events which have wrought our peace with God."[34]

### Literal Exegesis of Daniel's Seventieth Week Eliminates Gap Hypothesis

The established fact that Daniel's prophecy of the seventy weeks is written in the *poetic* style of synthetical parallelisms[35] should be considered as a hermeneutical guide in a responsible literary exegesis. Doctrinal presuppositions may never overrule or deny the truth of literary exegesis. The application of Daniel's style of parallelism leads to the messianic interpretation, in perfect harmony with the New Testament witness of the significance of the cross of Christ for Israel's covenant and its cultus. There is, therefore, no need to innovate a forced antichrist application with its unprecedented dissection of a prophetic time period.

The devastation of Jerusalem and its sanctuary by the Roman ruler is described twice:

> The people of the ruler who will come will destroy the city and the sanctuary. The end will come like a flood: War will continue until the end, and desolations have been decreed (Daniel 9:26b, NIV).

> And one who causes desolation will place abominations on a wing of the temple until the end that is decreed is poured out on him (Daniel 9:27b, NIV).

All conservative commentators agree that Daniel predicts the destruction of Jerusalem and its temple by the Roman ruler as fulfilled by General Titus in A.D. 70. This is the literal fulfillment of Daniel 9. Dispensationalism, however, declares with dogmatic certainty that Daniel refers to "a future Roman prince" who is identical with the "little horn" of chapters 7:8 and 8:23, with the lawless one of 2 Thessalonians 2:1-9, and with the beast of Revelation 13:10. He is going to make "a false covenant" with the future Jewish State for "one week" (of years) to allow them "the reestablishment of the Jewish sacrificial system."[36] After three and one-half years the Roman prince will suddenly "tear up his treaty with the Jewish people," because "by his very nature, the Man of Sin will be violently anti-Semitic." Then "he will actually take his seat in the temple of God and demand the honors and worship of God Himself."[37]

For the following three and one-half years this Roman antichrist will bring desolation and tribulation to the Jewish people
"until the end" (Daniel 9:27). This is the "time of Jacob's trouble" (Jeremiah 30:7). Christ also pointed to this period in the
future history of Israel when He warned the Jews about the
coming of the "abomination of desolation" and the "great tribulation" in Matthew 24:15-21. A. McClain reasons:

> Since it is now a matter of history that Jerusalem was destroyed
> in A.D. 70 by the Roman people, . . . it follows that "the prince
> that shall come" . . . is some great prince who will arise out of
> the Roman Empire.[38]

This interpretation suffers from three basic weaknesses, as
J. Barton Payne critiques:

> (1) It breaks up the sequence of the 70 weeks by intro-
> ducing an interval before this last part.
> (2) It assumes an unprecedented covenant-making by the
> Antichrist.
> (3) It transforms a past prince of Rome into a future
> deputy of the devil.[39]

While Daniel presents *one* prophecy of the coming destroyer of
Jerusalem, dispensationalism dissects this prophetic statement
into *two* different prophecies: one about the Roman people in
A.D. 70, and another about the end-time antichrist, "the ruler."
However, it is quite obvious that "the people" and "the ruler"
belong together as the army and its general. This is evident from
simple literal exegesis. The jump from the Roman army in
A.D. 70 to the end-time antichrist of other Bible prophecies is no
longer literal exegesis, but a forced dogmatic exegesis. E. J.
Young replies to this dispensational dissecting of Daniel 9:26,

> The emphasis in vs 26 is not upon a prince from the people, but
> upon the people who belong to the prince. . . . In other words,
> he must be their contemporary, alive when they are alive. . . .
> The people who destroyed the city and the prince that should
> come . . . are contemporaries. Otherwise, the language makes
> no sense. . . . This view, therefore, that a future Roman prince
> is to make a covenant with the Jews must be abandoned.[40]

It is clear that Daniel 9:26 has found its literal fulfillment
in Israel's history: a *literal* fulfillment in Christ's baptism (His
anointing) and atoning death (His being cut off); a *literal*

fulfillment in the subsequent destruction of Jerusalem and the sanctuary by the Roman armies led by Titus, in A.D. 70. This curse was the consequence of Israel's rejection of the Messiah's fulfillment of the sixfold goal of the seventy-weeks prophecy. The final phrase of Daniel 9:27 reads (in the translation of the NASB):

> And on the wing of abominations (will come) one who makes desolate, even until a complete destruction, one that is decreed, is poured out on the one who makes desolate.

This judgment of "a complete destruction" by divine decree on the desolator of Jerusalem parallels earlier descriptions of God's decreed judgments on Assyria and Jerusalem (see Isaiah 10:22-25; 28:21, 22). In Daniel 9:27 God decreed war and desolations "until the end" for Jerusalem after Israel had rejected the Messiah. God further decreed that a complete destruction shall be poured out on the desolator himself (Daniel 9:27). This last phrase seems to be a clear reference to the final Judgment Day, what the New Testament calls basically the second advent of Christ. If one prefers the King James Version, however, which translates the words "on one who makes desolate" as "upon the desolate," then the focal point of God's judgment only intensifies the abiding nature of God's curse on the temple and on Jerusalem.[41] The messianic prophecy of Daniel 9 placed upon Israel the ultimate test: either to remain God's theocracy by accepting Christ as her Messiah or to be judged by Christ Himself.

### Notes on Chapter 11

[1]A. J. McClain, *Daniel's Prophecy of the 70 Weeks* (Grand Rapids, Mich.: Zondervan, 1940), p. 9.

[2]E. J. Young, *The Prophecy of Daniel: A Commentary* (Grand Rapids, Mich.: Wm. B. Eerdmans Pub. Co., 1949), p. 191.

[3]*Sanhedrin* 97b (Soncino ed), p. 659.

[4]See G. R. Beasley-Murray, in *The New International Dictionary of New Testament Theology*, ed. C. Brown (Grand Rapids, Mich.: Zondervan, 1976), vol. 1, pp. 74, 75. F. F. Bruce, *Israel and the Nations* (Exeter, England: Paternoster Press, 1973), p. 224, refers to the "Roman custom of offering sacrifice to their standards."

[5]L. F. Hartman, *The Book of Daniel*, The Anchor Bible, vol. 23 (Garden City, N.Y.: Doubleday, 1978), p. 252.

[6]Joyce G. Baldwin, *Daniel: An Introduction and Commentary* (Downers Grove, Ill.: Inter-Varsity Press, 1978), p. 171; see also p. 174. Cf. G. McCready Price, *The Greatest of the Prophets* (Mountain View, Calif.: Pacific Press, 1955), p. 244, who points further to Matthew 22:7.

[7]G. F. Hasel, "The Seventy Weeks of Daniel 9:24-27," Insert D, *Ministry*, May 1976, p. 5. Two contextual observations corroborate this conclusion: (1) Daniel was thinking about time in terms of *years* only (chap. 9:2); (2) In chapter 10:2 Daniel adds to the expression "three weeks" the words "of days" (in Hebrew) to distinguish these three weeks as ordinary weeks, in apparent contrast with the year-weeks of chapter 9.

[8]Young, *The Prophecy of Daniel*, p. 216.

[9]Philip Mauro, *The Seventy Weeks and the Great Tribulation* (Boston: Hamilton Bros., 1923), p. 95. He refers to the predicted 430 years for Israel in Genesis 15:13 and Galatians 3:17; the seven years of plenty and the seven years of famine for Egypt in Genesis 45:6; the forty years for Israel in Numbers 14:34; and Jesus' resurrection within three days.

[10]J. F. Walvoord, *The Return of the Lord* (Grand Rapids, Mich.: Zondervan, 1971), p. 77.

[11]E. W. Hengstenberg, *Christology of the Old Testament* (Grand Rapids, Mich.: Kregel, 1956), vol. 3, p. 143.

[12]J. F Walvoord, *The Rapture Question* (Grand Rapids, Mich.: Zondervan, 1957), p. 24.

[13]McClain, *Daniel's Prophecy of the 70 Weeks*, p. 33.

[14]Walvoord, *The Rapture Question*, p. 25.

[15]The hermeneutical importance of the literary structure, with its poetic forms of parallelism and chiasm, in Daniel 9:24-27 is brought to light in three valuable studies: J. Doukhan, "The Seventy Weeks of Daniel 9: An Exegetical Study," *AUSS* 17:1 (Spring 1979): 1-22; W. H. Shea, "Poetic Relations of Time Periods in Daniel 9: 25," *AUSS* 18:1 (Spring 1980):59-63; J. B. Payne, "The Goal of Daniel's Seventy Weeks," *JETS* 21:2 (June 1978):97-115.

[16]Payne, "The Goal of Daniel's Seventy Weeks," p. 109.

[17]McClain, *Daniel's Prophecy of the 70 Weeks*, p. 35.

[18]Payne, "The Goal of Daniel's Seventy Weeks," p. 109.

[19]Ibid. See especially Doukhan, "The Seventy Weeks of Daniel 9," pp. 12-14.

[20]See Shea, "Poetic Relations of Time Periods in Daniel 9:25," pp. 59-63.

[21]McClain, *Daniel's Prophecy of the 70 Weeks*, p. 35.

[22]See Doukhan, "The Seventy Weeks of Daniel 9," pp. 1-12, especially p. 12.

[23]Young, *The Prophecy of Daniel*, p. 221.

[24]Baldwin, *Daniel: An Introduction and Commentary*, p. 177.

[25]McClain, *Daniel's Prophecy of the 70 Weeks*, p. 39.

[26]Ibid., p. 40.

[27]See *SDABC*, vol. 5, "Chronology of the Gospel of John," pp. 192, 193, 229-231; Payne, *Encyclopedia of Biblical Prophecy*, p. 387.

[28]McClain, *Daniel's Prophecy of the 70 Weeks*, p. 52.

[29]See Payne, "The Goal of Daniel's Seventy Weeks," p. 109; also his *Encyclopedia of Biblical Prophecy*, p. 388.

[30]Hasel, "The Seventy Weeks of Daniel 9:24-27," p. 17.

[31]McClain, *Daniel's Prophecy of the 70 Weeks*, p. 52.

[32]Ibid., p. 26. This date is arrived at by a complicated transformation of lunar years into solar years, which is rejected as incorrect in details by other dispensational writers. See Hasel, "The Seventy Weeks of Daniel 9:24-27."

[33]Payne, "The Goal of Daniel's Seventy Weeks," p. 101. Payne reckons the 69 weeks or 483 years from Artaxerxes' decree to Ezra in 458 B.C. till Christ's baptism in the fall of A.D. 26. Seventh-day Adventists prefer the dates 457 B.C. till A.D. 27 as more accurate; see Hasel, "The Seventy Weeks of Daniel 9:24-27."

[34]Young, *The Prophecy of Daniel*, p. 221.

[35]Doukhan, "The Seventy Weeks of Daniel 9," pp. 1-22; Shea, "Poetic Relations of Time Periods in Daniel 9:25," pp. 59-63.

[36]*NSRB*, p. 913; McClain, *Daniel's Prophecy of the 70 Weeks*, pp. 53, 58; Pentecost, *Things to Come*, p. 172.

[37]McClain, *Daniel's Prophecy of the 70 Weeks*, p. 61.

[38]Ibid., p. 50.

[39]Payne, *Encyclopedia of Biblical Prophecy*, pp. 388, 389. See the more detailed discussion by P. Mauro, *The Seventy Weeks and the Great Tribulation*, pp. 92-94.

[40]Young, *The Prophecy of Daniel*, pp. 211, 212; cf. Mauro, *The Seventy Weeks and the Great Tribulation*, p. 78. W. H. Shea (Andrews University), in an unpublished paper, prefers the possible exegesis that the phrase, "The people of the ruler who will come" in Daniel 9:26 refers to the Jewish people themselves, because they

caused the destruction of Jerusalem by the rejection of Christ as their ruler.

[41]E. J. Young and J. B. Payne prefer the KJV of Daniel 9:27.

# 12

## The Predicted Tribulation
## and Hope for the Church

---

The New Testament teaches that the Church, in spite of expecting apostasy and tribulation, should look forward to the blessed hope of Christ's second appearance. He will return from heaven in divine glory to resurrect the dead in Christ, to save the living righteous, and to destroy the oppressive antichrist:

> He will appear a second time, not to bear sin, but to bring salvation to those who are waiting for him (Hebrews 9:28).

> For the Lord himself will come down from heaven [*parousia*, verse 15], with a loud command, with the voice of the archangel and with the trumpet call of God, and the dead in Christ will rise first. After that, we who are still alive and are left will be caught up with them in the clouds to meet the Lord in the air. And so we will be with the Lord forever (1 Thessalonians 4:16, 17).

> God is just: He will pay back trouble to those who trouble you and give relief to you who are troubled, and to us as well. This will happen when the Lord Jesus is revealed from heaven in blazing fire with his powerful angels (2 Thessalonians 1:6, 7).

> And then the lawless one will be revealed, whom the Lord Jesus will overthrow with the breath of his mouth and destroy by the splendor of his coming [*parousia*] (2 Thessalonians 2:8).

> Listen, I tell you a mystery: We will not all sleep, but we will be changed—in a flash, in the twinkling of an eye, at the last trumpet. For the trumpet will sound, the dead will be raised imperishable, and we will be changed. . . . Then the saying

that is written will come true: "Death has been swallowed up in victory" (1 Corinthians 15:51-54).

According to dispensational eschatology, the second coming of Christ must be divided into two events: the secret rapture of the Church, which can happen at any moment, followed seven years later by the glorious second coming of Christ to destroy the antichrist. During these intervening seven years, the great tribulation for the Jewish people (national Israel) will take place. At the rapture, before this tribulation, Christ comes only for the saints (see John 14:3); at the glorious *parousia* or *epiphaneia* (appearing), Christ comes *with* the saints (see 1 Thessalonians 3:13). This is, in short, the program of events taught by pretribulation dispensationalists.

If this program is not based on responsible biblical exegesis but is imposed upon Holy Scripture by a preconceived doctrine of the separation of Israel and the Church, then a careful comparison of Scripture with Scripture should establish the true blessed hope of the people of Christ and their relation to the final tribulation. As soon as it is determined from Scripture that the "rapture" and the "glorious appearing" are not two separate events but a single, glorious advent, the doctrine of an imminent, pretribulation rapture is proven to be a defective view and a misdirected hope.

### The Blessed Hope of the Church

The New Testament employs three Greek terms to describe the second advent of Christ: *parousia* (coming), *apocalypsis* (revelation), and *epiphaneia* (appearing).

The *parousia* of Christ is described in 1 Thessalonians 3:13; 4:15-17; 2 Thessalonians 2:8; and Matthew 24:27. A comparison of these passages makes one thing clear: the *parousia* of Christ will cause not only the rapture of the Church and the resurrection of the righteous dead, but also the destruction of the antichrist, the lawless one. In 2 Thessalonians 2:8 Paul speaks of "the splendor of his coming" (literally: "the *epiphaneia* of his *parousia*"), thus pointing to the *parousia* as a dramatic and glorious event. This glorious appearing of Christ is, for the apostle, the blessed hope of the Church: "We wait for the blessed hope—the glorious appearing [*epiphaneia*] of our great God and Saviour, Jesus Christ" (Titus 2:13). Christ even likened his *parousia* to the flash of lightning from the east to the west, stressing again a visible event that will be evident to all people (see Matthew 24:27).

No trace of secret, invisible, or instantaneous rapture of the Church is to be found in the New Testament. On the contrary, 1 Thessalonians 4:15-17 suggests the very opposite: "A *loud* command," "the *voice* of the archangel," "the *trumpet call* of God," "the dead in Christ will rise" (emphasis added). The living saints will be "caught up" (raptured) together with the resurrected saints to meet the Lord in the air. No word about secrecy, or invisibility, or even about an instantaneous rapture is found here. Paul, in 1 Corinthians 15, reveals the mystery that the Church will be "changed" from mortality to immortality "in a flash, in the twinkling of an eye, at the last trumpet" (verse 52). It is this transformation that will be instantaneous, according to Paul, not the rapture from the earth to the air or to heaven. The *parousia* of Christ will be the most dramatic, earthshaking event in human history—salvation for all the saints, coupled with judgment for the impenitent world and the antichrist—and will take place at the last trumpet at God's own appointed time (see verses 51-55; Acts 1:6, 7).

The destruction of the wicked persecutors of Christ's Church will also take place at the *apocalypsis*, or revelation, of Jesus Christ in glory (see 2 Thessalonians 1:6, 7). It is at that revelation that the Church will receive relief, or rest, from her persecution, not at some "secret rapture" seven years before the glorious coming of Christ "from heaven in blazing fire with his powerful angels" (verse 7).

Paul taught the believers at Corinth that they should "eagerly wait for our Lord Jesus Christ to be revealed [*apocalypsis*]" (1 Corinthians 1:7). This makes the glorious *apocalypsis*, or revelation, the blessed hope of the Church. This event takes place on "the day of our Lord Jesus Christ" (verse 8). Also, Peter calls the hope of salvation for the Church, not a rapture, but a revelation of the glory of Jesus Christ (see 1 Peter 1:7, 13; 4:13). We arrive, therefore, at the conclusion that the New Testament makes no distinction between the *parousia*, the *apocalypsis*, and the *epiphaneia* of Jesus Christ. These terms signify one single, indivisible advent of Christ to bring salvation and glorious immortality to all believers, and judgment to their wicked persecutors.

The vocabulary of the New Testament does not allow for the idea of two comings, or two phases of Christ's coming, separated by a seven-year period of tribulation. It substantiates only one appearance of Christ in glory, to rescue the Church from the antichrist at the end of the tribulation.[1] Inspiration states He will appear "a second time" (Hebrews 9:28), not "two more times."

### The Predicted Tribulation for Israel and the Church

How, then, do dispensationalists get the "secret rapture" idea from the Bible? Basically, it is the result of the hermeneutic of a preconceived literalism for "Israel." C. C. Ryrie explains: "The distinction between Israel and the Church leads to the belief that the Church will be taken from the earth before the beginning of the tribulation (which in one major sense concerns Israel)."[2]

When one asks why the tribulation time will concern only literal Israel or the Jews, and not the Church, J. F. Walvoord states that the great tribulation is "a time of preparation for Israel's restoration (Deut 4:29, 30; Jer 30:4-11)."[3]

But what is the nature of this preparation time, according to Deuteronomy 4:29 and 30:1-10? A great tribulation? No! It is a time of seeking Yahweh with the whole heart and of a new obedience to His commandments! Moses made this spiritual preparation the explicit condition for a return to the promised land and a restored theocracy when Israel was in the distress of the scattering. The assurance that God would provide for a faithful, spiritual remnant during the Babylonian exile, the time of Jacob's trouble (see Jeremiah 30:7), did not negate or obscure the divine prerequisite of a true repentance before such a believing remnant could be restored to the land of blessing and prosperity (see Deuteronomy 30:1-10). A closer look at Jeremiah, chapters 30 and 31, reveals the well-known anthology of restoration promises for the twelve tribes in the Assyrian-Babylonian captivity. These passages include the new-covenant promise that Yahweh would provide a new spirit of willing obedience in the hearts of a repentant Israel and Judah (see Jeremiah 31:31-34, 18, 19; 30:9). Such was the spiritual nature of Israel's preparation time in her Babylonian tribulation before her restoration. The Bible presents no different program for

Israel today or in the future. These conditional promises of God are unchanged and irrevocable for Israel until the final Judgment.

Why, then, do some leading dispensational writers infer that the Church of Christ will not pass through the final tribulation, or suppression, by the antichrist? Why does the Church not need such a time of preparation for her glorification? Walvoord states, "None of the New Testament passages on the tribulation mention the Church (Matt 24:15-31; 1 Thess 1: 9-10; 5:4-9; Rev 4-19)."[4] However, surely all these passages are unquestionably addressed to the Church of Christ! The argument from silence proves nothing. R. H. Gundry appropriately replies:

> The Church is not mentioned as such in Mark, Luke, John, 2 Timothy, Titus, 1 Peter, 2 Peter, 1 John, 2 John, or Jude, and not until chapter 16 of Romans. Unless we are prepared to relegate large chunks of the NT to a limbo of irrelevance to the Church, we cannot make the mention or omission of the term "Church" a criterion for determining the applicability of a passage to saints of the present age.[5]

Moreover, the Revelation of John shows that a countless multitude of believers in the Lord Jesus Christ will pass through and "come out of the great tribulation; they have washed their robes and made them white in the blood of the Lamb" (Revelation 7:14). These "tribulation saints" have suffered heavily for the sake of Christ (see Revelation 7:16, 17). Can we assert that these Christians are from the Jewish race only, when John does not differentiate between tribulation saints and Christians? He even states explicitly that these victorious believers come "from every nation, tribe, people and language" (Revelation 7:9). This "great tribulation" does not refer to God's retributive wrath on the impenitent, but to the fierce persecution of the saints by the antichrist and the false prophet—in short, to the wrath of Satan (see Revelation 12:17; 13:15-17; 14:12).

Jesus warned His followers in advance that they would have trouble or tribulation for His sake and would even be killed because of religious fanaticism (see John 16:2, 33). To the church in Smyrna, the exalted Christ sent this consolation: "Do not be afraid of what you are about to suffer. I tell you, the devil will put some of you in prison to test you, and you will suffer persecution for ten days. Be faithful, even to the point of death, and I will give you the crown of life" (Revelation 2:10; cf. 1:9; Acts 14:22; Romans 5:3).

To escape the natural, normal interpretation of the saints as the Church of Christ in Revelation 6-20, the words from heaven to John in Revelation 4:1, "Come up here, and I will show you what must take place after this," are interpreted as teaching the rapture of the Church from earth to heaven. But such a forced exegesis is rejected even by some dispensational writers such as R. H. Gundry. He maintains that the literal exegesis requires that those words be applied to John the Revelator himself, and that the phrase "after this" (*meta tauta*) refers to the sequence in the personal experience of John's receiving a new vision. After his vision on earth, John is called to see a new vision in heaven. There is no reference to a succession of times or dispensations of fulfillments of these visions.[6]

We conclude, therefore, that the Church under Christ will go through fierce tribulations but will be victorious and withstand the final, great tribulation of the antichrist (see 1 Thessalonians 3:3; 1 John 2:18; 4:3; Matthew 16:18). Paul writes that the Church is destined for trials (see 1 Thessalonians 3:3). But he added that "God did not appoint us to suffer wrath but to receive salvation through our Lord Jesus Christ" (1 Thessalonians 5:9). Consequently, we need to distinguish between the tribulation of persecution by the antichrist and the retributive wrath of God appointed to the impenitent world.

During the seven apocalyptic plagues of Revelation 16, the Church on earth receives Christ's promise of divine protection, just as ancient Israel enjoyed God's protection when He struck Egypt with ten plagues (see Revelation 3:10, 11; 14:20; 16:15; Exodus 11:7). The Church of Christ will suffer persecution during the final tribulation of antichristian "Babylon," but she will not suffer the divine wrath. This wrath will be poured out from heaven on wicked Babylon during the final crisis, while God's people will be protected and rescued by the glorious second advent of Christ (see Revelation 16; 18:4; 19:11-21). The Apocalypse mentions no pretribulational rapture of the Church, but rather presents an exclusively posttribulation second coming of Christ. This conclusion is confirmed in other New Testament apocalyptic passages by Christ and Paul which portray the undeniable order of the great tribulation for the Church first, followed by her deliverance at Christ's glorious appearing. A pretribulational *parousia*, or secret rapture of the Church, is not a teaching of the New Testament (neither explicitly nor implicitly), but is based, rather, on the preconceived doctrine of a separation of Israelites and Christians. This separation is then forced upon the texts for the sake of the doctrine.

Any basic separation of the old- and new-covenant peoples has validity only if there is a biblical separation between Yahweh and Christ, between the Redeemer of Israel and the Redeemer of the Church. Christ, however, emphatically claimed to be the one Shepherd of both flocks, who had come to gather both Jews and Gentiles into one flock with one destiny—the New Jerusalem (see John 10:14-16; Revelation 21).

### Christ's Promise of Protection in the Tribulation

Christ never promised His Church a pretribulation rapture out of this world. On the contrary, in His supplication to His Father He said, "My prayer is not that you take them [His disciples and believers] out of the world but that you protect them from the evil one" (John 17:15). The contrast between a rapture "out of the world" and protection within the world "from the evil one" is clear. Christ explicitly rejects any thought of a rapture, either secret or public, that would remove His Church from the earth while leaving the world to continue its existence inhabited only by the unrighteous. He requests something else: that God will "protect them from [*terein ek*, "to guard," "to keep from"] the evil one." Jesus explained the necessity of God's keeping power: "I will remain in the world no longer, but they are still in the world, and I am coming to you. Holy Father, protect them by the power of your name" (verse 11). God's keeping or protecting power is necessary because the Church exists in the sphere of the evil one. In Revelation 3:10 Christ promises the Church in Philadelphia: "Since you have kept my command to endure patiently, I will also keep you from the hour of trial that is going to come upon the whole world to test those who live on the earth."

R. H. Gundry comments perceptively on these texts, both in John and in Revelation: "The plain implication is that were they absent from the world with the Lord, the keeping would not be necessary. Similarly, were the Church absent from the hour of testing, keeping would not be necessary."[7]

J. F. Walvoord disagrees. He argues: "The thought of the Greek [*terein ek*] is to 'keep from,' not to 'keep in,' so that the Philadelphia church is promised deliverance before the hour [of trial] comes."[8] This appeal to the meaning of the Greek is refuted, however, by Jesus' use of the same Greek verb in John 17:15, where He places this expression ("to keep from") in full contrast to the idea of removing the Church out of the world. Instead, Christ promises protection that results in a victorious rescue through God's keeping power. Concerning the great, countless multitude before the throne of God, one of the elders speaking to John declares, "These are they who have come out of the great tribulation" (Revelation 7:14). The emphasis is not on the period of tribulation, but on the victorious emergence of the saints out of it.

To say, as Walvoord does, that Christ's promise in Revelation 3:10 indicates a rapture of the Church before the hour, or time, of tribulation is to shift Christ's emphasis away from the experience of the Church during that time to the period of tribulation itself. But such a rationalistic distinction fails to catch the idiom in which an "hour" refers not to mere passage of time but to a prominent experience or trial (see John 2:4; 7:30; 8:20; 12:23, 27; 13:1).[9]

Christ promises to keep the Philadelphia church from the eschatological hour of trial. If this indicates a pretribulation rapture of the Church out of the world, why does not God's similar promise to ancient Israel concerning the Babylonian exile indicate a pretribulation rapture from the Babylonian trial? "It will be a time of trouble for Jacob, but he will be saved out of it" (Jeremiah 30:7). This text merely promises deliverance from the time of Jacob's distress after Israel has gone through the exile. Neither does Revelation 3:10 require a pretribulation rapture for the Philadelphia church, but rather it offers divine protection during the time of testing tribulation and persecution.

### The Posttribulation Parousia of Christ in Matthew 24

One of dispensationalism's main tenets is the doctrine of the imminence of the secret rapture and coming of Christ, "that is, it could happen any day, any moment."[10] Gundry explains more fully: "By common consent imminence means that so far as we know, no predicted event will *necessarily* precede the coming of Christ. The concept incorporates three essential elements: suddenness, unexpectedness or incalculability, and a possibility of occurrence at any moment."[11]

Obviously such a doctrine of imminency creates an unbearable tension with admonitions to watch for the apocalyptic signs heralding the approach of the day of the Lord. Walvoord even places us before the dilemma of looking either for the pretribulation coming of Christ or "for signs." He states: "The exhortation to look for 'the glorious appearing of Christ to His own' (Titus 2:13) loses its significance if the tribulation must intervene first. Believers in that case should look for signs."[12] The idea of an any-moment imminency seems to be incompatible with the belief in a posttribulation coming of Christ.

An expectant attitude toward the Lord's return, however, is in full harmony with the biblical admonitions to watch for the appointed signs. Luke, writing for the gentile Church, transmits Christ's forecast of future events from the fall of Jerusalem until His return, including signs in the sun, moon, and stars, as well as chaotic conditions and tribulation in the whole world (see Luke 21). Christ concludes: "When these things begin to take place, stand up and lift up your heads, because your redemption is drawing near" (Luke 21:28). Christ warns the Church that it must look for His coming while it watches the predicted signs and experiences distress. Such signs do not harmonize with the imminency doctrine, but stimulate an attitude of looking forward to Christ's *parousia* after the tribulation.

It may be a surprise to many to learn that, except for verses 40 and 41, dispensationalism applies the whole prophetic discourse of Jesus in Matthew 24 to national Israel and not to the Christian Church! Walvoord states, "The godly remnant of the tribulation are pictured as Israelites, not members of the Church."[13] However, Christ-believing Israelites become part of the Church through baptism into the death of Christ. In order to eliminate the force of this conclusion, dispensationalism simply declares the whole chapter applicable to the Jews only. Thus, according to this view, "this gospel of the kingdom" (verse 14) refers to the restoration of David's national kingdom; the tribulation of the saints (verses 15-22) applies to Jewish believers alone. Consequently, the rapture of the elect at the *parousia* of Christ (verse 31) involves only believing Israelites. The context of Matthew 24, however, clearly indicates that Christ addressed His prophetic discourse to His apostles, who stand unquestionably as representatives of His Church, not of national Israel. Consequently, the whole discourse of Matthew 24 relates to the Church, and the saints in the tribulation predicted there belong to the Church of which the apostles were the first witnesses. This is confirmed by the fact that both Mark and Luke repeat Christ's discourse for the gentile Church (Mark 13; Luke 21). The "gospel of the kingdom" is exactly the gospel Paul preached to both Gentiles and Jews (see Acts 20:25; 28:23, 31; Colossians 1:13).

Christ's prophetic perspective of future events in Matthew 24 does not contain a pretribulation rapture of the Church. On the contrary, the gathering of the elect by God's angels at Christ's *parousia*, at the sound of the trumpet (verse 31), is unmistakably the rapture of the Church, and comes after the tribulation. The text, "He will send his angels with a loud trumpet call, and they will gather his elect," refers to both Jewish and gentile Christians in the gospel Church who will be gathered at Christ's coming, after the preceding tribulation (Matthew 24:31; cf. Luke 21:28). The general term "elect" is not restricted to Jews (see 1 Peter 1:1; 2:9). It is remarkable that dispensationalism wants to apply Matthew 24 exclusively to national Israel and yet singles out verses 40 and 41 as applying to the rapture of the Church. But if one connects the expression in these verses, "one will be taken," to the rapture of the Church (which has linguistic support in John 14:1-3, where the root verb *paralambanein* is the same as that used in Matthew 24:40, 41), this rapture is still described in connection with the rapture of the elect (verse 31). In other words, it refers to the posttribulation *parousia* of Christ. We concur, therefore, with the conclusion of G. E. Ladd, "The Rapture of the Church before the Tribulation is an *assumption*; it is not taught in the Olivet Discourse."[14]

### How Does Christ Apply the Predicted "Abomination" of Daniel 9?

Do the words of Christ in Matthew 24:15-30 predict a religious persecution of the Jews in the modern State of Israel within seven years after the Church has been raptured from earth to heaven? The dispensationalists say they do, pointing to the Savior's references to the "abomination of desolation," and "great tribulation."[15] According to A. J. McClain, Christ placed the "abomination of desolation" (of Daniel 9:27) in the future, at the end of time, "just before His second coming in glory" (Matthew 24:29, 30).[16] J. F. Walvoord agrees that in Matthew 24:15-22 Jesus "had in mind the prediction of the climax of Israel's seventieth week or seventy sevens of years predicted in Daniel 9:27."[17] And a note with Matthew 24:15-20 in the *New Scofield Reference Bible* speaks of "a future crisis in Jerusalem after the manifestation of the 'abomination.'"[18]

Do the words of Jesus in Matthew 24 really refer to a future tribulation for Jews, after the Church has been raptured to heaven? Can such a position be sustained by objective exegesis? The dispensational exegesis of Matthew 24 is a striking example of a dogmatic futurism that denies the complementary function of the Synoptic Gospels — Matthew, Mark, and Luke. Jesus' prophetic discourse is recorded by all three Synoptic Gospels and therefore should be studied in the light of all three records.

However, dispensationalists exclude Luke from their interpretation of Christ's Olivet discourse because Luke's account does not favor their exegesis of the "abomination of desolation." Many New Testament students consider Luke's narrative to be historically more complete than either of the first two Gospels. Luke stands first in length and completeness.

The *New Scofield Reference Bible* even goes so far as to declare that Jesus' words in Luke 21:20-24 — the undeniable parallel of Matthew 24:15-22 — predict *the very opposite* of what He says in Matthew's account!

> The passage in Luke refers in express terms to a destruction of Jerusalem which was fulfilled by Titus in A.D. 70; the passage in Matthew alludes to a future crisis in Jerusalem after the manifestation of the 'abomination.' . . . In the former case Jerusalem was destroyed.[19]

Such a dualism is the result of an exegesis that breaks up the organic unity of the Synoptic Gospels in order to maintain a dogmatic concept. R. H. Gundry acknowledges that it is irresponsible to impose a Jewish application on Matthew's Gospel —

rather than applying it to the Church—or to relate Matthew 24 to a future dispensation, after the Church has been raptured from earth.[20] He states: "The Olivet discourse appears in substantially the same form in Mark and in a somewhat altered form in Luke, Consequently, it may still relate to the Church from the latter gospels."[21] Furthermore, Christ addressed the discourse to His apostles, who represented the Church, of course, rather than the Jewish nation.

All three Synoptic evangelists record Christ's warning that before the abomination would appear in Jerusalem, the Palestinian Christians must experience the trials of false christs, of wars and rumors of wars, of famines and earthquakes (see Matthew 24:4-8; Mark 13:5-8; Luke 21:8-11). These predictions became historical reality between A.D. 35 and A.D. 55.[22] Yet Christ had emphasized, "All these are the beginning of birth pains" (Matthew 24:8; cf. Mark 13:8).

Christ then mentioned a second kind of trial: persecution by both Jews and Gentiles, betrayal by relatives, and hatred by all for the sake of His name (see Matthew 24:9-14; Mark 13:9-13; Luke 21:12-19). Bo Reicke gives a detailed report of the fulfillment of all these trials before the destruction of Jerusalem in A.D. 70 and states, "The situation presupposed by Matthew corresponds to what is known about Christianity in Palestine between A.D. 50 and 64."[23] And in all these upheavals Paul affirmed that the gospel had "been proclaimed to every creature under heaven" (Colossians 1:23). These facts allow us to conclude that Matthew 24:1-14 and its parallels in Mark 13:1-13 and Luke 21:5-19 have found a literal fulfillment in the years between Christ's death and the destruction of Jerusalem.[24]

What, then, was Christ's purpose in giving all these signs, as "the beginning of birth pains"? It was to warn His disciples against the false prophets who would declare, "The time is near!" (Luke 21:8). He alerted His own disciples to the truth that His second advent would *not* occur soon: "The end will not come right away" (Luke 21:9). When Roman legions besieged Jerusalem, the Jewish Zealots were inflamed by predictions of apocalyptic rescue and maintained their resistance in the false expectation that God would supernaturally deliver the city as He had done in the time of King Hezekiah (701 B.C.).[25] Against these false prophets Christ urged His disciples not to expect His return in glory at the destruction of Jerusalem.

When they saw the desolating abomination in the holy place, they were to understand this as the signal to flee immediately from the city and Judea. They should not expect God to deliver Jerusalem as the prophets Joel (chapter 3), Daniel (12:1), and Zechariah (chapters 12 and 14) had envisioned. The reason should be clear: these apocalyptic prophecies presuppose a faithful remnant of Israel on Mount Zion. But this time the faithful remnant was the messianic flock that was called out of the doomed city. Jerusalem would be destroyed according to the prophecy of Daniel 9:26, 27, because the city had rejected the Messiah as her covenant God. In Matthew 24 Jesus points specifically to Daniel's prophecy of doom for Jerusalem:

> So when you see standing in the holy place "the abomination that causes desolation," spoken of through the prophet Daniel — let the reader understand — then let those who are in Judea flee to the mountains. . . . Pray that your flight will not take place in winter or on the sabbath. For then there will be great distress, unequaled from the beginning of the world until now — and never to be equaled again (Matthew 24:15-21).

There is no perspective here for Jerusalem's deliverance "by divine interposition," as the *Scofield Bible* claims. Just the opposite: the faithful remnant must flee out of Jerusalem and Judea when they saw the abominable invader coming into the land of Israel. Why flee? Because the Roman desolator functioned as God's decreed avenger on the city and the temple for her rejection of the Messiah and His apostles (see Daniel 9:26, 27, and Luke 21:22).

A close comparison of the parallel contexts in the Synoptic Gospels confirms this conclusion beyond any doubt. Mark's record of Jesus' warning states:

> When you see "the abomination that causes desolation" standing where it does not belong — let the reader understand — then let those who are in Judea flee to the mountains. . . . Pray that this will not take place in winter, because those will be days of distress unequaled from the beginning, when God created the world, until now — and never to be equaled again (Mark 13:14-19).

Luke's Gospel explains Mark's version of Christ's prophecy more elaborately for Theophilus (1:3):

When you see Jerusalem surrounded by armies, you will know that its desolation is near. Then let those who are in Judea flee to the mountains, let those in the city get out, and let those in the country not enter the city. For this is the time of punishment in fulfillment of all that has been written. . . . There will be great distress in the land and wrath against this people. They will fall by the sword and will be taken as prisoners to all the nations. Jerusalem will be trampled on by the Gentiles until the times of the Gentiles are fulfilled (Luke 21:20-24).

It seems impossible to interpret Luke's description as referring to anything other than the destruction of Jerusalem, which soon became historical reality in A.D. 70. Even the *New Scofield Reference Bible* admits this, as we have seen. Yet, the undeniable parallel passages in Matthew 24:15ff. and Mark 13:14ff. (all three Synoptic passages begin with "When you see . . .") are explained by dispensationalists as referring to a different, future dispensation when the Church is no longer on earth. Indeed, the *Scofield Bible* finds two different sieges of Jerusalem in the same words of Christ's Olivet discourse!

> Two sieges of Jerusalem are in view in the Olivet discourse, the one fulfilled in A.D. 70, and the other yet to be fulfilled at the end of the age. . . . The references in Matthew 24:15-28 and Mark 13:14-26 are to be the final siege, when the city will be taken by enemies but delivered by the return of the Lord to the earth (Rev 19:11-21; Zech 14:2-4).[26]

Apparently such an interpretation of Christ's words is guided, not by an exegesis that takes into account the context of the Synoptic Gospels, but by a preconceived futurism that forces a system of dispensationalism onto Christ's words. Such an interpretation is saying that Mark and Matthew wrote nothing about the impending desolation of Jerusalem that took place in A.D. 70, while Luke wrote nothing about the "final" abomination and tribulation that the antichrist has in store for the "finally regathered" Jews. Why, then, does Luke, who largely follows Mark's account, completely ignore such a horrible tribulation for future Jews? Why does he focus exclusively on the imminent desolation of Jerusalem by Titus and the resulting worldwide scattering of Jews at that time as the complete fulfillment of God's punishment for Jerusalem (see Luke 21:22; cf. Deuteronomy 28:44-59; Daniel 9:26, 27)? Why does Christ, in His Olivet discourse, give identical instructions about the desolating abomination to His apostles for the Church? The armies of Rome invading the "holy land" could be seen by all in Judea (see Matthew 24:15, 16; Mark 13:14). Both Matthew and Mark speak, not merely of a coming "abomination," but of a desolating abomination. Luke explains to his largely gentile readers that this horrible desolation would come to Jerusalem with the destroying heathen armies (see Luke 21:20).

If the three Synoptic Gospels describe one and the same event regarding Jerusalem — the approaching desolation of the city and the sanctuary — then Christ placed the fulfillment of Daniel 9:26, 27 in A.D. 70, within His own generation (cf. Matthew 24:34; 23:36; Luke 21:32, 22). Luke's emphatic declaration that the destruction of Jerusalem (by Titus in A.D. 70) was "the time of punishment in fulfillment of all that has been written" (Luke 21:22) is the sealing confirmation that Daniel's "seventieth week" has been completely fulfilled by Christ's mission to Israel and Jerusalem's horrible destruction by the Romans.[27]

G. G. Cohen has argued that the predicted "abomination of desolation" was *not* fulfilled in A.D. 70, because "history reveals no action by the Roman general, Titus, which can be identified as the abomination of desolation of Matthew 24:15 or 2 Thessalonians 2:3, 4."[28] But F. F. Bruce reports that

> . . . when the Temple area was taken by the Romans, and the sanctuary itself was still burning, the soldiers brought their legionary standards into the sacred precincts, set them up opposite the eastern gate, and offered sacrifices to them, there, acclaiming Titus as *imperator* (victorious commander) as they did so. . . . The offering of such sacrifice in the Temple court was the supreme insult to the God of Israel.[29]

Understood in this way, the Savior substantiates the fact that Daniel's seventy weeks end, not in a last-day post-Church persecution of Jews in Israel, but with the rejection of Christ and its consequences for Jerusalem.[30]

### Paul's Answer to the Imminency Expectation

A twofold confirmation of the posttribulation rapture can be found in Paul's words describing Christ's *parousia* as accompanied by "the voice of the archangel and . . . the trumpet call of God" (1 Thessalonians 4:16). The only archangel mentioned by name in the Bible is Michael (Jude 9), who is connected in Daniel 12:1, 2 with the resurrection of the saints *after* the time of distress or final tribulation. Walvoord is sufficiently impressed with this testimony of the posttribulation deliverance and resurrection of the saints in the Old Testament (cf. Isaiah 25:8; 26:14-21) that he concedes "the point that the resurrection of Old Testament saints is after the tribulation."[31] He feels compelled, however, to divorce this resurrection completely from the translation and resurrection of the Church, because "the Old Testament saints are never described by the phrase 'in Christ.'"[32]

This literalistic argument is untenable because Paul addresses most of his epistles to the saints, the typical Old Testament description for God's covenant people (cf. 1 Peter 2:9), and considers, as well, the Old Testament saints to be believers in the Messiah or Christ (see 1 Corinthians 10:1-4; cf. Hebrews 11:24-26). Paul's deliberate statement to the Thessalonians that at the time of the rapture of the Church the voice of the Archangel (Israel's Defender) will sound is a sufficiently clear confirmation that the resurrection of both the Old Testament and the New Testament saints will occur simultaneously as *one* resurrection (see John 5:28, 29). Walvoord calls this argument "not conclusive proof." But what else does Paul mean by saying that the voice of Israel's Defender, the Archangel, will be heard at the rapture and resurrection of Christ's Church? Paul's further statement in 1 Thessalonians 4:16 that "the trumpet call of God" will sound at that time is additional support for the same idea. Isaiah predicted that "a great trumpet will sound" (Isaiah 27:13) at the end of Israel's exile or tribulation, and "in that day . . . you, O Israelites, will be gathered up one by one" (verse 12). This prophecy will be gloriously fulfilled, suggests Paul, at the dramatic *parousia* of Christ and the rapture of His Church.

Walvoord also claims that 2 Thessalonians 2:1-12 is "no support for posttribulationism" because Paul was only "demonstrating that the predicted Day of the Lord was still future," and that the Thessalonian Christians should not worry "that their present persecutions were those anticipated for this period (of the Day of the Lord)."[33] A closer look at the biblical passage and its context reveals, however, that much more is involved. Paul writes explicitly to correct a false teaching (apparently set forth under Paul's own name) that the Day of the Lord had already begun or at least was so imminent that it could occur at any moment. This idea had alarmed some and led them to quit their daily work to become a burden on others (see chap. 3:6-15). Paul corrects this deception of an any-moment coming of the Day of the Lord, or *parousia*, by reminding the Church of his oral teaching about preceding signs of prophetic significance that must develop in history *before* the Day of the Lord will take place (chap. 2:3-5). He makes it clear that at "the coming of our Lord Jesus Christ" not only will the Church be "gathered to him" (verse 1) but also the lawless one (antichrist) will be destroyed "by the splendor of his coming" (verse 8). This clearly implies a posttribulation coming of Christ for His Church!

This conclusion is in perfect harmony with the conclusive testimony against a two-phase coming of Christ found in 2 Thessalonians 1:5-10. Yet dispensationalism teaches that the Church will be secretly gathered to Christ seven years before the antichrist is destroyed by Christ's *parousia*. Paul's clarifying remarks in 2 Thessalonians 2 effectively refute any such secret rapture. The occasion of our being gathered together to Christ, he says, will also involve simultaneously the destruction of the persecuting antichrist.

The efforts of dispensational writers to escape Paul's rather obvious teaching are curious. Some create an artificial distinction between "the day of Christ" (which they apply to the rapture) and "the day of the Lord" (in their view, the subsequent tribulation for Israel and the judgment of God). But how can the Day of the Lord include tribulation by the antichrist when Paul declares that the lawless one will bring his apostasy *before* the Day of the Lord?[34] "Let no one deceive you in any way; for that day will not come, unless the rebellion [*apostasia*] comes first [*protos*], and the man of lawlessness is revealed" (2 Thessalonians 2:3, RSV).

All accept the conclusion that this lawless one is the apocalyptic antichrist who will cause the great tribulation for the saints of God by his self-deification within the temple of God (verse 4). This apostasy is not an exclusive message for Jews, but is vitally relevant for Christians! Christians should know the antichrist so they need not be confused by a mistaken imminency of the *parousia*. Then they will watch and see the approach of the day beforehand and be ready for "the Day of the Lord."

Evidently the Thessalonians had understood from Paul's first epistle that they were to be raptured *before* the tribulation (chap. 4:13-18). Gundry states, "The Thessalonians errone-ously concluded that Christ's coming lay in the immediate future, with resultant cessation of work, fanatical excitement, and disorder."[35] Paul's answer in 2 Thessalonians 2 is a refuta-tion of such an imminency doctrine. The apocalyptic tribula-tion must come first, *before* the *parousia* and rapture.

Another effort to avoid the posttribulation advent of Christ is a forced exegesis of *he apostasia* in 2 Thessalonians 2:3 to denote *not* the apostasy or rebellion of the antichrist, but the departure or rapture of the Church from earth before the anti-christ and his tribulation arise. The simple fact is, however, that the term *apostasia* in the New Testament and in the Sep-tuagint is used exclusively for religious defection, a departure from the faith.[36] It never refers to the departure of the Church from earth. In 2 Thessalonians 2:3 it is correctly translated as "the rebellion" in both the Revised Standard Version and the New International Version. The definite article "the" before "rebellion" points to a well-known apostasy about which Paul had informed the Thessalonians earlier (verse 5) and which he now explains more fully in the following verses, especially verses 4, 9, and 10. *The* apocalyptic apostasy, says Paul, will be a deliberate departure from the apostolic faith, a rebellion against God, led by the antichrist. This is the time of the great tribulation for God's faithful people. Paul urges the Church to watch for this developing apostasy so that the *parousia*, or Day of the Lord, will *not* surprise her like a thief (1 Thessalonians 5:1-6).

Finally, some dispensationalists insist that the mysterious Restrainer of the antichrist (see 2 Thessalonians 2:6) must be the Holy Spirit working through the Church. Thus the Re-strainer being "taken out of the way" (verse 7) would point to the rapture of the Church out of the world before the antichrist brings his tribulation on the earth. But R. H. Gundry has convincingly shown that this dispensational exegesis has no foundation either in the immediate context or in the New Testament as a whole. Even if the Holy Spirit will be ultimately withdrawn from an impenitent, wicked world, this does not prove that the Church of Christ will be evacuated from earth to heaven "in a retrogressive step to the Old Testament economy."[37]

It is certainly a "fantastic assumption," as J. Wilmot says, for dispensational eschatology to assert that in the *absence* of the Holy Spirit and the Church, and within the "seven" years of the antichrist's reign, "a great multitude which no man can number" shall be converted to Christ from among all nations! Paul's eschatology in 1 and 2 Thessalonians places both the glorious rapture of the Church and the simultaneous destruction of the antichrist at the dramatic *parousia* (see especially 2 Thessalonians 2:1, 8). This is Paul's teaching of a posttribulation *parousia* and rapture, based on Christ's outline of events for the Christian dispensation in Matthew 24.[38]

When Christians trust in the teaching that they will be raptured to heaven *before* the persecution of the antichrist, how will they be prepared for the coming final test of faith? The danger of pretribulationism is that it instills in the hearts of God's people a false hope and thus fails to prepare the Church for her final crisis.

### Notes on Chapter 12

[1]See G. E. Ladd, *The Blessed Hope* (Grand Rapids, Mich.: Wm. B. Eerdmans Pub. Co., 1960), chapter 3, for a detailed study. The dispensational theologian Charles F. Baker, in *A Dispensational Theology*, 2d ed., admits after his analysis of the three words for the second coming, "We must conclude that the distinction between the coming of Christ at the time of the Rapture and His coming back to earth cannot be established simply by the words that are used" (p. 616).

[2]Ryrie, *Dispensationalism Today*, p. 159. Cf. Walvoord, *The Rapture Question*, p. 192, "Only pretribulationism distinguishes clearly between Israel and the church and their respective programs."

[3]Walvoord, *The Rapture Question*, p. 193.

[4]Ibid.

[5]R. H. Gundry, *The Church and the Tribulation* (Grand Rapids, Mich.: Zondervan, 1973), p. 78.

[6]See ibid., p. 64-66.

[7]Ibid., p. 58.

[8]Walvoord, *The Rapture Question*, p. 70.

[9]Gundry, *The Church and the Tribulation*, p. 60.

[10]Walvoord, *The Return of the Lord*, p. 80.

[11]Gundry, *The Church and the Tribulation*, p. 29. See chapter 3, "Expectation and Imminence," for an excellent response to the dispensational doctrine of imminency.

[12]Walvoord, *The Rapture Question*, pp. 195, 196.

[13]Ibid., p. 195.

[14]Ladd, *The Blessed Hope*, p. 73.

[15]Walvoord, *The Return of the Lord*, chapter 5.

[16]McClain, *Daniel's Prophecy of the 70 Weeks*, p. 40.

[17]Walvoord, *Israel in Prophecy*, p. 109.

[18]*NSRB*, p. 1034.

[19]Ibid.

[20]Gundry, *The Church and the Tribulation*, chapter 9, "The Olivet Discourse."

[21]Ibid., p. 130.

[22]See detailed report, with historical references, by B. Reicke, "Synoptic Prophecies on the Destruction of Jerusalem," in *Studies in New Testament and Early Christian Literature* (essays in honor of A. P. Wikgren), ed. D. E. Aune (Leiden: E. J. Brill, 1972), pp. 121-134; especially 130ff.

[23]Ibid., p. 133.

[24]See also the *SDABC* on Matthew 24:2-14, vol. 5, pp. 497, 498.

[25]Josephus, *Wars* VI 5.2, reports that "a large number of false prophets . . . announced to them [the people] that they should wait for deliverance from God." This caused the massacre of six thousand women and children in the temple court. Cf. Strack-Billerbeck, *Kommentar zum NT* (München: Beck, 1922) 4/2:1003.

[26]*NSRB*, p. 1114 (on Luke 21:20).

[27]Josephus writes that 1.1 million Jews perished and 97,000 were sold into slavery. He concludes: "Accordingly the multitude of those that perished therein exceeded all the destructions that either men or God ever brought upon the world" (*Wars*, VI 9.4).

[28]G. G. Cohen, "Is the Abomination of Desolation Past?" *Moody Monthly*, April 1975, pp. 31, 34.

[29]Bruce, *Israel and the Nations*, pp. 31, 34.

[30]See my further treatment of Mark 13 and Matthew 24 in the March 1983 issue of *Ministry* magazine.

[31]Walvoord, *The Rapture Question*, p. 154.

[32]Ibid.

[33]Ibid., pp. 164, 165.

[34]R. H. Gundry, in *The Church and the Tribulation*, pp. 96-99, shows conclusively that the variations "day of Christ" and "day of the Lord" have *no* different technical meanings. See, for example, 1 Corinthians 5:5.

[35]Ibid., p. 121.

[36]E. I. Carver, *When Jesus Comes Again* (Phillipsburg, N.J.: Presbyterian and Reformed Publishing Co., 1979), p. 271. For a more detailed study, see Gundry, *The Church and the Tribulation*, pp. 114-118.

[37]Gundry, *The Church and the Tribulation*, p. 128; see detailed discussion on pp. 122-128.

[38]See G. H. Waterman, "The Sources of Paul's Teaching on the Second Coming of Christ in 1 and 2 Thessalonians," *JETS* 18:2 (Spring 1975):105-113. He concludes, "The words of Jesus as recorded by Matthew were the source of Paul's teaching."

# Summary and Conclusion

Our fundamental starting point in this work has been the axiom of faith that the Bible is its own expositor by means of immediate and wider contexts. Because we accept Jesus Christ as the true Interpreter of the Hebrew Bible, we take our stand with the Church of the ages in confessing that the New Testament is God's authorized interpretation and authoritative application of the Old Testament. We have concluded that the New Testament teaches the fulfillment of the messianic prophecies in the life and death, and in the resurrection and exaltation of Jesus Christ. A striking element in this relationship between the Old and New Testaments is the fact that the New Testament considers even the history of ancient Israel as typological of Christ's mission (see chapter 5). Christ Himself initiated the new concept that with Him the time of the antitypes had arrived (see chapter 4).

Since Christ Himself created His Church, the inescapable consequence of the christological fulfillment is the fulfillment of Israel's mission in the mission of the Christian Church. This *ecclesiological* fulfillment concentrates especially on three Hebrew concepts: the survival of a faithful remnant of Israel, the promise of the new covenant in Jeremiah 31, and the promises of the vivifying Spirit of God in Ezekiel 36-37. These three interrelated promises are made the inaugural event of the messianic age and are applied ecclesiologically in the New Testament (see chapter 7).[1] The implication of the ecclesiological interpretation of Israel in the New Testament is unmistakably that the ethnic restrictions of God's promises to Israel are

207

fulfilled in Christ and His Church. The apostolic Church considered itself to be the new and the true Israel of the messianic age. Even in Romans 9-11 Paul does not look for a restored theocracy of national Israel in Palestine (see chapter 8). The restoration or gathering promises of the Old Testament are consistently applied christologically and, by extension, ecclesiologically in the New Testament, with the continued expectation of an apocalyptic consummation at the glorious second advent of Christ. This future eschatological fulfillment is again presented with an exclusively christocentric focus.

Another consequence of the christological fulfillment of Israel's covenant promises is the fact that the New Testament unmistakably *universalizes* Israel's territorial promises (see chapter 9). Although the New Testament occasionally employs the old ethnic and geographic imagery in the Gospels and Letters, the Middle East focus, or Palestinian restriction, is consistently eliminated in its ecclesiological and apocalyptic applications. The New Testament recognizes holy territory only where Christ is present, either by His physical presence, or His spiritual presence where two or three are gathered in His name.

At the apostolic council in Acts 15 the conclusion was reached that the apostolic Church was not instituted *beside* Israel but *as* the restored Israel (see chapter 10). The finality of Christ's decision to take the theocracy away from the Jewish nation (Matthew 21:43) and to bestow the new-covenant blessing and responsibility on the messianic community (Luke 12:32) is nowhere more impressively predicted than in the seventy-weeks prophecy of Daniel (see chapter 11). A gap hypothesis is neither needed nor justified on the basis of a literal exegesis. In his Olivet discourse, Christ applied the predicted abomination of desolation in the book of Daniel to the defilement of the temple and the destruction of Jerusalem in His own generation. But He did not stop with this application. In Mark 13 and Matthew 24 he blended the judgment on Jerusalem with the time of tribulation or distress of His own elect, the Church, throughout the Christian era until the time of the end (see chapter 12). The Church is commissioned to bear witness of Christ as the Messiah before all nations in spite of universal distress, so that the world will finally stand before the same bar of divine justice as Jerusalem faced in A.D. 70.

Christ's application of Daniel's prophetic outline is further developed by the apostle Paul in 2 Thessalonians 2, a perspective which calls for a more detailed study.[2] But most of all the Apocalypse of John needs a fresh approach on the basis of the christocentric hermeneutic. Once the principles of prophetic fulfillment have become clear, we may have renewed confidence in the sacred task of expounding the yet-unfulfilled prophecies of Holy Scripture. The same christocentric hermeneutic must be applied in both fulfilled and unfulfilled prophecy. All eschatological prophecies, including those which will find a specific end-time fulfillment, must pass through the transforming cross of Christ and His resurrection to a new life. This is true just as surely as the new covenant receives its present fulfillment and future consummation exclusively through the blood of Christ's self-sacrifice and His triumphant resurrection.

One of the most important results of this gospel hermeneutic—the christological-ecclesiological interpretation of Israel's covenants—is the conclusion that it is biblically unjustified to apply any old-covenant blessing unconditionally to the modern State of Israel in the Middle East, as if Christ had not yet appeared and the New Testament had not been written. No appeal to "natural" exegesis can be valid if it bypasses the cross of Christ (see 2 Corinthians 1:20). The biblical focus of prophecy is never on Israel as a people or a nation, as such, but on Israel as the believing, worshiping, covenant people, as the messianic community. The ultimate focus is on God and His Messiah. All eyes will finally be directed, not on Israel, but on Christ Jesus as the King of Israel and Lord of the Church (see Revelation 1:7; Zechariah 12:10; Isaiah 40:5). Biblical prophecy and apocalyptic is thoroughly theocentric and christocentric. This truth focuses on and glorifies the Creator and Redeemer of mankind. In the New Jerusalem there is no separation or compartmentalization of Israel and the Church. The apocalyptic Holy City unites all twenty-four names of Israel's patriarchs and Christ's apostles (Revelation 21:12-14). The center is "the throne of God and of the Lamb" (Revelation 22:1, 3). The saints who have passed triumphantly through the great tribulation will sing "the song of Moses the servant of God and the Song of the Lamb" (Revelation 15:3; cf. 7:9, 14).

It is encouraging to observe how some who call themselves "moderate dispensationalists" are prepared to acknowledge that through careful study of the interrelationship of the Old and New Testaments,

> the old sharp distinction between Israel and the Church begins to become somewhat blurred. . . . Strictly speaking, it is also incorrect to call Israel God's earthly people and the Church God's heavenly people, since in the eternal state we will all live together, sharing in the blessings of the New Jerusalem and the new earth. . . . We have compartmentalized too much.[3]

The link which establishes the basic unity and continuity between the Old and the New Testaments and their covenants is their common remnant concept. The apostles and disciples of Christ are called the faithful "remnant" of Israel (Romans 11:5), and the apostolic Church is referred to as the "Israel of God" (Galatians 6:15, 16; 3:29). It is not correct, therefore, to state that the Church has replaced Israel. Rather, the Church is the continuity of the Old Testament Israel of God; it has only replaced the Jewish nation. Gentile Christians do not constitute a different or separate entity from the faithful remnant of Israel. They are ingrafted into the messianic Israel. There is in the New Testament only one symbolic olive tree (Romans 11), one spiritual temple (Ephesians 2), one apocalyptic woman of God (Revelation 12), and one New Jerusalem (Revelation 21) for God's people in all dispensations or eras. For this purpose Christ came into the world: "I have other sheep that are not of this sheep pen. I must bring them also. They too will listen to my voice, and there shall be one flock and one shepherd" (John 10:16; cf. 11:51, 52). Christ's last prayer was aimed at this universal unity:

> My prayer is not for them alone. I pray also for those who will believe in me through their message, that all of them may be one, Father, just as you are in me and I am in you. May they also be in us so that the world may believe that you have sent me (John 17:20, 21).

### Notes on Summary and Conclusion

[1]On Ezekiel, see C. H. Bullock, "Ezekiel, Bridge Between the Testaments," *JETS* 25:1 (March 1982):23-31, especially 30.

[2]See my essay "Paul's Prophetic Outline in 2 Thessalonians 2," *AUSS* 21:2 (1983).

[3]K. L. Barker, "False Dichotomies Between the Testaments," *JETS* 25:1 (March 1982):3-16; quotation from p. 12.

# Bibliography

Allis, O. T. *Prophecy and the Church.* Philadelphia: The Presbyterian and Reformed Pub. Co., 1974.

Baker, C. F. *A Dispensational Theology.* Grand Rapids, Mich.: Grace Bible College Pub., 1972.

Baker, D. L. *Two Testaments: One Bible.* Downers Grove, Ill.: Inter-Varsity Press, 1977.

Barr, J. *Old and New in Interpretation.* New York: Harper & Row, 1966.

Bass, C. B. *Backgrounds to Dispensationalism.* Grand Rapids, Mich.: Baker, 1977 (reprint of 1960).

Beecher, W. J. *The Prophets and the Promise.* Grand Rapids, Mich.: Baker, 1975 (reprint of 1905).

Berkhof, L. *Principles of Biblical Interpretation.* Grand Rapids, Mich.: Baker, 1964.

Black, M. "The Christological Use of the Old Testament in the New Testament." *NTS* 18 (1972):1-14.

Boersma, T. *Is the Bible a Jigsaw Puzzle? An Evaluation of Hal Lindsey's Writings.* St. Catherines, Ontario, Canada: Paideia Press, 1978.

Bourke, M. *A Study of the Metaphor of the Olive Tree in Romans XI.* Washington, D.C.: Catholic University of America Press, 1947.

Bright, J. *The Authority of the Old Testament.* Grand Rapids, Mich.: Baker, 1977.

———. *Covenant and Promise.* Philadelphia: Westminster Press, 1976.

Brown, R. E. "Hermeneutics." In *The Jerome Biblical Commentary.* Englewood Cliffs, N.J.: Prentice-Hall, Inc., 1968, chapter 71.

———. *The Sensus Plenior of Sacred Scripture.* Baltimore: St. Mary's University, 1955.

211

Bruce, F. F. *New Testament Developments of Old Testament Themes.* Grand Rapids, Mich.: Eerdmans, 1970.

Chafer, H. S. "Dispensationalism." *BSac* 93 (1936):390-449.

_____. *Systematic Theology.* 8 vols. Dallas: Dallas Seminary Press, 1947.

Corley, B. "The Jews, the Future, and God (Romans 9-11)." *Scottish Journal of Theology* 19:1 (1976):42-56.

Danell, G. A. *Studies in the Name 'Israel' in the Old Testament.* Uppsala: Appelbergs Boktryckeri A-B, 1946.

Daniélou, J. *Sacramentum Futuri. Études sur les Origines de la Typologie Biblique.* Paris: Beauchesne, 1950. English translation: *From Shadows to Reality.* Westminster, Md.: Newman, 1960.

Davidson, A. B. *Old Testament Prophecy.* Edinburgh: T. and T. Clarke, 1905.

Davidson, R. M. *Typology in Scripture: A Study of Hermeneutical typos Structures.* Andrews University Seminary Doctoral Dissertation Series, Vol. 2. Berrien Springs, Mich.: Andrews University Press, 1981.

Davies, W. D. *The Gospel and the Land.* Berkeley, Calif.: University of California Press, 1974.

_____. "Paul and the People of Israel." *NTS* 24 (1978):4-39.

DeCaro, L. A. *Israel Today: Fulfillment of Prophecy?* Grand Rapids, Mich.: Baker, 1974.

DeYoung, J. C. *Jerusalem in the New Testament.* Kampen: Kok, 1960.

Diepold, P. *Israels Land.* BWANT NR 15. Stuttgart: Kohlhammer, 1972.

Dodd, C. H. *According to the Scriptures: The Sub-structure of New Testament Theology.* London: Nisbet, 1952.

_____. *The Old Testament in the New.* Facet Books BS3. Philadelphia: Fortress Press, 1971.

Doukhan, J. "The Seventy Weeks of Daniel 9." *AUSS* 17 (1979):1-22.

Ellis, E. E. *The Pauline Use of the Old Testament.* Grand Rapids, Mich.: Eerdmans, 1957.

_____. *Prophecy and Hermeneutics in Early Christianity.* Grand Rapids, Mich.: Eerdmans, 1978.

Epp, F. H. *Whose Land Is Palestine?* Grand Rapids, Mich.: Eerdmans, 1974.

Fairbairn, P. *Prophecy and Prophetic Interpretation.* Grand Rapids, Mich.: Guardian Press, 1976 (reprint of 1865).

_____. *The Typology of Scripture.* Grand Rapids, Mich.: Baker, 1975 (reprint of 1900).

Foulkes, F. *The Acts of God: A Study of the Basis of Typology in the Old Testament.* London: Tyndale, 1955.

France, R. T. *Jesus and the Old Testament*. London: Tyndale, 1971.

_____. "Old Testament Prophecy and the Future of Israel." *Tyndale Bulletin* 26 (1975):53-78.

Fritsch, C. T. "Biblical Typology: Typological Interpretation in the New Testament." *BSac* 104 (1946):87-100.

_____. "Principles of Biblical Typology." *BSac* 104 (1947):214-222.

_____. "To 'Antitypon'." In *Studia Biblica et Semitica*, Festschrift für Th.C. Vriezen. Wageningen: H. Veenman, 1966.

Fuller, D. P. *Gospel and Law: Contrast or Continuum? The Hermeneutics of Dispensationalism and Covenant Theology*. Grand Rapids, Mich.: Eerdmans, 1980.

Girdlestone, R. B. *The Grammar of Prophecy: A Systematic Guide to Biblical Prophecy*. Grand Rapids, Mich.: Kregel, 1955.

Goppelt, L. *Typos. Die Typologische Deutung des Alten Testaments im Neuen*. Darmstadt: Wissenschaftliche Buchgesellschaft, 1969 (reprint of 1939).

Goulder, M. D. *Type and History in Acts*. London: S.P.C.K., 1954.

Gundry, R. H. *The Church and the Tribulation*. Grand Rapids, Mich: Zondervan, 1973.

Gundry, S. N. "Typology as a Means of Interpretation: Past and Present." *JETS* 12 (1969):233-240.

Hagner, D. A. "The Old Testament in the New Testament." In *Interpreting the Word of God*. Edited by S. J. Schultz and M. B. Inch. Chicago: Moody Press, 1976.

Hasel, G. F. *New Testament Theology: Basic Issues in the Current Debate*. Grand Rapids, Mich.: Eerdmans, 1978.

_____. *The Remnant: The History and Theology of the Remnant Idea from Genesis to Isaiah*. 3d ed. Andrews University Monographs, Studies in Religion, Vol. 5. Berrien Springs, Mich.: Andrews University Press, 1980.

Hendriksen, W. *Israel in Prophecy*. Grand Rapids, Mich.: Baker, 1974.

Henry, C. F. H., ed. *Prophecy in the Making*. Carol Stream, Ill.: Creation House, 1971.

Hughes, P. E. *Interpreting Prophecy*. Grand Rapids, Mich.: Eerdmans, 1976.

Hulst, A. R. "Der Name 'Israel' in Deuteronomium." *OTS* 9 (1951):65-106.

Hummel, H. D. "The Old Testament Basis of Typological Interpretation." *Biblical Research* 9 (1964):38-50.

Jewett, P. K. "Concerning the Allegorical Interpretation of Scripture." *WTJ* 17 (1954):1-20.

Kac, A. W. *The Rebirth of the State of Israel*. Grand Rapids, Mich.: Baker, 1976.

Kaiser, W. C., Jr.. "Messianic Prophecies in the Old Testament." In *Handbook of Biblical Prophecy*. Edited by C. E. Amerding and W. W. Gasque. Grand Rapids, Mich.: Baker, 1978.

_____. *Toward an Old Testament Theology*. Grand Rapids, Mich.: Zondervan, 1978.

Kistemaker, S. *The Psalm Citations in the Epistle to the Hebrews*. Amsterdam: G. van Soest, 1961.

Kraus, H.-J.. *The People of God in the Old Testament*. World Christian Books No. 22. London: Lutterworth Press, 1963.

_____. *Psalmen*. BKAT Bande XV/1-2. Neukirchen-Vluyn: Neukirchener Verlag, 1972.

Ladd, G. E. *The Blessed Hope*. Grand Rapids, Mich.: Eerdmans, 1960.

_____. *Crucial Questions About the Kingdom of God*. Grand Rapids, Mich.: Eerdmans, 1961.

_____. *The Last Things*. Grand Rapids, Mich.: Eerdmans, 1978.

_____. *A Theology of the New Testament*. Grand Rapids, Mich.: Eerdmans, 1974.

Lampe, G. W. H., and Woollcombe, K. J. *Essays on Typology*. Studies in Biblical Theology, No. 22. Napierville, Ill.: A. R. Allenson, 1957.

Lenski, R. C. H. *The Interpretation of St. Paul's Epistle to the Romans*. Columbus, Ohio: Wartburg Press, 1945.

McClain, A. J. *Daniel's Prophecy of the Seventy Weeks*. Grand Rapids, Mich.: Zondervan, 1940.

Meyer, F. B. *Israel: A Prince With God*. Fort Washington, Pa.: Christian Literature Crusade, 1972.

Moule, C. F. D. "Fulfillment-Words in the New Testament: Use and Abuse." *NTS* 14 (1968):293-320.

Mowinckel, S. *He That Cometh*. Nashville, Tenn.: Abingdon, 1954.

Nixon, R. E. *The Exodus in the New Testament*. London: Tyndale, 1962.

Nygren, A. *Commentary on Romans*. Philadelphia: Fortress Press, 1978.

Payne, J. B. *Encyclopedia of Biblical Prophecy*. New York: Harper & Row, 1973.

_____. "The Goal of Daniel's Seventy Weeks." *JETS* 21:2 (1978): 97-115.

Pentecost, J. D. *Things to Come*. Findlay, Ohio: Dunham Publishing Co., 1961.

Preuss, H. D. *Jahweglaube und Zukunftserwartung*. BWANT 7. Stuttgart: Kohlhammer Verlag, 1964.

Ramm, B. *Protestant Biblical Interpretation*. Grand Rapids, Mich.: Eerdmans, 1975.

Reicke, B. *The Epistles of James, Peter, and Jude.* Anchor Bible, Vol. 37. Garden City, N.Y.: Doubleday, 1964.

Richardson, P. *Israel in the Apostolic Church.* Cambridge: Cambridge University Press, 1969.

Ridderbos, H. N. *The Epistle of Paul to the Churches of Galatia.* NICNT. Grand Rapids, Mich.: Eerdmans, 1957.

_____. *Paul: An Outline of His Theology.* Grand Rapids, Mich.: Eerdmans, 1975.

Robinson, H. W. *Corporate Personality in Ancient Israel.* Facet Books BS 11. Philadelphia: Fortress Press, 1967.

Rowley, H. H. *The Biblical Doctrine of Election.* London: Lutterworth Press, 1964.

_____. *The Missionary Message of the Old Testament.* London: Cary Kingsgate Press, 1955.

Ryrie, C. C. *The Basis of the Premillennial Faith.* Neptune, N.J.: Loiseaux Bros., 1966.

_____. *Dispensationalism Today.* Chicago: Moody Press, 1965.

Shea, W. H. "Poetic Relations of Time Periods in Daniel 9:25." *AUSS* 18:1 (1980):59-63.

Shires, H. M. *Finding the Old Testament in the New.* Philadelphia: Westminster Press, 1974.

Stendahl, K. *Paul Among Jews and Gentiles.* Philadelphia: Fortress Press, 1976.

Terry, M. S. *Biblical Hermeneutics.* New York: Eaton & Mains, 1890.

Trilling, W. *Das Wahre Israel. Studien zur Theologie des Mattaus-Evangeliums.* Studien zum Alten und Neuen Testament, Bd 10. München: Kösel Verlag, 1964.

Von Hofmann, J. C. K. *Interpreting the Bible.* Translated by Christian Preus. Minneapolis: Augsburg, 1972.

Vos, G. *Biblical Theology.* Grand Rapids, Mich.: Eerdmans, 1963, reprint.

Walvoord, J. F. *Israel in Prophecy.* Grand Rapids, Mich.: Zondervan, 1962.

_____. *The Millennial Kingdom.* Grand Rapids, Mich.: Zondervan, 1974.

_____. *The Rapture Question.* Grand Rapids, Mich.: Zondervan, 1957.

_____. *The Return of the Lord.* Grand Rapids, Mich.: Zondervan, 1971.

Waterman, G. H. "The Sources of Paul's Teaching on the Second Coming of Christ in I and II Thessalonians." *JETS* 18:2 (1975):105-113.

Wenham, J. W. *Christ and the Bible.* Downers Grove, Ill.: Intervarsity Press, 1973.

Were, L. F. *The Certainty of the Third Angel's Message.* Berrien Springs, Mich.: First Impressions, 1981, reprint.

Westermann, C. *Isaiah 40-66: A Commentary.* Philadelphia: Westminster Press, 1977.

_____. *The Old Testament and Jesus Christ.* Translated by Omar Kaste. Minneapolis: Augsburg, 1971.

Wolff, H. W. "The Old Testament in Controversy: Interpretative Principles and Illustration." *Interpretation* 12 (1958):281-291.

Wyngaarden, M. J. *The Future of the Kingdom.* Grand Rapids, Mich.: Baker, 1955.

Young, E. J. *The Prophecy of Daniel: A Commentary.* Grand Rapids, Mich.: Eerdmans, 1949.

# Index of Scriptural References

## Old Testament

217

## New Testament